General Equilibrium Option Pricing Method: Theoretical and Empirical Study

Jian Chen

General Equilibrium Option Pricing Method: Theoretical and Empirical Study

厦门大学出版社
XIAMEN UNIVERSITY PRESS

Springer

Jian Chen
Department of Finance, School
of Economics
Xiamen University
Xiamen, Fujian
China

ISBN 978-981-10-7427-1 ISBN 978-981-10-7428-8 (eBook)
https://doi.org/10.1007/978-981-10-7428-8

Jointly published with Xiamen University Press, Fujian Province, China

The print edition is not for sale in China Mainland. Customers from China Mainland please order the print book from: Xiamen University Press.

Library of Congress Control Number: 2017964427

Printed on acid-free paper

This Springer imprint is published by the registered company Springer Nature Singapore Pte Ltd.
part of Springer Nature
The registered company address is: 152 Beach Road, #21-01/04 Gateway East, Singapore 189721, Singapore

To My Daughter and Wife

Acknowledgements

I am sincerely grateful to everyone who helped me directly and indirectly during my work on this book. First of all, I would like to deeply thank my wife, Ling Ouyang, for her moral support during the challenging period of writing this book and giving me the confidence to go for my objectives. I also acknowledge my parents for their belief, encouragement, and support.

Further thanks go to my previous Ph.D. supervisor, Prof. Chenghu Ma. Chenghu provided me the first insights related to the general equilibrium topic and first motivated me to price jump risks implicit in the option market. His time, patience, guide, innovative idea, and constructive suggestions are invaluable. I am also greatly indebted to Haomiao Zuo who provides a great research assistant work for this book. In particular, he has done a lot of empirical investigations for the Part IV of this book.

Last but certainly not least, I am grateful to the support from Risk Management Institute (RMI) of National University Singapore. Part of the work is done during I was visiting the RMI. This book is also benefited from the financial support from the National Natural Science Foundation of China (No.71201136), and the support from the Xiamen University Press.

Contents

Part I
Introduction and Model

Chapter 1
Introduction

This book aims to (1) introduce the general equilibrium option pricing method and compare different models numerically and empirically; (2) investigate the jump risk and variance risk implicit in option prices, and highlight the important role of fanning preference in pricing European options; (3) construct the variance risk premium using option prices and test the predictability of variance risk premium for future excess stock returns.

1.1 Motivation for the Book

Since the tremendous success of Black and Scholes (1973) option pricing model, many papers find two empirical violations: the downwards sloping volatility smile across moneyness and the heavy-tailed asset return distribution implied by option prices. Both abnormalities are caused by the existence of rare disasters or tail events in asset returns. For example, Rubinstein (1994) finds that the implied volatility across moneyness becomes skewed since October 1987. This feature is often referred as "volatility smirk". On the other hand, Jackwerth (2000) shows that the option implied probability distribution is more left-skewed and changes from platykurtic to leptokurtic after the market crash in 1987.

The existence of extreme/rare events, such as the market crash in 1987, result in a development of option pricing models. Merton (1976) incorporates a Poisson process into the conventional Brownian motion of Black and Scholes (1973), so that the jump-diffusion process can characterize the dynamics of equity returns. Heston (1993) proposes a flexible square-root process to control the volatility of underlying returns, in contrast to the constant assumption in Black and Scholes (1973). Bakshi et al. (1997) and Bates (1996, 2000) show that incorporating both Poisson jump and stochastic volatility can fit real option data better than previous models. Thereafter,

J. Chen, *General Equilibrium Option Pricing Method: Theoretical and Empirical Study*, https://doi.org/10.1007/978-981-10-7428-8_1

based on this stochastic volatility model with jump (SVJ), many papers develop new pricing models, e.g. time-changed Lévy model of Carr and Wu (2004) and Huang and Wu (2004), and stochastic intensity jump model of Santa-Clara and Yan (2010).

Although these previous papers successfully explain the volatility smirk, they price options under a partial equilibrium framework and assume an underlying return dynamics given exogenously. As clearly pointed out by Naik and Lee (1990), there are three independent sources of uncertainty in the traditional diffusion-jump process, i.e. Brownian motion, Poisson jump process, and distribution of jump size. When the Poisson uncertainty is removed, the underlying process reduces to the Black and Scholes (1973) setup in which all claims can be priced by arbitrage. When the diffusion uncertainty is ignored and the jump size is predictable, the underlying process simplifies to the Cox and Ross (1976) setup where the market is complete. However, if both types of uncertainty exist simultaneously and the securities market consists of only two primitive securities: stocks and bonds, the financial market is incomplete and contingent claims cannot be priced by a replication argument alone. Therefore, the state price density and the pricing kernel are not unique.

In such an incomplete market, an alternative approach to pricing European options is the general equilibrium model built on the continuous time exchange economy of Lucas (1978). Naik and Lee (1990) first propose this method. In the pure exchange economy, they assume that there is a representative agent and only one company issuing stock. The representative agent obtains dividends from the company due to hold the equity and consume. The equilibrium derivative (option) price can be obtained when the representative agent maximizes his/her expected utility of lifetime consumption. In this model setting, the unique risk aversion parameter defined according to expected utility theory controls the representative agent's risk attitude towards economic uncertainty.

In the presence of jump, however, people obviously show more aversion to downside jump risk than that to normal market variation. The only risk aversion parameter cannot reconcile the premium implicit in deep OTM options with that in ATM options, and as a result, the implied volatility across moneyness is flat. This is inconsistent with the volatility smirk shown in previous studies. Thus, Bates (2008) argue that the representative agent shows different degrees of aversion to diffusive risk and market crash, so that he amplifies the agent's risk aversion to the rare event, and hence, disentangles the market price of the jump risk from that of the diffusive risk. Liu et al. (2005) suggest that the agent exhibits an extra layer of aversion toward the model uncertainty associated with the rare event, which is an addition to the standard risk aversion measure. Du (2011) adopts a time varying risk aversion induced by the habit formation of Campbell and Cochrane (1999) and Menzly et al. (2004). He finds that this setting amplifies consumption shocks, and as a result, the model is able to generate the excess volatility and a large jump risk premium which combine to produce pronounced volatility smirks. Another investigation for pricing options in the equilibrium framework is Benzoni et al. (2011), which is built on the long run risk model of Bansal and Yaron (2004) and the recursive utility of Epstein and Zin (1989). They specify the expected consumption growth rate to be driven by a persistent component (x) which is subject to the rare event. When the elasticity of intertemporal substitution is larger than one, a downward jump in x induces a stock market crash, and hence, results in a large premium implicit in OTM put options.

In contrast to previous studies, this book introduces the general equilibrium option pricing model based on a fanning preference. Allais (1953)'s experiment shows that people are not strictly risk averse to the tail event and their uncertainty choices depend on the extreme loss or gain of the lottery. This contradicts the independent axiom of the expected utility theory, and it is well known as *Allais Paradox*. To explain the Allais Paradox, Machina (1982, 1987) suggests that the indifference curves depart from the expected utility property of parallel straight lines in the direction of fanning out. The effect of fanning out reflects the extent to which an agent with the fanning preference deviates from the expected utility maximizer. Hess and Holthausen (1990) name it as eccentricity, and show that the risk premium is determined by both the risk aversion and the eccentricity. In the special case without fanning effect, the indifference curves are parallel and the model reduces to the conventional expected utility model.

With the equilibrium option pricing model, this book investigates the role of fanning preference in jump risk premium and variance risk premium. Specifically, both the jump and variance risk premiums can be decomposed into the component controlled by risk aversion parameter and that driven by the fanning effect. This separation can successfully explain the volatility smirk and also fit option data better than the conventional expected utility model. In addition, this book also tests the predictability of variance risk premium for future stock returns. Many studies find the predictive power of variance risk premium, e.g., Bollerslev et al. (2009), Bollerslev et al. (2013), Londono (2010), among many others. This book presents the international evidence and compares different variance risk premium measures.

1.2 Overview and Structure for the Book

This book is organized as follow:

Chapter 2 provides the general equilibrium option pricing model, in which the representative agent's risk preference is characterized by fanning preference. In equilibrium, the total equity risk premium is decomposed into diffusive risk premium, jump risk premium controlled by risk aversion, and additional jump risk premium driven by fanning effect. Similarly, the equilibrium variance risk premium also can be obtained. Lastly, in equilibrium, we can derive the option pricing model, in which the jump size distribution is general so that we can impose any distribution assumptions on it. The option pricing model degenerates to Naik and Lee (1990)'s model when the fanning preference is absent and reduces to Black and Scholes (1973)'s model without jump.

Chapter 3 numerically compares the difference between equilibrium option pricing model with those based on no arbitrage method. More specifically, the Monte Carlo simulation is applied to formulae of Ma (1992, 2006), Naik and Lee (1990), and Bates (1991), respectively in this chapter. In particular, Bates (1991)'s model is based on the no arbitrage pricing method and is used to compare with the general equilibrium option pricing model. In the Ma (1992, 2006)'s framework, the jump size can satisfy any distribution, e.g. log-normal distribution and uniform distribution. Mont Carlo experiment is also performed to emphasize the effect of different assumptions of jump size distributions on option prices. With the expected utility function, the Naik and Lee (1990)'s formula is tested in order to examine how the fanning preference affects the option prices.

Chapter 4 empirically compares the general equilibrium option pricing model and the model based on no arbitrage method. Specifically, based on the risk-neutral pricing rule, Bakshi et al. (1997)'s model with stochastic volatility is employed as the benchmark. For both models, the mean squared errors (MSE) estimation method is applied to FTSE-100 index options in order to compare their in-sample fits. The jump risk premium is hence extracted from the differences between the risk-neutral and the physical estimates, and the risk aversion is also estimated. On the other hand, the out-of-sample performance of these two types of pricing models is investigated by constructing the absolute and percentage pricing errors.

Chapter 5 shows the effect of fanning preference on the volatility smirks. In this chapter, we separate the jump risk premium into the component controlled by fanning effect and that driven by risk aversion. The former indeed plays an important role in generating pronounced volatility smirks. Specifically, in the absence of fanning effect, the equilibrium model reduces to Naik and Lee (1990)'s model and the generated volatility smirk is flat. This is inconsistent with empirical findings of Pan (2002) and Jackwerth and Rubinstein (1996). They find that the deep OTM option prices contain larger premiums than those implicit in ATM options, so that the implied volatility is skewed to left. However, incorporating the fanning preference is able to produce pronounced volatility smirks consistent with results of previous papers.

Chapter 6 analyzes the effect of jump size distribution on option pricing. In the conventional jump-diffusion process of Merton (1976) for equity returns dynamics, the pattern of jump size distribution is inherited by that of stock return distribution. In other words, if the log return of stock follows a normal distribution, the logarithm of jump size will be normally distributed as well. However, empirical findings show that the log return distribution for stock displays a high peak and asymmetric heavy tails. Consequently, the distribution for logarithm of jump size could also exhibit such an leptokurtic feature. This is inconsistent with the log-normal distribution assumed by Merton (1976). This chapter examines the volatility smirks and risk-neutral implied distribution of underlying returns, when normal and Laplace distributions are imposed on jump sizes, respectively.

Chapter 7 moves the research focus to the volatilities of index returns. This chapter calculates the realized volatility by summing the squared daily index returns, and then constructs the risk-neutral counterpart using FTSE-100 index options according to the discrete model-free measure of Jiang and Tian (2005). As a result, we obtain the volatility spreads defined as the difference between volatilities under risk-neutral measure and physical measure. Lastly, we estimate the volatility spreads via GMM and infers the estimates of risk aversion implicit in the volatility risk premium.

Chapter 8 shows the predictability of variance risk premium for future excess stock returns. Bollerslev et al. (2009) find the strong predictive power of variance risk premium at monthly and quarterly horizons. This chapter follows this idea and shows the Hong Kong evidence. The variance risk premium is constructed by the difference between realized variance and risk-neutral variance. According to the model-free method of Jiang and Tian (2005), the variance under risk-neutral measure can be obtained from 30-days ATM options. Then we test the predictability of variance risk premium for Hong Kong stock market returns.

Chapter 9 provides other international evidences of the predictability of variance risk premium. This chapter considers nine stock markets, including US, UK, France, Germany, Belgium, Netherlands, Switzerland, Euro zone, and Japan. The in-sample predictive regressions are used to test the forecasting ability. The variance risk premium is calculated according to Bollerslev et al. (2009) and Drechsler and Yaron (2011).

Chapter 10 compares the predictability of different variance risk premium measures for the international stock markets. The variance risk premium measure is defined as the difference between the expected future return variance under the risk-neutral and physical measures. According to Carr and Madan (1998) and Britten-Jones and Neuberger (2000), the model free implied variance (MFIV) can provide an unbiased empirical analog to the risk neutral expectation of total return variation. However, methods of constructing the expectation under the physical measure vary in empirical studies. Basically, according to the information used to construct the expected variance, they can be classified into two categories. One category is based on the realized variance. The other category is based on the past realized variance and the MFIV information. Therefore, this chapter compares total nine measures of variance risk premium and tests their predictability for excess stock market returns.

Finally, Chap. 11 concludes this book, and provides the possible future research directions.

Chapter 2
General Equilibrium Option Pricing Models

2.1 The Economy and Utility Functions

This section briefly introduces the market structure, the optimal choice problem, and the non-expected recursive utility in a continuous-time pure exchange economy.

Assume a filtered probability space $\{\Omega, \mathcal{F}, P\}$ with an increasing and right continuous filtration $\mathcal{F} = \{\mathcal{F}_t\}_{t\geq 0}$. In a pure exchange economy of Lucas (1978), there exists a single consumption good and, for simplicity, one state variable (x_t) which is determined by the following jump-diffusion process,

$$\mathrm{d}x_t = b(t, x_{t-})\mathrm{d}t + a(t, x_{t-})\mathrm{d}B_t + \int_{u\in R} k(t, x_{t-}, u)N(\mathrm{d}t,\ \mathrm{d}u)\ , \tag{2.1}$$

where x_0 is given, b and a are respectively the average growth rate and the constant diffusive volatility, B is the standard Brownian motion, and the Poisson random measure N is characterized by the jump intensity λ and a distribution Π for the logarithm of jump size u. When a rare event occurs at time t with size of u, the state variable jumps from x_{t-} to $x_t = x_{t-} + k(t, x_{t-}, u)$, and the effect on x_t of all possible jump sizes over the time interval $(t, t + \mathrm{d}t]$ is aggregated through the integral in Eq. (2.1). In such a setting, the economy has two independent sources of uncertainty, namely the standard Brownian motion and the random Poisson process.

There are $n + 1$ assets available for trading in the market at each point of time. Asset 0 is a risk free bond with interest rate $r_f(t, x_t)$, and assets 1 through n are risky with dividend rates $\delta^j(t, x_t)$, $j = 1, \ldots, n$. The interest rate and dividend rates are all expressed in units of the consumption good. The movement of the jth asset price is $\{x_t\}$-adapted, which solves the following SDE:

$$\begin{aligned}\mathrm{d}\, S_t^j &= [\nu^j(t, x_{t-}) + r_f(t, x_{t-}) - \delta^j(t, x_{t-})/S_{t-}^j]S_{t-}^j\ \mathrm{d}t +\\ &\quad \sigma^j(t, x_{t-})S_{t-}^j\mathrm{d}B_t + S_{t-}^j\int_{u\in R} \theta(t, x_{t-}, u)N(\mathrm{d}t,\ \mathrm{d}u)\ ,\end{aligned} \tag{2.2}$$

J. Chen, *General Equilibrium Option Pricing Method: Theoretical and Empirical Study*, https://doi.org/10.1007/978-981-10-7428-8_2

with S_0 given. ν^j, δ^j, and θ^j determine the compensation for future risk, the dividend rate, and the jump size for security j, respectively.

The representative agent is endowed with an initial positive wealth, $W_0 > 0$, and chooses a consumption and portfolio policy $\{(c_t, z_t)\}_{t\geq 0}$ to maximize his/her life-time utility subject to the flow budget constraint:

$$\begin{aligned} \mathrm{d}W_t = & [W_{t-}(\nu_{t-} \cdot z_{t-} + r_{ft-}) - c_{t-}]\mathrm{d}t + W_{t-}z_{t-} \cdot \sigma_{t-}\mathrm{d}B_t + \\ & W_{t-} \int_R z_{t-} \cdot \theta_{t-} N(\mathrm{d}t,\ \mathrm{d}u) \,, \end{aligned} \tag{2.3}$$

where W_t is the time t wealth. c_t and z_t represent the consumption and portfolios holding of risky assets at the time, respectively.

In this book, the representative agent's risk preference is of the continuous-time intertemporal recursive utility, which satisfies the following stochastic Koopmans equation in the presence of jump (see Duffie and Epstein 1992a, b for the case of Brownian information, and Ma 2000 for an extension to the jump-diffusion structure),

$$\begin{aligned} U_t = E_t \Bigg\{ \int_t^T \Bigg[& f(c_{s-}, U_{s-}) + \lambda \int_R [M(U_{s+}, U_{s-}) - U_{s+} + \\ & U_{s-}]\Pi(\mathrm{d}u) \Bigg] \mathrm{d}s + U_T \Bigg\} \,, \end{aligned} \tag{2.4}$$

where Π is the jump size distribution, λ is the jump intensity, and the pair of (f, M) is named as the utility generator which is an analogue of the discrete-time recursive utility of Epstein and Zin (1989).[1] In particular, f is a differential counterpart of the utility aggregator and M corresponds to a Gateaux derivative of the certainty equivalent.

With respect to the form of (f, M), Ma (2000, 2006) consider the betweenness generator studied by Chew (1989) and Dekel (1986). The homothetic betweenness function satisfies following conditions:

$$f(kc, k^\eta v) = k^\eta f(c, v) \,, \qquad M(x, y) = y\phi(\frac{x}{y}) \,, \tag{2.5}$$

where η and ϕ measure the representative agent's *local* and *global* risk aversions, respectively.

We further specifies the Duffie and Epstein (1992a, b)'s aggregator function and the weighted utility's certainty equivalent (see Epstein 1992; Epstein and Zin 2001). As a result, the pair of (f, M) in Eq. (2.5) is given by

[1] In fact, according to Ma (2011), Eq. (2.4) can be regarded as a limit of the Epstein and Zin's discrete-time version, when the time lag is close to zero.

$$f(c, v) = \frac{\beta\,[c^{\zeta} - (\eta v)^{\frac{\zeta}{\eta}}]}{\zeta\,(\eta v)^{\frac{\zeta}{\eta}-1}}\,, \qquad \phi(z) = \frac{\eta}{\eta - 2\varphi}[z^{1-\frac{\varphi}{\eta}} - z^{\frac{\varphi}{\eta}}] \quad \forall z > 0\,, \tag{2.6}$$

where ζ controls the elasticity of intertemporal substitution, β determines the subjective rate of time preference, and φ governs the shape of indifference curves, which characterizes the fanning effect in the sense of Machina (1982, 1987). Appendix A shows the detailed derivation of Eq. (2.6).

The setting for $f(c, v)$ in Eq. (2.6) is exactly the same as that of Liu et al. (2005) (see Eq. D.10 in p.157 of their paper), as both studies adopt the Duffie and Epstein (1992a, b)'s aggregator function. However, in contrast to their pure Brownian information, we use Ma (2000, 2006)'s mixed Brownian and Poisson structure given in Eq. (2.4). Evidently, the jump affects the representative agent's utility through the M function, which is excluded in the pure Brownian framework.

In the determinants of M function, coefficient φ controls the fanning direction of indifference curves. $\varphi < 0$ represents the indifference curves fan out, while $\varphi > 0$ indicates fan in. In the special case of $\varphi = 0$, the indifference curves are parallel and the utility generator (2.6) reduces to the conventional expected utility.

To highlight the conceptual significance of fanning characteristic for indifference curves, we take the common consequence effect of Allais Paradox for instance. The independent axiom of expected utility theory guarantees linear and parallel indifference curves, and $CE(x) = \Sigma p_i U(x_i)$. Consider the case of three potential outcomes (x_1, x_2, x_3) with associated probabilities (p_1, p_2, p_3). We can derive $p_1 = p_3 \frac{U(x_2)-U(x_3)}{U(x_1)-U(x_2)} + \frac{CE-U(x_2)}{U(x_1)-U(x_2)}$. Thus, in the Machina's triangle as depicted in the panel (a) of Fig. 2.1, the indifference curves are linear and parallel in probabilities. However, results of Allais (1953) violate the independent axiom.

More specifically, in Allais's experiment, the lotteries are described as follows:

$$\begin{aligned}
&\text{Set 1} : a_1 = (\$0m, 0; \$1m, 1; \$5m, 0), a_2 = (\$0m, 0.01; \$1m, 0.89; \$5m, 0.1);\\
&\text{Set 2} : a_3 = (\$0m, 0.89; \$1m, 0.11; \$5m, 0), a_4 = (\$0m, 0.9; \$1m, 0; \$5m, 0.1).
\end{aligned}$$

Plotting these outcomes in the panel (a) of Fig. 2.1, we can conclude that a preference for a_1 over a_2 and a_3 over a_4 should be derived according to the additive expected utility. But surprisingly, results show that people prefer a_1 to a_2 in the first set, and a_3 to a_4 in the second set. It implies a risk averse manner in set 1, but a weak risk aversion or even a risk prone attitude in set 2. This contradicts the independent axiom of expected utility theory, as people's decisions depend on the extreme loss of all money. It seems plausible that people weight the outcomes of extreme events differently in comparison to the normal events.

To explain the Allais Paradox, Machina (1982, 1987) suggest that the indifference curves display a fanning out pattern, as shown in the panel (b) of Fig. 2.1. Clearly, at the southeastern corner, the probabilities of extreme losses get large and the indifference curves become flatter than those exhibited in panel (a). As is known, flat indifference curves indicate a moderate degree of risk aversion to the extreme event.

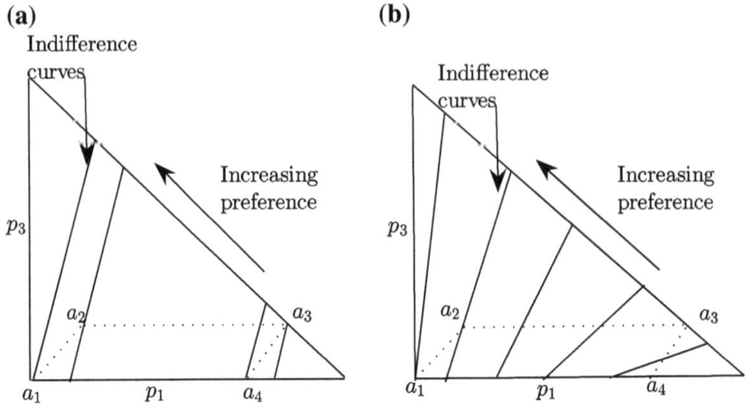

Fig. 2.1 Machina's probability triangle This figure plots the Machina's probability triangle. Panel **a** and **b** represent the case of expected utility and that of fanning out preference, respectively. a_1, a_2, a_3, and a_4 are the lotteries documented in the Allais Paradox. In each lottery, three outcomes (x_1, x_2, x_3) are associated with probabilities (p_1, p_2, p_3). Since $p_2 = 1 - p_1 - p_3$, Machina (1982) plots all outcomes in a probability triangle that is described only by the pair of probabilities (p_1, p_3)

To measure the agent's risk preference, we use the weighted utility's certainty equivalent, and $CE(x) = \frac{\Sigma p_i w(x_i) U(x_i)}{\Sigma p_i w(x_i)}$, in which $w(\cdot)$ is a weighting function and $w(x) = x^{\varphi}$ in our paper (see Epstein 1992; Epstein and Zin 2001). Clearly, in the numerator of the weighted utility's certainty equivalent, the probabilities are weighted by the weighting function, and the denominator normalizes *CE* by the expected weighting function.[2] When $\varphi \neq 0$, the indifference curves are nonparallel in probabilities. While, when $\varphi = 0$, the certainty equivalent of weighted utility degenerates to that of expected utility.

After clarify the utility function, we formulate the representative agent's optimal choice problem. Let J be the value function of the representative agent,

$$J(t, x, W) = \sup_{(c,z)} U_t. \tag{2.7}$$

According to Ma (2006), Eq. (2.7) satisfies the following Bellman equation,

$$\begin{aligned} 0 = \sup_{(c,z)} & \mathcal{A}J(t, x, W) + f(c, J(t, x, W)) \\ & + \lambda \int_R M(J(t, x_+, W_+), J(t, x, W)) \Pi(\mathrm{d}u) \end{aligned} \tag{2.8}$$

[2]Hess and Holthausen (1990) argue that the probability is weighted by the weighting function as though it has been distorted, and they further demonstrate that the distortion depends on the economic state. In the presence of rare event, this distortion has a significantly large impact on the agent's behavior, leading to a choice of the apparently very risky lottery.

with terminal condition $J(T, x, W) = 0$, where f and M correspond to the utility generator defined in Eq. (2.4), and $\mathcal{A}$ is the infinitesimal generator for (x, W) that is given by

$$\begin{aligned}\mathcal{A}J \equiv\ & J_t + J_x \cdot b + J_W[W(\nu \cdot z + r) - c] + \frac{1}{2}tr(\Sigma)\\ & +\lambda \int_R (J_+ - J)\Pi(\mathrm{d}u),\end{aligned} \tag{2.9}$$

in which

$$\Sigma \equiv \begin{bmatrix} a \\ Wz \cdot \sigma \end{bmatrix}^T \begin{bmatrix} J_{xx} & J_{xW} \\ J_{Wx} & J_{WW} \end{bmatrix} \begin{bmatrix} a \\ Wz \cdot \sigma \end{bmatrix} \tag{2.10}$$

and $J_+ \equiv J(t, x + k(t, x, u), W + Wz \cdot \theta(t, x, u))$.

2.2 Market Risk Premium

This section derives the market prices of risks, including total equity risk premium, jump risk premium, variance risk premium, and covariance risk premium. Consider that the representative agent in the exchange economy is endowed with one share of each risky security, and the aggregate dividend rate process (δ_t) is a geometric Lévy process that satisfies the following SDE:

$$\frac{\mathrm{d}\delta_t}{\delta_{t-}} = b\,\mathrm{d}t + a\,\mathrm{d}B_t + \int_0^\infty (u-1)\,N(\mathrm{d}t,\ \mathrm{d}u), \tag{2.11}$$

where b, a, B_t, and N are defined as in Eq. (2.1).

In equilibrium, the interest rate (r) and the dividend-equity ratio (ℓ) are determined by

$$r = b + \ell + (\eta - 1)a^2 + \lambda \int_0^\infty (u-1)u^{\eta-1}\phi'(u^\eta)\Pi(\mathrm{d}u), \tag{2.12}$$

$$\ell = \frac{f_c(1, k)}{\eta k}, \tag{2.13}$$

where k takes the same sign as η and solves

$$\frac{f(1,k)}{k} + b\eta + \eta(\eta - 1)a^2/2 + \lambda \int_0^\infty \phi(u^\eta)\Pi(\mathrm{d}u) = 0.$$

Here, we assume that there exists a real $s^* < -1$ such that, for all real $s^* < t \leq -1$, $\int_0^\infty \phi'(u^\eta)u^{\eta-t-1}\Pi(\mathrm{d}u)$ takes finite values.

According to Eqs. (2.12) and (2.13), the total market risk premium, denoted by π, is given by

$$\begin{aligned}\pi &= b + \ell - r + \lambda \int_0^\infty (u-1)\Pi(du) \\ &= (1-\eta)a^2 + \lambda \int_0^\infty (u-1)\Pi(du) - \lambda \int_0^\infty (u-1)u^{\eta-1}\phi'(u^\eta)\Pi(du)\,,\end{aligned} \tag{2.14}$$

in which, the term of $(1-\eta)a^2$ is the diffusive risk premium, denoted by π_D, and corresponds to the market risk premium when there is no jump in the economy. The difference between the two integrals in Eq. (2.14), denoted by π_J^*, represents a total jump risk premium, when there exists only two types of uncertainty in the economy: the diffusive risk and the jump risk.

In order to highlight the effect of fanning out preference on the jump risk, π_J^* can be decomposed into the Naik and Lee (1990)'s jump risk premium determined by the risk aversion exclusively and an extra jump risk premium driven by the fanning effect. For the purpose of distinguishing these two jump risk premiums, the former is denoted as π_J and the latter as π_F. This derivation is given in Appendix B. As a result, the total market premium is decomposed into three components: the diffusive risk premium, the Naik and Lee's jump risk premium, and an additional jump risk premium determined by the fanning effect,

$$\pi = \pi_D + \pi_J + \pi_F\,. \tag{2.15}$$

The first two premiums are measured by the risk aversion exclusively, and the last one is controlled by the fanning out preference.

Remarkably, incorporating the fanning effect can reconcile the high market risk premium implicit in options with a moderate degree of risk aversion. According to the pricing kernel puzzle, the agent is risk prone and exhibits a moderate risk averse manner when a crash arrived. The low degree of risk aversion results in a small amount of compensation paid for the jump risk, as indicated by the expected utility theory. However, the actual market risk premium is quite high in the presence of jump. To reconcile the high risk premium with a low degree of risk aversion, either the risk aversion measure is modified,[3] or the true probability distribution of uncertain economic states is adjusted to the agent's subjective view. In our model, the objective probability is weighted by a weighting function driven by the fanning effect. As a result, a portion of the total market risk premium is captured by the agent's fanning out preference.

In addition, in Eq. (2.14), $K = \int_0^\infty (u-1)\Pi(du)$ is the mean percentage jump size of the aggregate endowment, and λ is the jump intensity. Their risk-neutral counterparts are given by,

[3]Bates (2008) amplifies the risk aversion to the rare event, Liu et al. (2005) add an extra layer of aversion to the model uncertainty, Du (2011) uses a time varying risk aversion.

$$\widehat{\lambda} = \lambda \int_0^\infty u^{\eta-1}\phi'(u^\eta)\Pi(\mathrm{d}u)\,, \tag{2.16}$$

$$\widehat{K} = \frac{\int_0^\infty (u-1)u^{\eta-1}\phi'(u^\eta)\Pi(\mathrm{d}u)}{\int_0^\infty u^{\eta-1}\phi'(u^\eta)\Pi(\mathrm{d}u)} = \frac{u^{\eta-1}\phi'(u^\eta)\,K}{\int_0^\infty u^{\eta-1}\phi'(u^\eta)\Pi(\mathrm{d}u)}\,. \tag{2.17}$$

With the utility function defined in Eqs. (2.6), (2.16) and (2.17) can be solved,

$$\widehat{\lambda} = \lambda \frac{1}{\eta - 2\varphi}[(\eta-\varphi)g(\eta-\varphi-1) - \varphi g(\varphi-1)]\,, \tag{2.18}$$

$$\widehat{K} = \frac{(\eta-\varphi)[g(\eta-\varphi) - g(\eta-\varphi-1)] - \varphi[g(\varphi) - g(\varphi-1)]}{(\eta-\varphi)g(\eta-\varphi-1) - \varphi g(\varphi-1)}\,. \tag{2.19}$$

where $g(\cdot)$ is the moment generating function of jump size distribution (Π). Moreover, $K = g(1) - g(0)$.

In particular, when $\varphi = 0$, results in Eqs. (2.18) and (2.19) then degenerate to those of expected utility model,

$$\bar{\lambda} = \lambda\, g(\eta-1)\,, \qquad \bar{K} = \frac{g(\eta) - g(\eta-1)}{g(\eta-1)}\,, \tag{2.20}$$

in which $\bar{\lambda}$ and $\bar{K}$ are the counterparts of $\widehat{\lambda}$ and $\widehat{K}$ when the fanning effect (φ) is set to zero.

Next, the equilibrium variance risk premium is provided. According to Eq. (2.13), the time t equilibrium price for the aggregate equity is proportional to the aggregate dividend rate, $S_t = \ell^{-1}\delta_t$. In particular, S_t follows the same motion as δ_t except for the term of drift. Therefore, the underlying stock return is controlled by

$$\frac{\mathrm{d}S_t}{S_{t-}} = b'\,\mathrm{d}t + a\,\mathrm{d}B_t + \int_0^\infty (u-1)\,N(\mathrm{d}t,\ \mathrm{d}u)\,, \tag{2.21}$$

where S_0 is given, b' and a are respectively the average growth rate and the constant diffusive volatility, B is the standard Brownian motion, and the Poisson random measure N is characterized by the jump intensity λ and a distribution Π for the logarithm of jump size u.

Let $QV_{[t,\ t+1]}$ denote the quadratic variation of the log-price process over the $[t,\ t+1]$ time interval,

$$\begin{aligned} \mathrm{QV}_{[t,\ t+1]} &= \int_t^{t+1} (\mathrm{d}\ln R_s)^2\ \mathrm{d}s \\ &= \int_t^{t+1} a^2\,\mathrm{d}s + \int_t^{t+1}\int_R (\ln u)^2\ N(\mathrm{d}u,\ \mathrm{d}s)\,, \end{aligned} \tag{2.22}$$

where R_t is the stock return S_t/S_{t-1}, and $y = \ln(u)$ follows normal distribution.

The variance risk premium (VRP) is defined as the difference between the quadratic variation under physical measure P and that under the risk-neutral measure Q,

$$VRP_t = E_t^P(\mathrm{QV}_{[t,\,t+1]}) - E_t^Q(\mathrm{QV}_{[t,\,t+1]})\,. \tag{2.23}$$

According to the recursive utility, in equilibrium, the variance risk premium is determined by

$$\begin{aligned} VRP_t &= \int_t^{t+1}\int_R (\ln u)^2\, N(\mathrm{d}u,\ \mathrm{d}s) - \int_t^{t+1}\int_R (\ln u)^2\, N^Q(\mathrm{d}u,\ \mathrm{d}s) \\ &= \lambda \int_R (\ln u)^2\, \Pi(\mathrm{d}u) - \lambda \int_R (\ln u)^2 \phi'(u^\eta)\, u^{\eta-1}\, \Pi(\mathrm{d}u)\,. \end{aligned} \tag{2.24}$$

The solutions to the integrals in Eq. (2.24) are given in Appendix C.

Similarly, we can also obtain the equilibrium covariance risk premium, which is the market price for the covariance risk. Here, we only consider the covariance between individual equity with the aggregate market. Assume that the individual equity return is controlled by

$$\frac{\mathrm{d}S_j(t)}{S_j(t-)} = b_j'\,\mathrm{d}t + a_j\,\mathrm{d}B_t + \int_0^\infty (u_j - 1)\, N(\mathrm{d}t;\ \mathrm{d}u_i,\ \mathrm{d}u_m) \qquad j = i,\ m\,, \tag{2.25}$$

where $j = i,\ m$ represent the individual equity and market portfolio, respectively, $S_j(0)$ is given, b_j' and a_j are respectively the average growth rate and the constant diffusive volatility, B_t is the standard Brownian motion, and the Poisson random measure N is characterized by the jump intensity λ and a joint distribution $\Pi_{i,m}$ for the logarithm of jump size u_j.

The covariance between individual stock and market portfolio is given by

$$\mathrm{Cov}_{i,m} = \int_0^t a_m a_i\,\mathrm{d}s + \lambda \int_0^t \left\{\int\int_{R+} \ln u_m\, \ln u_i\, \Pi_{i,m}(\mathrm{d}u_i,\ \mathrm{d}u_m)\right\}\mathrm{d}s\,. \tag{2.26}$$

The covariance risk premium (*CRP*) is defined as

$$\begin{aligned} CRP &= \mathrm{E}_t^P\left[\mathrm{Cov}_{i,m}\right] - \mathrm{E}_t^Q\left[\mathrm{Cov}_{i,m}\right] \\ &= \lambda\Big\{\int\int_{R+} \ln u_m\, \ln u_i\, \Pi_{i,m}(\mathrm{d}u_i,\ \mathrm{d}u_m) - \\ &\qquad \int\int_{R+} \ln u_m\, \ln u_i\, \phi'(u_m^\eta)\, u_m^{\eta-1}\, \Pi_{i,m}(\mathrm{d}u_i,\ \mathrm{d}u_m)\Big\}\,. \end{aligned} \tag{2.27}$$

The solution to Eq. (2.27) is given in Appendix D.

2.3 Option Pricing Model

In this section, the equilibrium price for a European call option (C) written on the aggregate equity can also be obtained (see Ma 2006 for details),

$$C = Ke^{-r(T-t)}\mathcal{L}^{-1}\left\{\frac{\Theta^{T-t}(s)}{s(s+1)}\right\}\left(\ln\frac{K}{S}\right), \tag{2.28}$$

where K is the strike price, T is the maturity, r represents the risk-free interest rate, S is the underlying stock price, $\mathcal{L}^{-1}$ indicates the inverse bilateral Laplace operator, and $\Theta(\cdot)$ can be interpreted as the risk-neutral moment generating function for the distribution of aggregate equity returns at the maturity. In particular,

$$\begin{aligned}\ln\Theta(s) &= -[b+(\eta-1.5)a^2]s + 0.5a^2s^2 + \int_0^\infty (u^{-s}-1)\widehat{N}(\mathrm{d}t,\ \mathrm{d}u)\\ &= \ell s - (r-0.5a^2)s + 0.5a^2s^2 + \frac{\lambda}{\eta-2\varphi}\{(\eta-\varphi)\\ &\quad [g(\eta-\varphi-s-1) + sg(\eta-\varphi) - g(\eta-\varphi-1)\\ &\quad -sg(\eta-\varphi-1)] - \varphi[g(\varphi-s-1) + sg(\varphi)\\ &\quad -g(\varphi-1) - sg(\varphi-1)]\}\,,\end{aligned} \tag{2.29}$$

where $Re(s) \in (s^*, -1)$ for $s^* < -1$ is restricted to a vertical stripe in the complex plane, and $g(\cdot)$ is the moment generating function for the distribution (Π). In Eqs. (2.28) and (2.29), the distribution for logarithm of jump size is general and any assumption can be imposed, e.g. the commonly used normal distribution, and hence $g(x) = \exp\{\mu_J x + \frac{1}{2}x^2\sigma_J^2\}$, in which μ_J and σ_J are the average size and the standard deviation of normal distribution, respectively. In the absence of fanning effect, this pricing formula (2.28) reduces to that of Naik and Lee (1990). It can also generate a number of other option pricing models in the literature, under various particular specifications of the utility function and the underlying process, e.g., Black and Scholes (1973) and Cox and Ross (1976).

According to the models (2.28) and (2.29), we can compare the equilibrium option price process corresponding to the non-expected utility with that to the conventional expected utility. This is the so-called observational equivalence, which is initially advocated by Kocherlakota (1990).

Further to Kocherlakota (1990), Wang (1993), and Ma (1998)'s studies in a discrete time framework, this paper demonstrates that the non-expected recursive utility is observationally distinguishable from the additive expected utility function in pricing options in continuous time. Consider the additive expected utility generator with a constant discount rate $\hat{\beta}$ and a constant elasticity of intertemporal substitution $\hat{\eta}$.[4] Therefore, $f(c, v) = \frac{c^{\hat{\eta}}}{\hat{\eta}} - \hat{\beta}v$, and the corresponding option pricing is $\hat{C}_t(T, S, K)$

[4]In our utility generator (2.6), the elasticity of intertemporal substitution is controlled by ζ. In the special case of additive expected utility, $\varphi = 0$ as well as $\zeta = \eta$ (see Epstein 1992).

characterized by $(\hat{\beta}, \hat{\eta})$. On the other hand, $C_t(T, S, K)$ represents the counterpart for the non-expected recursive utility (η, ϕ).

Definiton An equilibrium option price process corresponding to a non-expected recursive utility generator (η, ϕ) is said to be replicated by specifying an additive expected utility function if there exists K and $(\hat{\beta}, \hat{\eta})$ such that $\hat{C}_t(T, S, K) = C_t(T, S, K)$. The non-expected recursive utility and the additive expected utility are said to be observationally equivalent, if any recursive utility generator is replicated by the additive expected utility function.

Denote y as the logarithm of random jump size, and the support of $\Pi(\cdot)$ as $supp\{\Pi(\cdot)\}$.

Theorem *Suppose that $\phi(x) \neq 1$ for all $x \neq 1$, and that $\Pi(\mathcal{R}_+) > 0$. Then, the equilibrium option price process generated by the non-expected utility generator (2.6) cannot be replicated by any specification of the additive expected utility functions, if and only if, either*

(i) $a^2 > 0$, or
(ii) $a^2 = 0$ and $\exists\, y_1, y_2 \in supp\{\Pi(\cdot)\}$ such that

$$\frac{\ln\phi'(e^{\eta y_1})}{y_1} \neq \frac{\ln\phi'(e^{\eta y_2})}{y_2}. \tag{2.30}$$

The proof is given in Appendix E. Clearly, according to the theorem, it is observational non-equivalent between the non-expected recursive utility and the additive expected utility in pricing options.

Remarkably, according to Eq. (E.3) in the Appendix E, the non-expected recursive utility can be replicated by the additive expected utility, when $\Pi(\mathcal{R}_+) = 0$, i.e., a pure Brownian motion. In other words, these two classes of utility are observationally equivalent, by setting $\hat{\eta} = \eta$ and $\hat{\beta} = Q(\eta - 1) + r$. This is the reason why Liu et al. (2005) find that the recursive utility generates the same market prices of risks as the expected utility, when they use Duffie and Epstein (1992a, b)'s pure Brownian structure.

$\Theta(\cdot)$ in Eq. (2.29) is the characteristic function for the instantaneous risk-neutral growth rate $\frac{1}{T}\left(\ln \widehat{S}_T - \ln S_0\right)$, we may refer it to be the risk-neutral moment generating function for the distribution of aggregate equity returns at the maturity. Appendix F provides a proof. Note, in Eq. (2.29), the assumption for jump size distribution is general and we can impose any forms of distribution on jump sizes. In the literature, Zhang et al. (2012) also consider a general setting on the jump size, which is a special case of our models (2.28) and (2.29) in the absence of fanning effect.

According to Eq. (2.29), we can obtain the risk-neutral skewness ($skew$) and kurtosis ($kurt$) of aggregate equity return distribution at the maturity, as follows

$$skew = \frac{\mathrm{E}[\widehat{S}_T - \mathrm{E}(\widehat{S}_T)]^3}{\{\mathrm{E}[\widehat{S}_T - \mathrm{E}(\widehat{S}_T)]^2\}^{3/2}} = \frac{\mathrm{E}(\widehat{S}_T^3) - 3\mathrm{E}(\widehat{S}_T)\,\mathrm{E}(\widehat{S}_T^2) + 2[\mathrm{E}(\widehat{S}_T)]^3}{\{\mathrm{E}(\widehat{S}_T^2) - [\mathrm{E}(\widehat{S}_T)]^2\}^{3/2}}$$
$$= \frac{\Theta(-3) - 3\Theta(-1)\,\Theta(-2) + 2[\Theta(-1)]^3}{\{\Theta(-2) - [\Theta(-1)]^2\}^{3/2}}\,, \tag{2.31}$$

$$kurt = \frac{\mathrm{E}[\widehat{S}_T - \mathrm{E}(\widehat{S}_T)]^4}{\{\mathrm{E}[\widehat{S}_T - \mathrm{E}(\widehat{S}_T)]^2\}^2}$$
$$= \frac{\mathrm{E}(\widehat{S}_T^4) - 4\mathrm{E}(\widehat{S}_T)\,\mathrm{E}(\widehat{S}_T^3) + 6[\mathrm{E}(\widehat{S}_T)]^2\,\mathrm{E}(\widehat{S}_T^2) - 3[\mathrm{E}(\widehat{S}_T)]^4}{\{\mathrm{E}(\widehat{S}_T^2) - [\mathrm{E}(\widehat{S}_T)]^2\}^2}$$
$$= \frac{\Theta(-4) - 4\Theta(-1)\,\Theta(-3) + 6[\Theta(-1)]^2\,\Theta(-2) - 3[\Theta(-1)]^4}{\{\Theta(-2) - [\Theta(-1)]^2\}^2}\,. \tag{2.32}$$

As demonstrated in Appendix G, the risk-neutral skewness and kurtosis of log return distribution for aggregate equity are proportional to the counterpart of jump size distribution. According to Eqs. (2.31) and (2.32), the risk-neutral skewness ($skew^*$) and kurtosis ($kurt^*$) of log return distribution are given by

$$skew^* = \Psi\, skew_u + \Lambda\,, \tag{2.33}$$
$$kurt^* = \Upsilon\, kurt_u + \Gamma\,, \tag{2.34}$$

where $skew_u$ and $kurt_u$ are risk-neutral skewness and kurtosis of jump size distribution, respectively, Ψ and Υ are the coefficients, and Λ and Γ, respectively, represent all remaining terms that affect the skewness and kurtosis of stock return distribution.

Bakshi et al. (2003) find that the slope of implied volatility is determined by the skewness and kurtosis of stock return distribution. Therefore, the jump size distribution also affects the volatility smirk.

Part II
Comparison Between Models

Chapter 3
Simulation Comparison

3.1 Introduction

In the presence of jumps, the financial market is no longer complete, and option payoffs cannot be replicated by a portfolio of primitive assets. The state price density and the pricing kernel are not unique. In order to price options in an incomplete market, either a candidate pricing kernel is used for the risk-neutral evaluation approach, or a general pricing framework built on the equilibrium exchange economy of Lucas (1978) is required.

Early effort to price options with jump risk starts from Merton (1976). He assumes the jump risk is diversifiable and uncorrelated with aggregate market returns, therefore the jump risk is not priced. The argument no longer holds when the underlying asset for the options is the market index itself. Jarrow and Rosenfeld (1984) reject the hypothesis of diversifiable jump risk. Applying the maximum likelihood estimation, they demonstrate that the market portfolio does contain a jump component and the jump risk should be priced.

To take into account of jump risk, various models have been developed. These include Ball and Torous (1983), Bates (1996, 2000), Cox and Ross (1976), Duffie et al. (2000), Merton (1976), to name a few. Different processes have been assumed to describe the jumps, including the variance-gamma jump model of Madan et al. (1998), the log stable model of Carr and Wu (2003), and the popular Lévy process of Carr and Wu (2004), Huang and Wu (2004), and Cont et al. (2004). By incorporating jumps into the asset price dynamics, these models can develop a multitude of volatility smile patterns observed in the market.

Along the line of risk-neutral evaluation approach, Bates (1991, 2000) and Bakshi et al. (1997) explicitly incorporate both volatility risk and jump risk under the risk-neutral measure. However, they make a simplifying and rather restrictive assumption that the premium for each risk factor is a constant proportion to the amount of risk. Adopting a more mathematical tool, Carr and Wu (2004) and Huang and Wu (2004) try to unify various stochastic volatility and jump-diffusion models via the use of time-changed Lévy process. More recently, empirical evidences from Pan (2002),

J. Chen, *General Equilibrium Option Pricing Method: Theoretical and Empirical Study*, https://doi.org/10.1007/978-981-10-7428-8_3

Eraker et al. (2003), and Eraker (2004) show that jumps take place not only in the underlying asset price dynamics but also in the volatility process.

On the other hand, to use a more flexible pricing framework, Naik and Lee (1990) (hereafter NL), Ma and Vetzal (1997) (hereafter MV), and Ma (1992, 2006) resort to the general equilibrium framework in which both the diffusion risk and the jump risk are priced, and the risk aversion parameters explicitly incorporated. Built upon an exchange economy of Lucas (1978), Ma (1992, 2006) assumes recursive utility in the presence of Lévy jumps, and solves for a general pricing formula. The recursive utility proposed by Epstein and Zin (1989) and Duffie and Epstein (1992a, b) allows a separation between the intertemporal substitution and the risk aversion, while the Lévy jumps are general enough that the jump frequency and the magnitude of jumps may follow any distribution with finite moments.

In the special case of lognormal jump sizes distribution, the general model of Ma (1992, 2006) reduces to that of Ma and Vetzal (1997), which still belongs to the family of equilibrium model. When the recursive utility takes the special form of expected utility function, it can further reduce to the framework of Naik and Lee (1990), who set up a fully stated equilibrium to price diffusion and jump risks in the index options market, and show that the risk premium is equal to the covariance of option payoff with the change in the marginal utility of equilibrium aggregate wealth.[1] The MV model also has a number of other well-known models as special cases. These include the Black-Scholes model when the underlying stock follows a pure diffusion process; the Merton (1976) model when restrictions on the preference parameters lead to a risk-neutral representative agent[2]; and the Cox and Ross (1976) model when the same restrictions on the preference parameters apply and the underlying price dynamics follows a pure jump process.

In this chapter, Monte Carlo simulations are applied to demonstrate the important difference that the jump risk in the risk-neutral measure and the jump risk in a fully stated equilibrium have on option prices. In particular, we make comparison in three aspects discussed below and we assume lognormal distribution for the jump size following MV (denoted MV(L)) in the first and second comparisons.

First, this chapter compares option prices from the equilibrium models of NL and MV(L) with those from the risk-neutral measure of Bates (1991) (hereafter BA). We find that, unlike the fully stated equilibrium framework, the risk-neutral measure can only capture mild risk aversion. It consistently overprices options when there is moderate or high level of risk aversion embedded in option prices. As a result, investors are only partially compensated for undertaking the risk.

Next, this chapter examines the effect that different utility functions have on option prices. We compare option prices from NL with expected utility and from MV(L) with recursive utility. The fanning parameter φ in MV(L) controls the shape of

[1] With S&P 500 index options, Santa-Clara and Yan (2010) come to a similar conclusion that the risk premium is a function of both the stochastic volatility and the jump intensity.

[2] There is a difference in that the jump risk priced in Merton's model is not priced because it is assumed to be diversifiable. Here it is not priced because the representative agent is risk-neutral given the restrictions on utility function.

indifference curve and results from non-expected utility certainty equivalent. When $\varphi < 0$, the indifference curve displays fanning out, which leads to a resolution to the well-known Allais paradox in experimental economics (see Epstein (1992) and Machina (1982)). When φ moves towards zero the fanning out effect is minimized. As a result, the recursive utility reduces to the expected utility and both NL and MV(L) give very similar option prices.

Finally, this chapter makes a comparison between the lognormal and the uniform distributions that jump sizes follow, according to the specifications of Ma and Vetzal (1997). The option prices are denoted as MV(L) and MV(U) when the jump size follows the lognormal and the uniform distribution, respectively. We find that when the standard deviation of the jump size distribution is small, the choice between the two makes little difference. However, if the standard deviation of jump sizes is large, employing uniform distribution leads to significantly higher option prices.

The rest of this chapter proceeds as follows. Section 3.2 discusses the theoretical relationship between risk-neutral and physical jumps in the context of pricing European options. Section 3.3 presents simulation results from four alternative option pricing models across time to maturity, strike prices, and level of risk aversion. Finally, Sect. 3.4 concludes this chapter.

3.2 Methodology

When the diffusive volatility is constant, the underlying asset return is controlled by

$$\frac{\mathrm{d}S_t}{S_{t-}} = \mu \,\mathrm{d}t + \sigma \,\mathrm{d}B_t + \int_0^{\infty} (u-1)\, N(\mathrm{d}t,\ \mathrm{d}u)\,, \tag{3.1}$$

where μ and σ are the average growth rate and the constant diffusive volatility, respectively, B_t is a standard Brownian motion, and N is a Poisson random measure that is characterized by a jump intensity λ and a distribution Π for the logarithm of jump size u. When a rare event occurs at time t with size of u, the stock return jumps from S_{t-} to $S_t = uS_{t-}$, and the effect on S_t of all possible jump sizes over the time interval $(t, t + \mathrm{d}t]$ is aggregated through the integral in Eq. (3.1). Consequently, the mean percentage jump is $K = \int_0^{\infty} (u-1)\,\Pi(\mathrm{d}u)$. In such a setting, the economy has two independent sources of uncertainty, namely the standard Brownian motion and the random Poisson process. Note, Eq. (3.1) is consistent with Eq. (2.25) in Chap. 2, and the only difference is the denotations for drift term and diffusive volatility in order to be in line with the literature.

The risk-neutral counterpart of Eq. (3.1) is given by

$$\frac{\mathrm{d}S_t}{S_{t-}} = (r - \ell - \lambda^{Q} K^{Q})\,\mathrm{d}t + \sigma \,\mathrm{d}B_t^{Q} + \int_0^{\infty} (u-1)\, N^{Q}(\mathrm{d}t,\ \mathrm{d}u)\,, \tag{3.2}$$

where r is the risk-free rate, ℓ is the dividend yield, Q represents the risk-neutral probability measure, B^Q is a standard Brownian motion, and N^Q is a Poisson process with intensity λ^Q and jump size distribution Π^Q.

Based on Eq. (3.2), the Bates (1991) pricing model for a European call option is given by

$$C_t(S_t, T, X) = \mathrm{e}^{-rT} \sum_{n=0}^{\infty} \left[\frac{\mathrm{e}^{\lambda^Q T} (\lambda^Q T)^n}{n!} \right] [S_t \, \mathrm{e}^{h(n)T} N(d_{1n}) - X \, N(d_{2n})] \quad (3.3)$$

where

$$h(n) = -\lambda^Q \mu_J^Q + \frac{n}{T} \ln(1 + \mu_J^Q)$$

$$d_{1n} = \frac{\ln(S_t/X) + h(n)T + \frac{1}{2}(\sigma_T^2 + n(\sigma_J^Q)^2)}{\sqrt{\sigma^2 T + n(\sigma_J^Q)^2}}$$

$$d_{2n} = d_1 n - \sqrt{\sigma^2 T + n(\sigma_J^Q)^2}$$

and μ_J^Q is the risk-neutral jump size mean and σ_J^Q is the risk-neutral standard deviation of jump size distribution.

For the general equilibrium option pricing model, Eq. (2.28) in Chap. 2 gives the details. In particular, when the fanning effect in recursive utility (2.6) is zero, our model reduces to the expected utility model,

$$f(c, v) = \frac{c^\gamma}{\gamma} - bv \,, \qquad \phi(z) = z - 1 \,, \quad (3.4)$$

where γ is the risk aversion parameter and equal to η in Eq. (2.6). As a result, our option pricing model degenerates to Naik and Lee (1990)'s model (see Ma (2007) for a proof). In addition, the option pricing model (2.28) imposes a general assumption on the jump size distribution. this chapter evaluates the performance of normal and uniform jump size distribution. Their moment generating functions ($g_U(x)$ and $g_N(x)$) are given by

$$g_U(x) = \frac{1}{x+1} \frac{\mathrm{e}^{U_H(x+1)} - \mathrm{e}^{U_L(x+1)}}{U_H - U_L} \quad (3.5)$$

$$g_N(x) = \exp\{\mu_J x + \frac{1}{2} x^2 \sigma_J^2\} \,, \quad (3.6)$$

where, U_H and U_L are the upper and lower bounds for uniform distribution; and μ_J and σ_J are the mean and standard deviation of normal distribution.

3.3 Simulations

In this section, we perform Monte Carlo simulation to demonstrate the differences that the following pairs have on option prices.

- the risk-neutral and physical jumps;
- the recursive utility function and the expected utility function;
- the lognormal and the uniform distributions for jump sizes.

We carry out 100,000 simulations in each exercise. We specify that the long-term, medium-term, and short-term options have two years, nine months, and three months to maturity, respectively.

The underlying stock price S_t follows a stochastic differential equation with random jumps which follow the lognormal distribution as in (3.1),

$$\frac{\mathrm{d}S_t}{S_t} = \alpha \,\mathrm{d}t + \sigma \,\mathrm{d}Z_t + \int_0^{\infty} (u - 1)\, \Pi(\mathrm{d}t,\ \mathrm{d}u).$$

The annual expected rate of return and volatility[3] for the stock are assumed to be 0.06 and 0.17, respectively. The riskless interest rate r is set at 3% with zero dividend yield for simplicity, mean jump size μ_J and the standard deviation of jump size σ_J are −0.05 and 0.07, respectively; and jump intensity is 0.5, indicating 1 jump every 2 years.

Figure 3.1 plots one simulation for the pure diffusion process and the jump-diffusion process over a 2-year period. The stock price starts at 3379 and ends at 3783.5 for the jump-diffusion process, and 4100 for the pure diffusion process due to a crash around time 0.3, roughly on the 110th day. The magnitude of this crash is approximately 263.8 points, 8.35% of the starting value.

3.3.1 *Risk-Neutral and Physical Jumps*

In Fig. 3.2 we apply the BA model with the risk-neutral jump, and the NL model with the physical jump. In addition to the parameter values mentioned, we specify the option strike price to be 3200, and the risk aversion parameter γ for NL to be 0.42.

Throughout the time series, option values from BA are clearly higher than those from NL, reflecting lower option returns and lower compensation for the jump risk. The price differences mainly come from four sources, all of which result directly from the differences between the risk-neutral and physical measures in pricing options. First, the expected return on the stock is the risk-free interest rate in the risk-neutral

[3]The continuous diffusion volatility is unchanged when moving from the risk-neutral measure to the physical measure. See for example Liu et al. (2007). For simplicity, the stochastic volatility is replaced by a constant volatility.

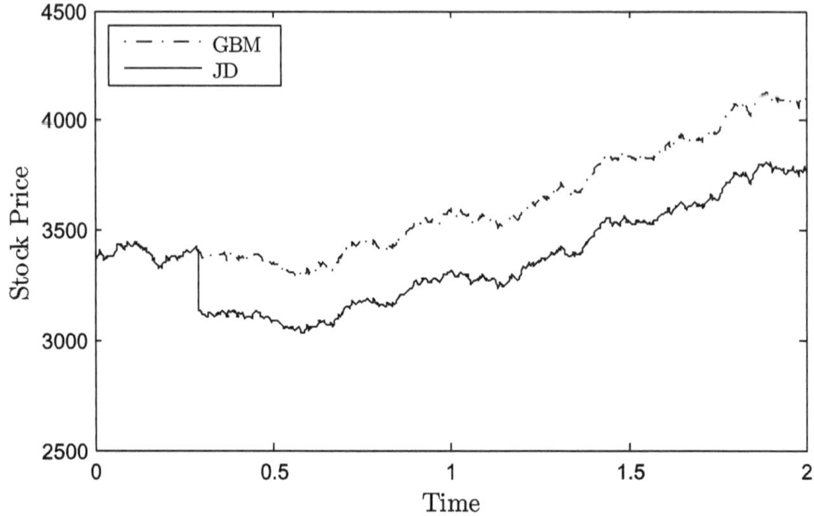

Fig. 3.1 Stock Processes With and Without Jumps. The drift and volatility of the geometric Brownian motion (GBM) and the jump-diffusion (JD) process are 0.03 and 0.17, respectively. For the jump-diffusion process, the jump intensity is 0.5, and the jump sizes follow lognormal distribution with mean −0.05 and volatility 0.07

measure, but incorporates risk premium in the physical measure; Second, investor's risk attitude plays a role. In NL, risk aversion is captured by γ and affects option prices when $\gamma \neq 1$; Third, the jump intensity is different as shown in (2.16); Fourth, the mean jump size is different as shown in (2.17). However, the divergence decreases as the time to maturity shortens. For three-month options, the difference between BA and NL is negligible. This is intuitive, as we expect the market risk dominates the jump risk when options are close to expiry.

The general equilibrium framework by Naik and Lee (1990) and Ma (1992, 2006) is considered to be more flexible because risk aversion parameter enters into the pricing formulae. This makes it easier to explicitly recover investors' risk preferences from the options market. The effect of investor's risk aversion on option prices is illustrated in Fig. 3.3.

All option prices in Fig. 3.3 are generated by NL across time to maturity and risk aversion. The values of 0.18, 0.42 and 0.84 for γ indicate strong, moderate, and mild risk aversion. Not surprisingly, the highest level of risk aversion correspond to the lowest option prices in each graph, and the effect is much less dominant for short-term options.

Calibrated option prices from BA and NL are also presented in Table 3.1 in the columns headed BA (column 1) and NL (columns 2–4). We report call option prices across a range of moneyness, time to maturity, and risk aversion levels. Under the header NL, the letters I, II, and III correspond to strong, moderate, and mild risk aversion when γ is 0.18, 0.42, and 0.84, respectively. For BA model, the option prices

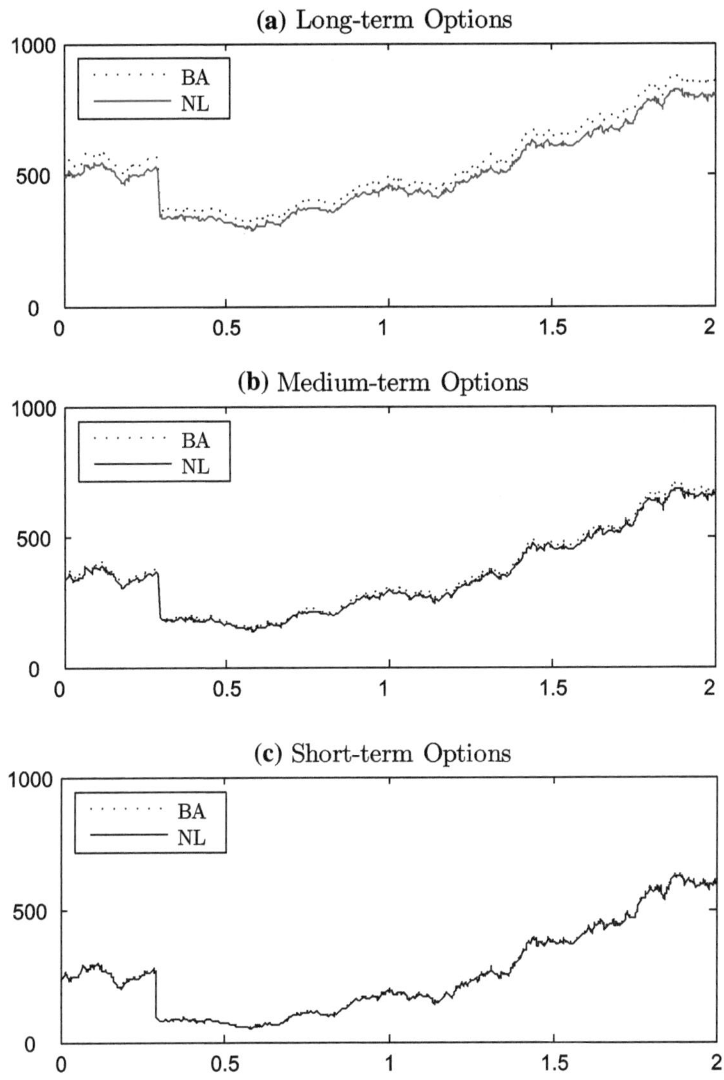

Fig. 3.2 Option Prices with Risk-neutral or Physical Jumps across Maturity Option prices come from the BA model with risk-neutral jumps and the NL model with physical jumps. For NL, risk aversion parameter γ is 0.42. The option strike is 3200

are lower than those from NL when there is mild jump risk aversion. This indicates that the BA model is unable to capture moderate to strong jump risk aversion even if this preference is embedded in the option prices.

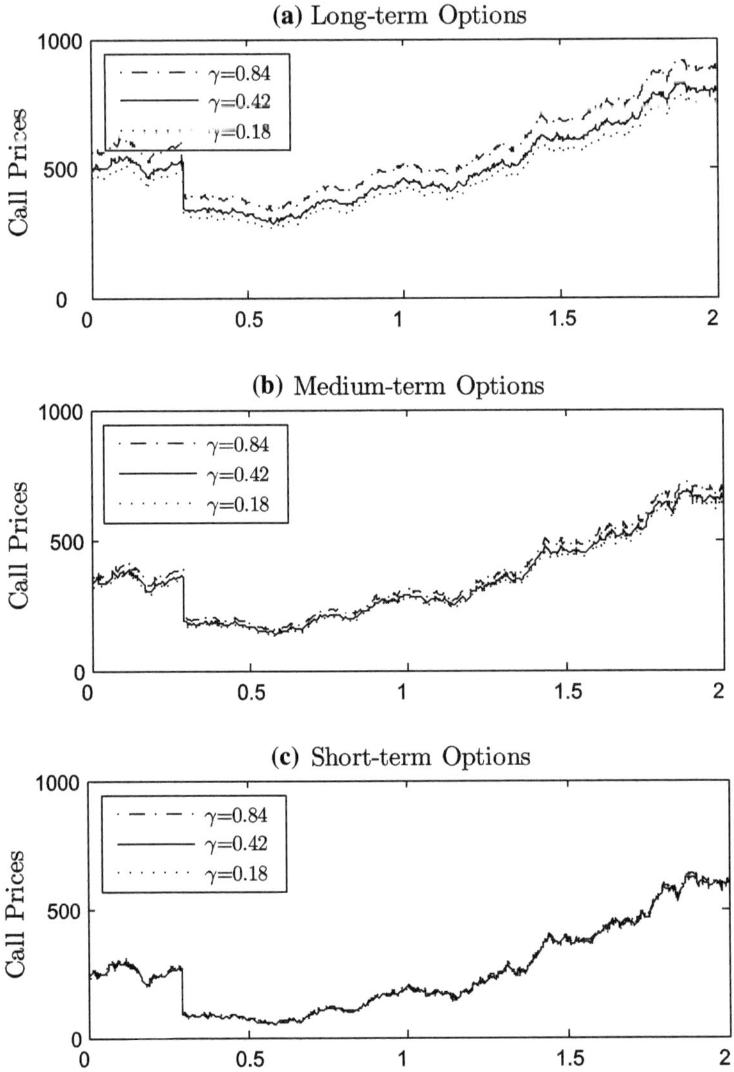

Fig. 3.3 Option Prices across Different Levels of Risk Aversion Option prices come from the NL model. The risk aversion parameter γ takes three different values, 0.18, 0.42, and 0.84 for strong, moderate and mild risk aversions

3.3.2 *Recursive and Expected Utility Functions*

Both NL and MV(L) models are special cases of the general pricing model (2.28), with the former assuming expected utility function while the latter recursive utility function. In the recursive utility function (2.6), $\eta \equiv \alpha + 2\varphi \leq 1$, α changes with η when φ is set to be -0.01 for fanning out.

Subsequently, the difference between the option prices from NL and MV(L) are determined by the value of φ. Ma and Vetzal (1997) illustrate that the effect of fanning φ on option prices is not significant when φ is close to zero, and option values increase sharply when φ moves away from zero in either direction.[4]

In Fig. 3.4, we keep η constant at a moderate risk aversion level of 0.42 and set the range for φ from -5.5 to 0 and from 0.43 to 5.5 so as to ensure $\frac{\alpha}{\varphi} < -1$ and $\alpha + 2\varphi \leq 1$. We value long-term ATM options when the strike price is 3400 and the underlying index is 3402.44. With the specified parameter values, option prices from NL are constant at 408.22 regardless of φ as φ does not enter into NL model. As demonstrated in Fig. 3.4, when φ is very close to 0, say at -0.01, the recursive utility function almost reduces to the expected utility function so that the curve of MV(L) prices is tangent to the horizontal line of NL prices. However, the price of MV(L) declines sharply when φ moves away from zero and the differences between NL and MV(L) increase. The pattern is the same for medium-term, short-term, ITM, or OTM options.

The pattern has also been tabulated in Table 3.1. Under the header of MV(L), there are three columns (5–7) of call option prices with different risk aversion when φ is equal to -0.01 and three columns (8–10) of prices when φ is equal to -2.50. We can see that regardless of the risk aversion levels, the prices from MV(L) when $\varphi = -0.01$ are the same to those estimated by NL to the second decimal point, reflecting the fact that the recursive utility is very close to the expected utility. When φ moves away from zero to -2.50, call prices from MV(L) are lower for the same time to maturity and risk aversion. It is worth noting that in the last six columns of Table 3.1 (columns 11–16), when the jump size follows uniform distribution, the same pattern holds. Option prices from the model when φ is equal to -2.50 are lower than those when φ is -0.01.

3.3.3 *Lognormal and Uniform Jump Size Distributions*

All option prices in Fig. 3.5 come from the NL model where the jump sizes follow either the lognormal distribution (MV(L)) or the uniform distribution (MV(U)) across different time to maturity, a range of risk aversion levels, and a range of standard deviation for jump sizes. The bounds U_H and U_L for the uniform jump sizes

---

[4]The impact of fanning φ shown here is opposite to the conclusion of Ma and Vetzal (1997) because we assume a negative jump while they assume a positive jump.

Table 3.1 Option Price Differences between Different Models

Moneyness	BA	NL			MV(L)						MV(U)					
	1	2	3	4	5	6	7	8	9	10	11	12	13	14	15	16
					$\varphi = -0.01$			$\varphi = -2.50$			$\varphi = -0.01$			$\varphi = -2.50$		
		I	II	III	I	II	III	I	II	III	I	II	III	I	II	III
Panel A: Long-term Options																
0.22	828.75	735.31	779.28	859.39	735.31	779.27	859.38	726.91	769.99	848.54	762.55	806.55	886.63	756.22	799.55	878.42
0.07	554.35	478.90	514.73	581.27	478.90	514.72	581.26	472.61	507.66	572.79	499.63	535.82	602.90	494.76	530.35	596.32
−0.05	347.82	292.23	318.87	369.45	292.23	318.87	369.44	287.96	314.00	363.42	306.51	333.65	385.04	303.13	329.78	380.25
−0.14	206.18	168.46	186.69	222.09	168.46	186.69	222.09	165.81	183.60	218.16	177.48	196.18	232.41	175.32	193.67	229.20
Panel B: Medium-term Options																
0.22	683.19	645.30	663.43	695.57	645.30	663.43	695.57	641.86	659.72	691.39	656.35	674.27	706.03	653.78	671.48	702.87
0.07	367.89	339.77	353.67	378.73	339.77	353.67	378.73	337.58	351.28	375.96	339.77	353.67	378.73	345.35	359.05	383.72
−0.05	159.18	143.18	151.34	166.39	143.18	151.34	166.39	142.16	150.21	165.04	146.71	154.91	170.02	145.87	153.97	168.90
−0.14	55.34	48.38	52.01	58.87	48.39	52.01	58.87	48.03	51.61	58.38	49.61	53.27	60.18	49.31	52.92	59.74
Panel C: Short-term Options																
0.22	625.23	611.59	618.12	629.54	611.59	618.12	629.54	610.32	616.76	628.04	615.61	622.01	633.23	614.66	621.00	632.10
0.07	264.30	254.52	259.59	268.57	254.52	259.59	268.56	253.85	258.87	267.75	256.87	261.90	270.79	256.33	261.32	270.13
−0.05	55.88	52.48	54.36	57.76	52.48	54.36	57.76	52.35	54.22	57.60	52.98	54.85	58.24	52.86	54.72	58.09
−0.14	5.14	4.65	4.91	5.39	4.65	4.91	5.39	4.65	4.91	5.39	4.62	4.87	5.35	4.61	4.86	5.33

it Note This table reports the calibrated option prices from three models: Bates (1991) (BA), Naik and Lee (1990) (NL), and Ma and Vetzal (1997) with log-normally distributed jump sizes (MV(L)) and uniformly distributed jump sizes (MV(U)) across moneyness, maturity, fanning and risk aversion. Long-/medium-/short-term options have 2 years/9 months/3 months before expiry. The underlying asset price is 3402. The letters I, II, and III correspond to strong, moderate and weak risk aversions at 0.18, 0.42, and 0.84, respectively

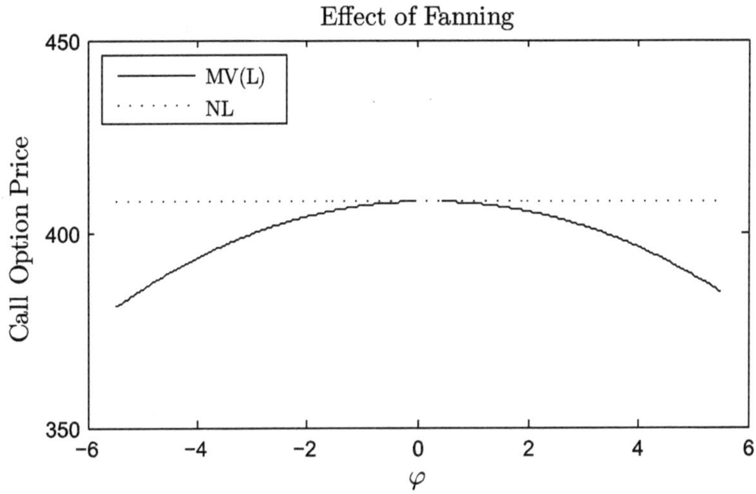

Fig. 3.4 Effect of Fanning on Option Prices The prices of long-term ATM option with strike price 3400 and underlying index level at 3402.44 are plotted when the fanning parameter φ is between −5.5–0, and between 0.43–5.5 using MV(L). For each value of φ, α is chosen to fix η at 0.42. The prices of the same option from NL are constant at 408.22 with changes of φ

distribution are set such that the uniform distribution has the same first and second moment as the lognormal distribution.

First, regardless of the distributional assumption for the jump sizes, higher level of risk aversion leads to lower option values, consistent with previous figures. When the standard deviation of the jump sizes σ_J is small in the region $[0.01, 0.1]$, option prices from the two models are fairly similar across risk aversion levels with the option prices from MV(U) slightly higher than those from MV(L). It implies that to choose either the lognormal or the uniform distribution for the jump size has little impact on option prices. However, when σ_J increases up to 0.4 the differences become very clear, especially for low level of risk aversion. For long-term options when η is equal to 1 and σ_J is equal to 0.4, the price from MV(L) is 824.52 while the price from MV(U) is 1,594.71, almost twice as much as that for MV(L). It shows that if there is high variation in the jump size, caution must be exercised to choose an appropriate distribution to model the jump size.

Simulation results are also reported in Table 3.1. For long-term deep ITM options with moderate risk aversion when $\varphi = -0.01$, option is valued at 779.27 for MV(L) (panel A column 6) but 806.55 for MV(U) (panel A column 12). The difference is greatly reduced for the same option with short-term maturity to 618.12 for MV(L) (panel C column 6) and 622.01 for MV(U) (panel C column 12). For OTM call options, the differences are even smaller.

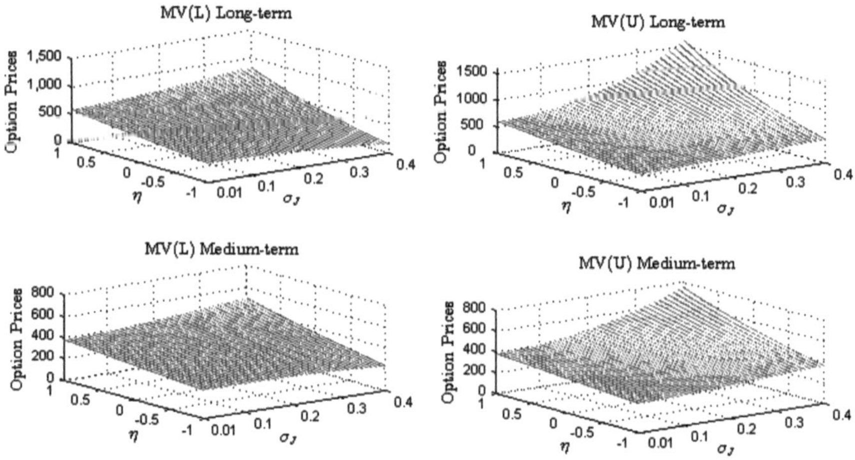

Fig. 3.5 Option Prices with Different Jump Size Distributions The option prices come from either MV(L) with lognormal jump size distribution or MV(U) with uniform jump size distribution, with η and σ_J denoting risk aversion and the volatility of the jump size distribution

3.4 Conclusions

This study uses Monte Carlo simulations to make a careful distinction between how jump risk enters into the option valuation models and how it affects option prices. In particular, in the risk-neutral framework jump risk premium is assumed to be a constant proportion of the risk factor in order to simplify modeling. In the more flexible general equilibrium models, a risk aversion parameter explicitly takes into account of jump risk.

Option prices are simulated over time along a number of lines. These include different time to maturity, moneyness, level of risk aversion, utility function assumed, and the underlying distribution for jump sizes, in order to highlight the effect of jump risk on option prices. Results show that when jump risk premium is assumed to be proportional to the risk factor itself in the risk-neutral measure, as in Bates (1991) and Bakshi et al. (1997), the model overprices options across board, and it is able to capture only a mild to moderate level of risk aversion embedded in option prices. Therefore investors are not fully rewarded for taking the risk. With a more flexible pricing model as Naik and Lee (1990) and Ma (1992, 2006), a risk aversion parameter enters into the model to account for the risk. In addition, using either the expected or the recursive utility function similarly reflects investor's aversion to jump risk when the fanning parameter φ is very close to zero. When φ moves away from zero, pricing model with expected utility tends to overprices options. Moreover, for jump sizes distribution the choice between the lognormal or the uniform distribution makes a big difference when the standard deviation of jump sizes is high. However, as time to expiry shortens, all the effects different choices mentioned above on option prices diminish as the aggregate market risk dominates option prices.

Chapter 4
Empirical Comparison

4.1 Introduction

To better explain the behavior of option prices across moneyness and maturities, many existing literatures incorporate both the stochastic volatility of Heston (1993) and the Poisson jump of Merton (1976). See for example, Bates (1996, 2000) and Bakshi et al. (1997). Huang and Wu (2004) and Carr and Wu (2004) further introduce a time-changed Lévy process that can be used to generate a wide class of jump-diffusion stochastic volatility models such as the variance-gamma jump model of Madan et al. (1998) and the log stable model of Carr and Wu (2003).

Despite specifying a variety of the underlying dynamics, these models are constructed under the risk-neutral probability measure. However, in the presence of jumps the additional sources of uncertainty including the random jump size, jump frequency, and jump timing make the market incomplete. Consequently, the state price density and the pricing kernel are not unique. Incorporating additional risk components in the underlying process, Pan (2002) and Santa-Clara and Yan (2010) price different market risks in terms of a candidate pricing kernel. In particular, following Bates (2000), Pan (2002) uses a pricing model that has a square-root process for the diffusive variance and jump intensity proportional to the diffusive variance. She finds a significant jump risk premium of roughly 3.5% per year and diffusive risk premium of 5.5% per year. Allowing the jump intensity to follow its own stochastic process, Santa-Clara and Yan (2010) further develop Pan's framework so as to extract the jump intensity process autonomously from the diffusive volatility process. Using more recent option data, they find an average ex ante premium of 11.8% that compensates the investor for the volatility and jump risks implicit in option prices.

An alternative approach to pricing options in the incomplete market is the preference-based equilibrium models, in which the state price density arises from the marginal rate of substitution evaluated at equilibrium consumption streams. Built upon a representative agent economy of Lucas (1978), Naik and Lee (1990) use the general equilibrium framework to price options on the market portfolio with

J. Chen, *General Equilibrium Option Pricing Method: Theoretical and Empirical Study*, https://doi.org/10.1007/978-981-10-7428-8_4

discontinuous returns. They show that the risk premium is equal to the covariance of option payoff with the change in the marginal utility of equilibrium aggregate wealth.[1]

Ma (1992, 2006) further generalize the model by assuming an intertemporal recursive utility function that describes individual preference over the life-time consumption streams and the Markovian uncertainty of state variables. In addition, he adopts the Lévy process to model the jumps. His option pricing formula is expressed in terms of the inverse Laplace transformation of a complex function $\Theta(\cdot)$, through which the preference parameters and other aggregate risk factors of the economy affecting the option prices are explicitly modeled.

In the special case of the jump size following lognormal distribution, the general model of Ma (1992, 2006) simplifies to the model in Ma and Vetzal (1997), which still belongs to the family of general equilibrium models. It can further reduce to the model in Naik and Lee (1990) when the recursive utility takes the special form of the expected utility. There also exists a number of other well-known models as special cases of Ma (1992, 2006). These include the Black-Scholes model when the underlying stock follows a pure diffusion process, the Merton (1976) model when certain restrictions on the preference parameters apply, and the Cox and Ross (1976) model with restrictions on the preference parameters and the underlying price dynamics being a pure jump process.

This chapter investigates the jump risk implicit in the FTSE-100 index options by comparing the general equilibrium model of Ma and Vetzal (1997) (MV) and the stochastic volatility model with jumps of Bakshi et al. (1997) (SVJ). As discussed above, MV model is based on a fully stated equilibrium framework and hence able to capture the full extent of the jump risk.[2] For the SVJ model that built upon the risk-neutral framework, the risk premium is assumed to be a constant proportion of the risk.

In the empirical estimation, daily FTSE-100 index options during the period from 3 January to 30 September, 2005 are used. When the mean squared errors (MSE) on each trading day between the theoretical option prices of MV or SVJ and the traded market prices are minimized, estimates of parameters can be obtained. Results show that the in-sample fitting error of the MV model is larger than that of the SVJ model for the medium- and the long-term options, probably due to the absence of the stochastic volatility factor. However, incorporating the jump risk enables the MV model to fit the short-dated options well with smaller MSE than that of the SVJ model. For longer-term options, the jumps extracted from the MV model occurs less frequently but with a larger size than the estimates from the SVJ model, indicating more significant market crashes. The parameters revealed by the SVJ model show that the jump intensity drops in magnitude across the time to expiry but the jump size is stable.

---

[1] With S&P 500 index options, Santa-Clara and Yan (2010) come to a similar conclusion that the risk premium is a function of both the stochastic volatility and the jump intensity.

[2] As we focus on the jump risk in this chapter, we assume for simplicity that the diffusion risk is not priced and the diffusive volatility is constant.

Next the out-of-sample forecasting exercise of the models is carried out. The parameters estimated on the previous trading day are used to forecast options prices for today and compare them with the corresponding traded option prices today. Daily data from 3rd October to 31st December, 2005 are used. Empirical results indicate that the SVJ model has lower absolute forecasting errors but the MV model has lower percentage pricing errors. Moreover, the implied volatilities across moneyness illustrate that the MV model better explains the short-term OTM call options while the SVJ model tends to underprice them. For near-the-money options, we also depict the implied volatilities across maturity and find that the MV model performs better than the SVJ model to price short-term options.

Finally, the jump risk premium can be extracted directly from the estimated parameters in the risk-neutral measure and the equilibrium framework. Results show that the jump-size uncertainty is significant in the short term and the jump intensity uncertainty dominates in the long term. Our estimates of the risk aversion coefficient is 1.829 in the short term, 1.361 in the medium term, and 2.243 in the long run.

The rest of this chapter is organized as follows: Sect. 4.2 outlines the theoretical relationship between the risk-neutral and the general equilibrium jumps in the context of pricing European options. Section 4.3 discusses data and the empirical results, including the in-sample fit, the out-of-sample performance, and the jump risk premium implicit in option prices. Finally, Sect. 4.4 concludes this chapter.

4.2 Option Pricing Models

In this chapter, two models are employed to characterize the stock return dynamics. One is the risk-neutral model of Bakshi et al. (1997) and the other is the general equilibrium model of Ma (1992, 2006). The risk-neutral probability measure builds on the theorem of no arbitrage and values all risky assets as if they are risk-free. On the other hand, the general equilibrium model is based on the individual risk preference and able to capture the risk aversion embedded in the asset prices. In the risk-neutral environment, the underlying non-dividend-paying stock price S_t is assumed to follow the stochastic jump diffusion process

$$\frac{\mathrm{d}S_t}{S_t} = \alpha^Q\,\mathrm{d}t + \sqrt{V_t}\,\mathrm{d}Z_s^Q + \int_0^\infty (u-1)\Pi^Q(\mathrm{d}t,\ \mathrm{d}u) \tag{4.1}$$

$$\mathrm{d}V_t = [\theta_v^Q - k_v^Q\,V_t]\,\mathrm{d}t + \sigma_v\sqrt{V_t}\,\mathrm{d}Z_v^Q \tag{4.2}$$

where Q refers to the risk-neutral probability measure; α^Q is the expected return conditional on jumps occurring and equal to $r - \lambda^Q\mu_J^Q$ in Bakshi et al. (1997); V_t is the diffusion component of the return variance conditional on no jump occurring; the risk-neutral jump distribution Π^Q is assumed to be lognormal with mean jump sizes μ_J^Q and jump intensity λ^Q; k_v^Q, θ_v^Q/k_v^Q, and σ_v are respectively the speed of mean reversion, the long-run mean, and variation coefficient of the risk-neutral diffusion volatility V_t; Z_s^Q and Z_v^Q are each a standard Brownian motion under Q with $\mathrm{Cov}_t[dZ_s^Q, dZ_v^Q] \equiv \rho dt$.

Based on the above parameterization, the risk-neutral return variance can be decomposed into two components, the diffusion variance V_t and the instantaneous jump variance V_J,

$$\frac{1}{dt}\mathrm{Var}_t\left(\frac{dS_t}{S_t}\right) = V_t + V_J \tag{4.3}$$

$$V_J = \lambda[\mu_J^2 + (e^{\sigma_J^2} - 1)(1 + \mu_J)^2] \tag{4.4}$$

In the risk-neutral framework, all systematic risks including the volatility risk, the diffusion risk, and the jump risk are internalized, and further assumed to earn a risk premium proportional to the risk factor itself in Bakshi et al. (1997) and Bates (1996). Building on the risk-neutral measure in Eqs. (4.1) and (4.2), the model of stochastic volatility with jumps (SVJ) is derived as follows in Bakshi et al. (1997),

$$C_t(S_t, T, X) = S_t P_1(T, S_t, r, V_t) - K\, e^{-rT} P_2(T, S_t, r, V_t) \tag{4.5}$$

where

$$P_j(T, S_t, r, V_t) = \frac{1}{2} + \frac{1}{\pi}\int_0^\infty \mathrm{Re}\left[\frac{e^{-i\phi\, ln(K)} f_j(T, S_t, r, V_t, \phi)}{i\phi}\right] d(\phi)$$

with the characteristic functions f_j $(j = 1, 2)$. Consequently, the risk-neutral probabilities P_1 and P_2 are derived from reverting the characteristic functions f_1 and f_2, respectively.

For the general equilibrium option pricing model, Eq. (2.28) in Chap. 2 gives the details. In particular, when the fanning effect in recursive utility (2.6) is zero, our model reduces to the expected utility model,

$$f(c, v) = \frac{c^\gamma}{\gamma} - bv\,, \qquad \phi(z) = z - 1\,, \tag{4.6}$$

where γ is the risk aversion parameter and equal to η in Eq. (2.6). As a result, our option pricing model degenerates to Naik and Lee (1990)'s model (see Ma (2007) for a proof). Assume that the jump sizes follow the log-normal distribution, the moment generating function for the corresponding normal distribution is as follows,

$$g(x) = \exp\left[\left(\ln(1 + \mu_J) - \frac{1}{2}\sigma_J^2\right)x + \frac{1}{2}\sigma_J^2 x^2\right]\,, \tag{4.7}$$

then Eq. (2.29) in Chap. 2 becomes

$$\begin{aligned}\ln \Theta^T(s) = {} & \ell\, s\, T - (r - 0.5\,\sigma^2)\, s\, T + 0.5\,\sigma^2 s^2\, T + \frac{\lambda\, T}{\alpha}\{(\alpha + \varphi)\\ & [g(\alpha + b - s - 1) + s\, g(\alpha + \varphi) - g(\alpha + \varphi - 1)\\ & - s\, g(\alpha + \varphi - 1)] - \varphi\,[g(\varphi - s - 1)\\ & + s\, g(\varphi) - g(\varphi - 1) - s\, g(\varphi - 1)]\}\end{aligned} \tag{4.8}$$

In the empirical investigation we use the FTSE-100 index futures as the underlying asset and treat index options as if they are written on the index futures. Hence the dividend price ratio ℓ is equal to 0 and Eq. (4.8) simplifies to

$$\begin{aligned}\ln \Theta^T(s) = {} & -(r - 0.5\,\sigma^2)\, s\, T + 0.5\,\sigma^2 s^2\, T + \frac{\lambda\, T}{\alpha}\{(\alpha + \varphi)\\ & [g(\alpha + b - s - 1) + s\, g(\alpha + \varphi) - g(\alpha + \varphi - 1)\\ & - s\, g(\alpha + \varphi - 1)] - \varphi\,[g(\varphi - s - 1)\\ & + s\, g(\varphi) - g(\varphi - 1) - s\, g(\varphi - 1)]\}\end{aligned} \tag{4.9}$$

As a result, the general equilibrium pricing model (2.28) becomes to

$$C(S_t, T, X) = X\, \mathrm{e}^{-rT} H\,, \tag{4.10}$$

where

$$H = \frac{1}{2\pi}\int_{-\infty}^{\infty} \mathrm{Re}\left[\frac{X\, \mathrm{e}^{x+iy}}{S_t(x+iy)(x+iy+1)}\Theta^T(x+iy)\right] \mathrm{d}y.$$

and $\Theta(s)$ is given by Eq. (4.9).

4.3 Data and Methodology

The data used in this study are European-style options and futures both written on the FTSE-100 index. They are traded on the London International Financial Futures and Options Exchange (LIFFE). The index options and index futures expire at the same time at 10:30 a.m. on the third Friday of the expiry month. The future price is equal to the underlying spot index when the option expire therefore the index options can be viewed as if they are written on the index futures. Hence the spot index itself and dividend payments are not needed.

Our sample period is from 3rd January to 31st December, 2005. Standard filter rules are applied to exclude infrequently traded options. First, the time to expiration is greater than seven days and less than 540 days. Second, the options whose prices are less than 0.5 are eliminated to mitigate microstructure problems. Third, only the out-of-money (OTM) options are employed for the empirical study as ITM options are less frequently traded. The moneyness is defined as $F/X - 1$ for call options and $1 - F/X$ for put options. Options that are 40% or more OTM are excluded as they have poor liquidity. In total, we have 60,642 options over 257 business days. Table 4.1 tabulates the summary statistics for the number and percentage of strikes across moneyness and maturity and the number of option strikes per day. On average, we have more put options than call options per day. In addition, more than 40% of the put options are more than 20% OTM across board compared to call options that are seldom more than 20% out of the money. The risk-free interest rates used in this study are Euro-Sterling rates obtained from the DataStream. We match interest rates and options that share the same maturity.

To examine the in-sample pricing accuracy and the out-of-sample forecasting performance of the models, we divide the data into two parts. The in-sample data is from 3rd January to 30th September, 2005. There are 44,397 traded option prices over 193 business days to estimate the structural parameters. The out-of-sample data is from 3rd October to 31st December, 2005. There are 16,247 traded option prices over 64 business days to test the forecasting ability of models.

In the empirical investigation, we minimize the mean squared errors (MSE) between the traded prices and theoretical option prices. The same loss function has been adopted by most existing literatures, including Bakshi et al. (1997), Bates (1996, 2000), and Huang and Wu (2004). The loss function is defined as

$$\mathrm{MSE}_t(\vartheta) \equiv \frac{1}{N_t}\sum_{i=1}^{N_t}(C_{it}(\vartheta) - \hat{C}_{it}(\vartheta))^2 \tag{4.11}$$

where ϑ is the vector of unknown parameters, c_{it} is the observed option prices on day t, $\hat{c}_{it}$ is the theoretical price determined by the SVJ option pricing model (4.5) or the MV model of (4.10), $i = 1, ..., N_t$, and N_t is the total number of options on

Table 4.1 Summary statistics for FTSE-100 options

	Short-term options		Medium-term options		Long-term options	
Moneyness	call	put	call	put	call	put
[−0.4, −0.3)	0 (0)	18 (20.45%)	0 (0)	18 (20.69%)	0 (0)	9 (20%)
[−0.3, −0.2)	0 (0)	21 (23.86%)	0 (0)	20 (22.99%)	6 (16.67%)	11 (24.44%)
[−0.2, −0.1)	20 (39.22%)	23 (26.14%)	24 (45.28%)	23 (26.44%)	15 (41.67%)	12 (26.67%)
[−0.1, 0)	31 (60.78%)	26 (29.55%)	29 (54.72%)	26 (29.88%)	15 (41.67%)	13 (28.89%)
Total	51 (100%)	88 (100%)	53 (100%)	87 (100%)	36 (100%)	45 (100%)
Strikes per day	12	27	16	27	12	15

Note There are 60,642 options over 257 business days in our sample from 3rd January to 31st December, 2005. Option strikes are categorized according to time to maturity and moneyness for both call and put contracts. The moneyness is defined as $F/K - 1$ for calls and $1 - F/K$ for puts. Short-term options have less than 90 days to maturity, medium-term between 90 and 270 days, and long-term between 270 and 540 days day t. As the underlying asset is the index future in this chapter, we replace the stock price S in the two pricing models by the future price F according to $S = Fe^{-rt}$. Since the difference between c_{it} and $\hat{c}_{it}$ is a function of the parameter vector ϑ to be estimated, minimizing the mean squared pricing errors provides us with an estimate of the implied model parameters.

4.4 Empirical Results

4.4.1 Parameter Estimates and In-Sample Fit

Parameter estimates of the Black–Scholes (BS) model, the stochastic volatility model with jumps (SVJ), and the equilibrium model of MV are presented in Table 4.2 for different maturities. It is clear that there are evident differences for the parameters among different maturities.

First, we look at the risk-neutral diffusion volatility. As the time to expiry increases, the speed of volatility mean reversion k_v^Q slows down. On the other hand, the variation coefficient σ_v exhibits an upward tendency. For parameters θ_v^Q and ρ they increase slightly from short-term options to medium-term options then drop for long-term options. Long-term options have the most negative correlation between the asset price process and the volatility process at -0.632. In addition, according to Heston (1993), the increase in the magnitude of σ_v over time is associated with a more leptokurtic return distribution, and the estimate for ρ at -0.632 for the long-term options indicates that the return distribution is more left-skewed than that for the medium- and short-term options. Part of the negative skewness and excess kurtosis are attributed to the jump component incorporated in the option pricing model.

Second, we examine the jump related parameters. The magnitude of jump intensity λ and volatility of the jump risk σ_J inferred from the SVJ model increase across maturity while the estimate of the mean jump size μ_J is rather stable between -15 and -14%. For the MV model, the estimates for the mean jump size μ_J and jump volatility σ_J increase in magnitude whereas the jump intensity λ decreases in magnitude across maturity.

According to Table 4.2, for the long-term options the jump implied by SVJ model may occur at a higher frequency with λ at 0.432 times per year, higher than 0.325 for the medium-term options and 0.132 for the short-term options. At the same time, the jump size is log-normally distributed with a relatively stable mean of -14.3% for long-term options, compared with -14.8% for medium-term options and -14.2% for short-term options. However, for the MV model the jump frequency increases from 0.132 in the long term to 0.245 in the medium term and 0.502 for the short-term options. The average jump magnitude decreases from -13.9% for long-term options to -11.3% for medium-term options, and dramatically to -6.6% for short-term options.

Table 4.2 Parameter estimation and in-sample fit

	Short-term Options			Medium-term Options			Long-term Options		
Parameters	BS	MV	SVJ	BS	MV	SVJ	BS	MV	SVJ
λ		0.502 (0.15)	0.132 (0.14)		0.245 (0.07)	0.325 (0.84)		0.132 (0.05)	0.432 (1.08)
μ_J		−0.066 (0.02)	−0.142 (0.07)		−0.113 (0.02)	−0.148 (0.12)		−0.139 (0.05)	−0.143 (0.11)
σ_J		0.067 (0.008)	0.061 (0.04)		0.107 (0.008)	0.126 (0.11)		0.156 (0.01)	0.174 (0.15)
$\sqrt{V_J}$		0.065 (0.01)	0.05 (0.02)		0.073 (0.01)	0.042 (0.02)		0.072 (0.02)	0.050 (0.03)
η		−0.829 (2.15)			−0.361 (1.58)			−1.243 (1.99)	
α		−3.037 (2.01)			−2.477 (1.41)			−2.789 (1.65)	
σ	0.098 (0.008)	0.076 (0.005)		0.108 (0.007)	0.078 (0.004)		0.121 (0.006)	0.077 (0.003)	
σ_v			0.286 (0.17)			0.373 (0.22)			0.383 (0.22)
θ_v			0.036 (0.03)			0.043 (0.03)			0.031 (0.02)
k_v			4.725 (3.95)			2.662 (2.99)			1.548 (2.11)
ρ			−0.473 (0.17)			−0.438 (0.42)			−0.632 (0.11)
V_t			0.095 (0.002)			0.089 (0.003)			0.100 (0.005)
MSE	27.52	1.25	1.60	169.51	11.50	3.59	869.79	21.14	7.82

Note BS stands for the Black-Scholes model, MV stands for the equilibrium model of Ma and Vetzal (1997), and SVJ stands for the stochastic volatility model with jumps of Bakshi et al. (1997). Short-term options have less than 90 days of maturity, medium-term options between 90 and 270 days, and long-term options between 270 and 540 days. Standard errors are reported in parentheses

As far as the MV model is concerned, the results indicate less frequent but more significant market crashes in the long-term option prices. For the SVJ model, the implicit market crashes for long-term options are as significant but more frequent. The instantaneous variance of the jump component V_J is calculated in Eq. (4.4). The average spot $\sqrt{V_J}$ for the MV model stays around 7% across the time to expiration, but its SVJ counterpart is much smaller around 5% and exhibits U-shape as the maturity extends from the short term to the long term. The time series of $\sqrt{V_J}$ for the MV and SVJ models are depicted in Fig. 4.2. Clearly, the instantaneous volatility fluctuates less under the MV model than under the SVJ model but the volatility stays at a lower level in the SVJ model. In comparison, the daily FTSE-100 index returns during the period from 3rd January to 30th September, 2005, are plotted in Fig. 4.1.

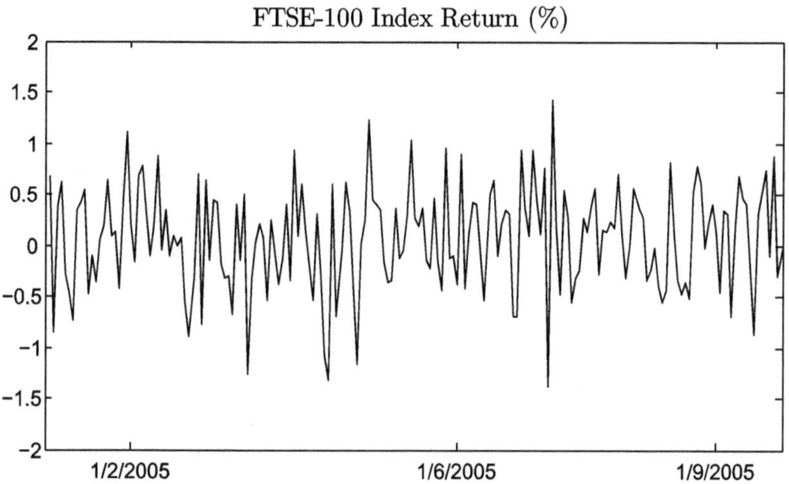

Fig. 4.1 Daily FTSE-100 index returns
Time series of the daily FTSE-100 index returns for the period from 3rd January to 30th September, 2005

Third, the in-sample MSE as defined in Eq. (4.11) is reported at the bottom of Table 4.2. Not surprisingly, the BS model has the largest MSE for all maturities. Due to the absence of the stochastic volatility factor, the MSE for the MV model is much larger than that of SVJ model for the medium- and long-term expiries. However, incorporating the jump risk enables the MV model to fit the short-dated options well with a smaller MSE. According to Heston (1993), Bakshi et al. (1997, 2000), and Bates (2000), the stochastic volatility primarily affects longer-term options whereas jump plays a more important part in pricing the short-dated options. Our results support this argument.

We also calculate the t-statistic for the estimates to gauge the statistical robustness of the two models following Huang and Wu (2004). The t-test is defined as

$$t\text{-statistic} = \frac{\overline{\text{MSE}}_i - \overline{\text{MSE}}_j}{\text{stdev}(\overline{\text{MSE}}_i - \overline{\text{MSE}}_j)} \tag{4.12}$$

where the overline on MSE denotes the sample average and stdev$(\cdot)$ denotes the standard error of the sample. The t-statistic for the SVJ model against the MV model for the short-, medium-, and long-term options are respectively 0.269, -1.446, and -1.052. Hence it is difficult to conclude which model performs significantly better at the 90% significance level.

In Fig. 4.3, we plot the BS spot volatilities and the dynamics of the MSE implied by the BS model, the SVJ model, and the MV model. As illustrated, the BS implied volatilities are more volatile for the short-term options than for the long-term options. There appears to be an upward jump with a magnitude of 3.58% in April, 2005.

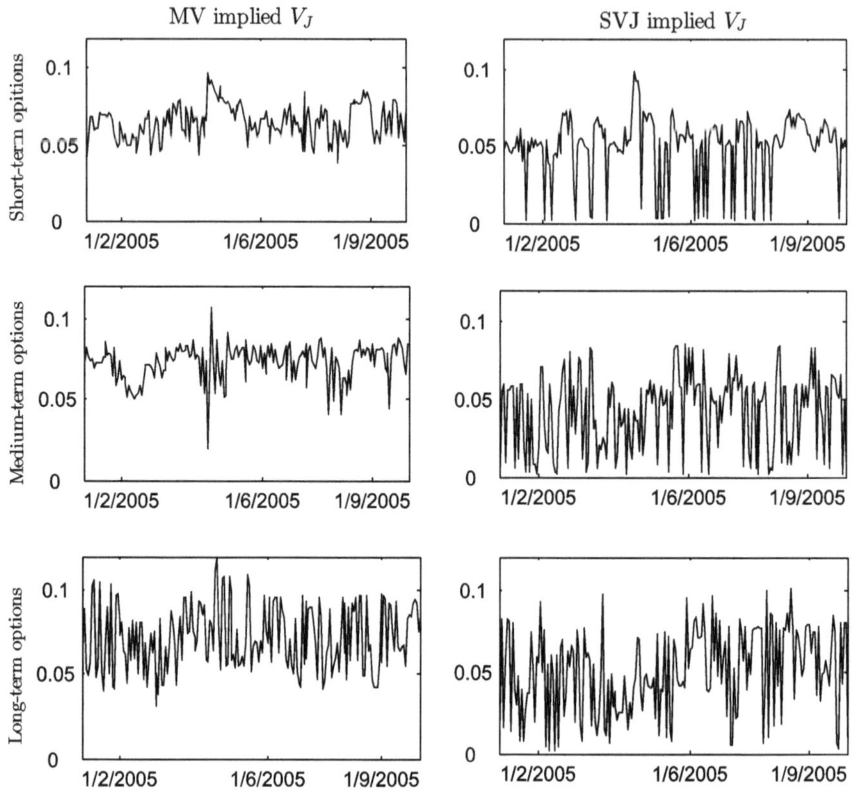

Fig. 4.2 Instantaneous St.d. for jump component
The standard deviation (st.d.) for the jump component is determined by Eq. (4.4). Parameter estimates are reported in Table 4.2

However, the jump size falls to 2.07% for the medium-term options and further to 1.06% for the long-term options. The existence of jumps in the stochastic volatility process has also been found in Pan (2002)'s heteroskedasticity-corrected test results. In particular, Eraker (2004) finds these volatility jumps with a positive mean jump size of 1.5 for short-dated S&P 500 options from 1st January, 1987 to 31st December, 1990.

4.4.2 *Out-of-Sample Performance*

Following Bakshi et al. (1997), the out-of sample performance for each model is examined in terms of both the absolute pricing error and the percentage pricing error. The absolute pricing error is the daily average of the absolute difference between the observed price and the model implied price calculated using the parameters

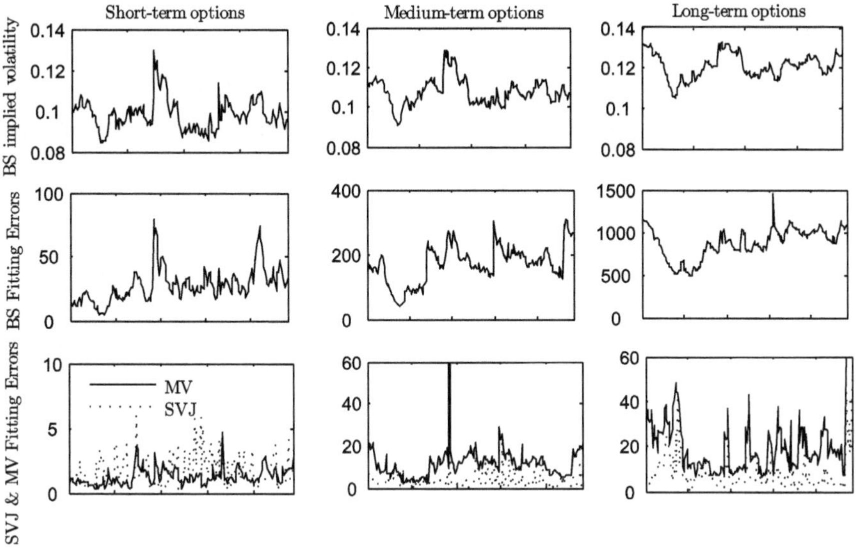

Fig. 4.3 Dynamic in-sample pricing errors
The dynamic in-sample pricing errors for the BS, the MV, and the SVJ models and the option implied volatilities are plotted across different time to maturity

Table 4.3 Out-of-sample forecasting performance

Short-term options			Medium-term options			Long-term options		
BS	MV	SVJ	BS	MV	SVJ	BS	MV	SVJ
Panel A. Average absolute pricing errors								
5.014	1.810	1.425	14.284	3.533	2.185	32.247	4.313	3.421
(4.39)	(1.91)	(1.56)	(9.10)	(3.29)	(2.85)	(14.47)	(3.75)	(3.42)
Panel B. Average percentage pricing errors								
−0.242	0.014	−0.029	−0.536	−0.046	−0.054	−0.388	−0.013	−0.029
(0.64)	(0.21)	(0.45)	(1.52)	(0.31)	(0.34)	(0.90)	(0.08)	(0.14)

Note the absolute pricing error is the absolute difference between the market price and the model implied price calculated using the parameters estimated in the previous day. The percentage pricing error is the difference between the market price and the model implied price, divided by the market prices. The standard errors are reported in parentheses

estimated from the previous day. The percentage pricing error is the daily average of the difference between the market price and the model implied price, divided by the market price. Results for each model are reported in Table 4.3.

In panel A, according to the absolute pricing error measure the SVJ model ranks first, followed by the MV model and the BS model. For each model, because long-dated options are more expensive, the absolute pricing errors are largest for the long-term options. In panel B, the daily average percentage error measure indicates that, except for the MV model for the short-term options, all the models on

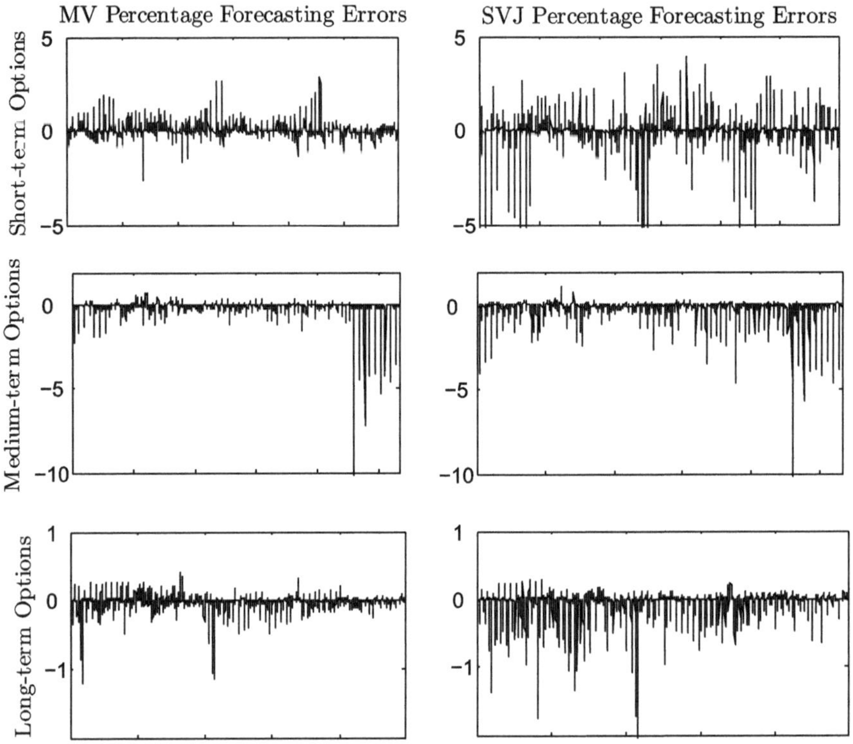

Fig. 4.4 Percentage forecasting errors across maturities
The out-of-sample percentage forecasting errors of the MV and the SVJ models are plotted for short-, medium-, and long-term options

average underprice OTM options with negative relative pricing errors. The MV model performs best with the smallest percentage errors across the time to expiry.

In Fig. 4.4, we plot the daily percentage pricing errors for the two models across three maturities. A close examination of the time series of percentage pricing errors reveal that the forecasting errors by the MV model fluctuate more frequently across the X-axis and distribute more symmetrically on both sides of zero than the SVJ model whose percentage forecasting errors are always negative.

Following Pan (2002) we are going to examine the implied volatilities on a trading day when the volatility is high, a trading day when the volatility is low, and a trading day when the volatility is at a medium level. In Fig. 4.5, we plot the implied volatilities from short-, medium-, and long-term options on three such trading days, 3rd October, 19th October, and 16th November when the volatility level is low, high, and medium. The option implied volatilities are plotted along side those derived from the forecasted prices by the SVJ model and the MV model. Incorporating the jump risk allows the MV model to capture the volatility smile for short-term options, while for medium- and long-term options the SVJ model does a better job in pricing the cross section

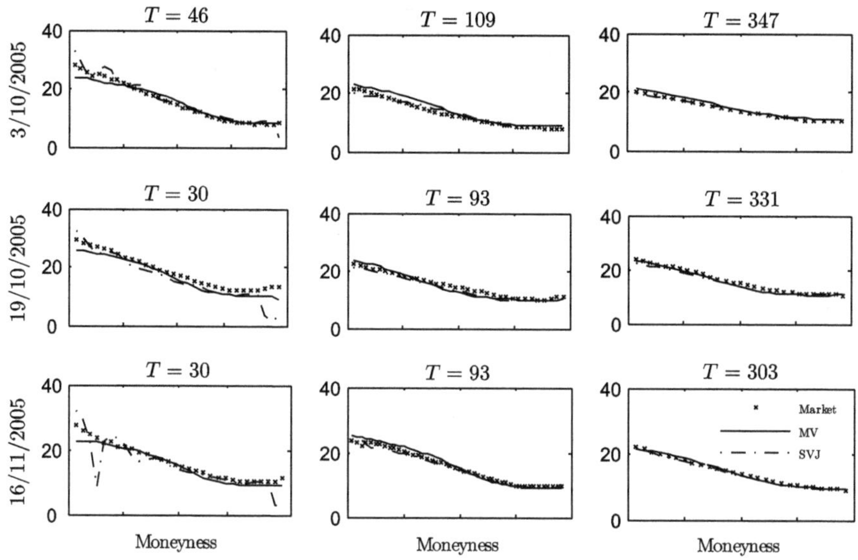

Fig. 4.5 Option implied and fitted volatilities across moneyness
The option implied and the fitted volatilities are plotted on 3rd October, 19th October, and 16th November, 2005, which exhibit low, high, and medium volatility levels, respectively. On each day, the fitted volatilities are derived from the SVJ model and the MV model

of options with both the stochastic volatility and jump factors. However, the SVJ model severely underprices the deep out-of-money calls that are close to maturity. The undervaluation is severe when the market implied volatilities are at a high or medium level. In contrast, the MV model fits the smile curve of those short-term calls better, although it still underprices them when the volatilities are at high or medium level. In addition, the MV model appears to underprice the deep out-of-money puts in the short term and overprices those options in the medium term.

Our investigation shows that the SVJ model is able to explain the medium- and long-term options across moneyness. But for short-term options, the MV model evidently performs better. This can also been seen in Fig. 4.6, in which we depict the near-the-money options with increasing time to maturity. The fitted volatility curve implied by the MV model is closer to the market volatilities of short-term options whereas the SVJ model overprices options with less than five months to maturity but better explains options with longer term to expiration.

4.4.3 Jump Risk Premium

In this section, we investigate the jump risk premium embedded in the option prices. The risk premium for the jump timing risk and the jump size uncertainty are measured

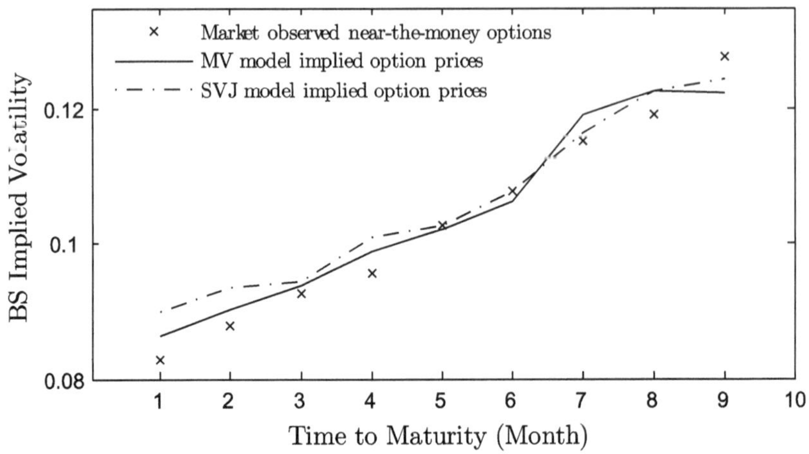

Fig. 4.6 Market and fitted implied volatilities across maturity
The implied volatilities are inferred from near-the-money option prices across different time to maturity on 3rd October, 2005

Table 4.4 Jump risk premium

	Short term	Medium term	Long term
λ^Q/λ	0.268 (0.27)	1.450 (4.13)	3.892 (10.37)
$\mu_J^Q - \mu_J$	−7.55% (0.07)	−3.56% (0.12)	−0.39% (0.12)

Note the jump risk premium for the jump-timing and jump-size uncertainties are measured by λ^Q/λ and $\mu_J^Q - \mu_J$, respectively. Standard errors are reported in the parentheses

by the difference between the risk-neutral parameters and their physical counterparts. In specific, the premium for the jump timing risk is obtained by λ^Q/λ and the premium of the jump size risk is estimated by $\mu_J^Q - \mu_J$. The risk premium estimates, which are obtained from the parameters tabulated in Table 4.2, are reported in Table 4.4.

We find that $\lambda^Q < \lambda$ in the short term, which is consistent with the finding of Pan (2002). She attributes the result to the existence of different types of jumps coexisting in the short-term data. For medium- and long-term options, the jump-timing risk premium is 1.45 and 3.89, respectively. Meanwhile, the jump size risk premium is significant in the short term at −7.55%. Pan (2002) finds −17.6%, but the result artificially absorbs all jump risk premium as she assumes $\lambda^Q = \lambda$. Santa-Clara and Yan (2010) obtain −2.1% for the jump risk by imposing a risk aversion parameter of 2 for the representative agent. The jump size risk premium implicit in the medium- and long-term options drop to −3.56 and −0.39%, respectively.

Figure 4.7 illustrates the difference between the physical and the risk-neutral jump sizes distributions. Clearly, the difference decreases as option time to maturity increases.

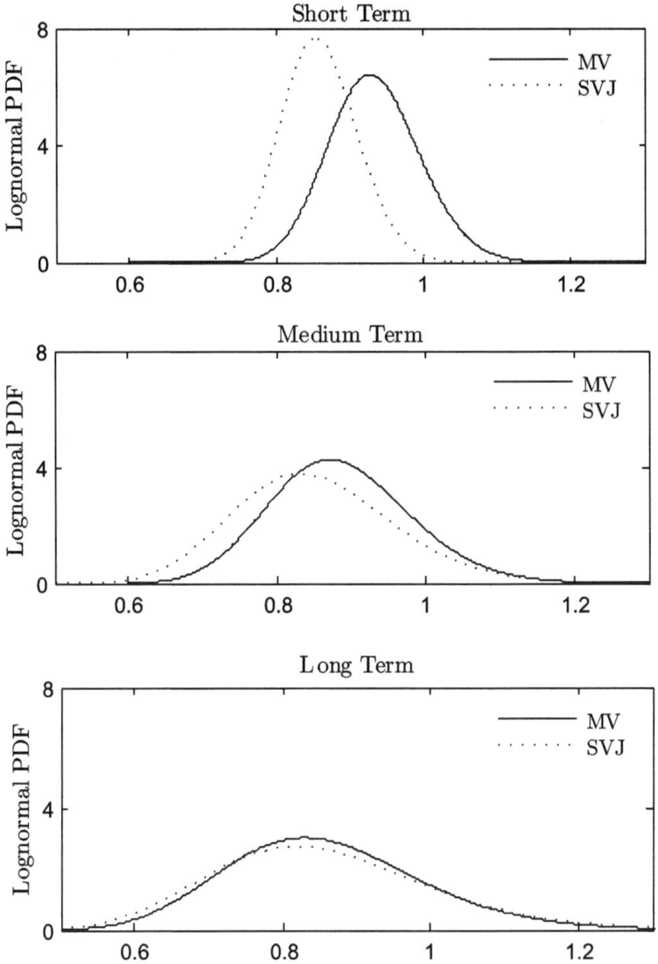

Fig. 4.7 Jump size distributions
The jump size distributions inferred from short-, medium-, and long-term options are plotted. The mean and standard deviation of the distributions are reported in Table 4.2

We also obtain an estimate for the jump risk aversion parameter. According to estimates of η in table 2, the local risk aversion measured by $1 - \eta$ is 1.829, 1.361, and 2.243 for short-, medium-, and long-term options, respectively. It is clear that the risk aversion under the medium-term is the smallest. This relates to the jump risk premia reported in Table 4.4. For the short-term options, the jump size risk is significant at -7.55% whereas for the long-term options, the jump timing risk premium is significant at 3.892. For the medium-term options, neither is significant, leading to the risk measure of 1.361.

Moreover, the risk aversion coefficient η is jointly determined by two parameters α and φ, and $\eta \equiv \alpha + 2\varphi$. Therefore, the estimate of parameter φ is equal to 1.104, 1.058, and 0.773 for short-, medium-, and long-term options, respectively. The positive coefficients indicate the fanning-in in the indifference curves. The increasing time to expiry coupled with decreasing magnitude of φ indicates that the indifference curves within the context of Marschak-Machina (M-M) triangle tend to be parallel.

4.5 Conclusions

This chapter examines the jump risk implicit in the FTSE-100 index options by comparing the in-sample and out-of-sample performances between the stochastic volatility model with jumps (SVJ) of Bakshi et al. (1997) and the fully specified equilibrium model of Ma and Vetzal (1997) (MV) and inferring the risk aversion from option prices across different time to maturity.

In particular, we minimize the mean squared error (MSE) to estimate the unknown parameters in the SVJ and the MV models. We obtain the jump risk premium from the differences between the risk-neutral and the physical jump coefficients. We measure the forecasting performance using the absolute and percentage pricing errors which are constructed by utilizing the parameter estimates of the previous day. Empirical results show that when the jump risk premium is assumed to be proportional to the risk factor itself in the risk-neutral measure, the SVJ model overprices the short-term near-the-money options and underprices the short-term deep OTM call options. Allowing individual utility function to capture the jump risk, the MV model performs better to price short-dated options. In the absence of the stochastic volatility to capture the diffusive risks, however, the MV model overprices the long-term options.

Part III
Jump Risk Premium

Chapter 5
Fanning Out Preference and Option Pricing

5.1 Introduction

As is well known, the major critique on Black-Scholes model is its failure to explain the volatility smirk observed in the real financial market. To better price the cross-sectional index options, a vast literature suggests more general models incorporating the stochastic volatility and the jump (see, for example, (Bates 1996, 2000; Bakshi et al. 1997; Pan 2002; Huang and Wu 2004; Carr and Wu 2004; Santa-Clara and Yan 2010)). These previous papers, however, price options under a partial equilibrium framework and assume an underlying return dynamics given exogenously.

Alternatively, Naik and Lee (1990) propose a general equilibrium model based on the pure exchange economy of Lucas (1978). They derive the equilibrium option price when the representative agent maximizes his/her expected utility of lifetime consumption. However, Liu et al. (2005) find that this model fails to generate the pronounced volatility smirk consistent with the post-1987 evidence on S&P500 index options. Results show that the only constant risk aversion can not differentiate the representative agent's risk attitudes toward the diffusive uncertainty and the rare event.

This chapter also explores the equilibrium model in the aspect of pricing the cross-sectional index options. In contrast to Naik and Lee (1990)'s expected utility model, we use the non-expected recursive utility that displays the characteristics of Machina (1982)'s fanning out preference. This setting is motivated by the *Allais Paradox* and a number of evidences on the option market.

First, Allais (1953)'s experiment shows that people are not strictly risk averse to the tail event and their uncertainty choices depend on the extreme loss or gain of the lottery. This contradicts the independent axiom of the expected utility theory. To explain this phenomenon, (Machina 1982, 1987) suggests that the indifference curves depart from the expected utility property of parallel straight lines in the direction of fanning out. Thereafter, non-expected utilities showing the fanning out characteristic are developed, e.g., the weighted utility of Chew and MacCrimmon (1979a), Chew and MacCrimmon (1979b), Chew (1983), the rank dependent utility of Quiggin

J. Chen, *General Equilibrium Option Pricing Method: Theoretical and Empirical Study*, https://doi.org/10.1007/978-981-10-7428-8_5

(1982), Yaari (1987), and the cumulative prospect theory of Tversky and Kahneman (1992), among many others.[1] Recently, there is a growing literature on applications of non-expected utilities in finance. For example, Epstein and Zin (2001) utilize the weighted utility to explain the behavior of consumption and stock returns, (Barberis and Huang 2008a, b) use the prospect theory to examine the equity premium puzzle and the cross-sectional risk premium, and Polkovnichenko and Zhao (2013) employ the rank dependent utility to solve the pricing kernel puzzle.

Second, in the option market, (Pan 2002; Santa-Clara and Yan 2010) note that the compensation demanded for the jump risk are significantly larger than that for the diffusive risk. This finding implies the representative agent's risk sensitivities towards the normal uncertainty and the rare event are different. Clearly, it violates the only constant relative risk aversion defined in the expected utility.

On the other hand, in accordance with the expected utility, the larger jump risk premium implicit in options indicates a more risk aversion to the rare event. However, Jackwerth (2000) finds that the risk aversion function implied by S&P500 index returns and options in the post-1987 crash period is partially negative and increasing in wealth. In other words, the agent is risk prone and exhibits a moderate risk averse manner when a downward jump is arrived. This is the famous *pricing kernel puzzle* and similar results are presented in Aït-Sahalia and Lo (2000), Rosenberg and Engle (2002), Bakshi et al. (2010).

Furthermore, Dierkes (2009) points out that the option market is particularly susceptible to the irrationality. To price deep OTM put options, traders must deal with rather tail events and extreme outcomes, which people are particularly miscalibrated. Interestingly, resorting to the fMRI technique, neuroeconomists suggest that the expected reward from gambles is nonlinear in probabilities and this originates in the human brain (see (Hsu et al. 2009)). Thus, it is not surprised that even professional option traders may exhibit this bias.

To characterize the representative agent's risk preference as dictated by the findings of this literature, we use the (Epstein and Zin 1989)'s recursive utility function, in which the certainty equivalent is specified to satisfy the weighted utility's form. This setting allows the indifference curves to fan out, and hence, is able to explain the Allais Paradox. The effect of fanning out reflects the extent to which an agent with the fanning preference deviates from the expected utility maximizer.[2] In the special case without fanning effect, the indifference curves are parallel and our model reduces to the conventional expected utility model.

Incorporating the fanning out preference, our model decomposes the total market premium into three parts: the diffusive risk premium, the jump risk premium as defined in Naik and Lee (1990), and a premium associated with the fanning out preference. The first two components are driven by the risk aversion exclusively, and the last one is determined by the fanning effect. Thus, the agent's attitude toward the

---

[1]Starmer (2000), Weber and Camerer (1987) are good sources for a review of the development of the non-expected utility.

[2]Hess and Holthausen (1990) name it as eccentricity, and show that the risk premium is determined by both the risk aversion and the eccentricity.

risks is characterized not only by the risk aversion but also the fanning out preference, which is distinct from the only risk aversion measure in the expected utility model.

Numerical results show that the fanning effect captures a significant portion of the total market premium and it also can reconcile the premium implicit in the ATM options with that implicit in the deep OTM puts. In simulating the cross-sectional index options, the model incorporating fanning effect generates significant higher premiums implicit in the 10% OTM put options than that implicit in ATM options, and hence, results in pronounced volatility smirks.

We also carry out an empirical test for the model incorporating the fanning out preference over the period extending from January 2002 through December 2011. In particular, we estimate the implied fanning effect to -21.59 with a standard error of 3.141. This result empirically verifies the fanning out preference implicit in the option market.

With the estimated parameters, we construct the time series of the market premium, the diffusive risk premium, the jump risk premium, and the fanning effect premium across the market implied volatility for the one-month ATM options. Our empirical results show that, on average, the market premium is equal to 25.3%, in which a proportion of 65.2% is attributed to the fanning effect premium. Clearly, the fanning out preference captures a significant portion of the premiums implicit in options. While the risk aversion estimated to be 3.264 in our sample only accounts for 5.5% of the total premiums.

In the aspect of explaining the in-sample data and forecasting the out-of-sample option prices, our model performs better than the conventional expected utility model with smaller errors. For the ability to fit the market implied volatilities, both models predict the options well on the low volatile day. But they perform differently on high volatile days. More specifically, the fanning model produces downward sloping volatility smirks which are close to the market observations, while the expected utility model only exhibits flat patterns for the plots of implied volatilities against the moneyness. During the episode of recent financial crisis, the fanning model nearly fits all cross-sectional index options with varying degrees of moneyness, whereas the expected utility model severely underprices those data.

This study is closely related to the literature that investigates the option volatility smirk from an equilibrium setting. For example, Bates (2008) incorporates a crash aversion component into the standard power utility, so that he amplifies the agent's risk aversion to the rare event, and hence, disentangles the market price of the jump risk from that of the diffusive risk. In contrast to Bates (2008) who emphasizes the heterogeneous attitude, (Liu et al. 2005) argue that the agent exhibits an extra layer of aversion towards the model uncertainty associated with the rare event, which is an addition to the standard risk aversion measure. The authors further examine the robustness of this result when employing the recursive utility, and find that it provides exactly the same market prices of risks as the conventional expected utility model in the absence of uncertainty aversion.

Different from Bates (2008), Liu et al. (2005) which are subject to the expected utility rule, (Du 2011) adopts a time varying risk aversion induced by the habit formation of Campbell and Cochrane (1999), Menzly et al. (2004). He finds that this setting amplifies consumption shocks, and as a result, the model is able to generate the excess volatility and a large jump risk premium which combine to produce pronounced volatility smirks. Another investigation for pricing options in the equilibrium framework is Benzoni et al. (2011), which is built on the long run risk model of Bansal and Yaron (2004) and the recursive utility of Epstein and Zin (1989). They specify the expected consumption growth rate to be driven by a persistent component (x) which is subject to the rare event. When the elasticity of intertemporal substitution is larger than 1, a downward jump in x induces a stock market crash, and hence, results in a large premium implicit in OTM put options.

Unlike these prior studies which focus on the adjustment of risk aversion, our research modifies the probabilities of uncertain economic states in order to coincide with the agent's subjective probability distribution. Reference Kogan et al. (2006) find that the agent's subjective probability distribution deviates substantially from the true distribution. This could occur, for instance, if the agent believes that the future cash flow to risky financial assets have far higher growth rates and/or lower risks than that dictated by the true distribution. In our model, the objective probability is adjusted by the fanning effect and the agent maximizes his/her utility using the weighted probabilities. As a result, an additional premium implicit in the option market is assigned to the fanning out preference.

In addition, our setting for the recursive utility function is different from that of Liu et al. (2005). They adopt the (Duffie and Epstein 1992a, b)'s continuous-time intertemporal recursive utility which is based on the pure Brownian information. In contrast, we use (Ma 2000, 2006)'s version in which the information structure is allowed to be driven by a jump-diffusion process. We further demonstrate that the non-expected recursive utility and the standard expected utility are observationally equivalent in the pure Brownian framework, which is in line with (Liu et al. 2005)'s conclusion. In the presence of jump, however, they are observationally nonequivalent.

The rest of this chapter is organized as follows. Section 5.2 sets up models. Section 5.3 carries out a numerical experiment to examine the important role of fanning effect played in both the equity and the option markets. Section 5.4 contains the estimation for models and empirical results including the explanation for jump risk premium and the fitting for volatility smirks. Section 5.5 concludes this chapter.

5.2 Model Setup

In equilibrium, the interest rate (r) and the dividend-equity ratio (ℓ) are determined by

$$r = b + \ell + (\eta - 1)a^2 + \lambda \int_0^\infty (u-1)u^{\eta-1}\phi'(u^\eta)\Pi(du),$$

$$\ell = \frac{f_c(1,k)}{\eta k},$$

where k takes the same sign as η and solves

$$\frac{f(1,k)}{k} + b\eta + \eta(\eta - 1)a^2/2 + \lambda \int_0^\infty \phi(u^\eta)\Pi(du) = 0.$$

Here, we assume that there exists a real $s^* < -1$ such that, for all real $s^* < t \leq -1$, $\int_0^\infty \phi'(u^\eta)u^{\eta-t-1}\Pi(du)$ takes finite values.

As shown in Eq. (2.14), the total market risk premium, denoted by π, is given by

$$\begin{aligned}\pi &= b + \ell - r + \lambda \int_0^\infty (u-1)\Pi(du) \\ &= (1-\eta)a^2 + \lambda \int_0^\infty (u-1)\Pi(du) - \lambda \int_0^\infty (u-1)u^{\eta-1}\phi'(u^\eta)\Pi(du),\end{aligned}$$

in which, the term of $(1-\eta)a^2$ is the diffusive risk premium, denoted by π_D, and corresponds to the market risk premium when there is no jump in the economy. The difference between the two integrals, denoted by π_J^*, represents a total jump risk premium, when there exist only two types of uncertainty in the economy: the diffusive risk and the jump risk.

π_J^* can be further decomposed into the Naik and Lee (1990)'s jump risk premium determined by the risk aversion exclusively and an extra jump risk premium driven by the fanning effect. As a result, the total market premium is decomposed into three components: the diffusive risk premium, the Naik and Lee's jump risk premium, and an additional jump risk premium determined by the fanning effect,

$$\pi = \pi_D + \pi_J + \pi_F .$$

The first two premiums are measured by the risk aversion exclusively, and the last one is controlled by the fanning out preference.

Remarkably, incorporating the fanning effect can reconcile the high market risk premium implicit in options with a moderate degree of risk aversion. According to the pricing kernel puzzle, the agent is risk prone and exhibits a moderate risk averse manner when a crash arrived. The low degree of risk aversion results in a small amount of compensation paid for the jump risk, as indicated by the expected utility theory. However, the actual market risk premium is quite high in the presence of jump. To reconcile the high risk premium with a low degree of risk aversion, either the risk aversion measure is modified,[3] or the true probability distribution of uncertain economic states is adjusted to the agent's subjective view. In our model, the objective probability is weighted by a weighting function driven by the fanning effect. As a result, a portion of the total market risk premium is captured by the agent's fanning out preference.

---

[3]Bates (2008) amplifies the risk aversion to the rare event, Liu et al. (2005) add an extra layer of aversion to the model uncertainty, Du (2011) uses a time varying risk aversion.

The equilibrium price for a European call option (C) written on the aggregate equity can also be obtained (see (Ma 2006) for details),

$$C = K\mathrm{e}^{-r(T-t)}\mathcal{L}^{-1}\{\frac{\Theta^{T-t}(s)}{s(s+1)}\}(\ln\frac{K}{S}) ,$$

where K is the strike price, T is the maturity, r represents the risk-free interest rate, S is the underlying stock price, $\mathcal{L}^{-1}$ indicates the inverse bilateral Laplace operator, and $\Theta(\cdot)$ can be interpreted as the risk-neutral moment generating function for the distribution of aggregate equity returns at the maturity. In particular,

$$\begin{aligned}\ln\Theta(s) &= -[b + (\eta - 1.5)a^2]s + 0.5a^2s^2 + \int_0^{\infty}(u^{-s} - 1)\widehat{N}(\mathrm{d}t,\ \mathrm{d}u)\\ &= \ell s - (r - 0.5a^2)s + 0.5a^2s^2 + \frac{\lambda}{\eta - 2\varphi}\{(\eta - \varphi)\\ &\quad [g(\eta - \varphi - s - 1) + sg(\eta - \varphi) - g(\eta - \varphi - 1) -\\ &\quad sg(\eta - \varphi - 1)] - \varphi[g(\varphi - s - 1) + sg(\varphi) -\\ &\quad g(\varphi - 1) - sg(\varphi - 1)]\} ,\end{aligned}$$

where $\mathrm{Re}(s) \in (s^*, -1)$ for $s^* < -1$ is restricted to a vertical stripe in the complex plane, and $g(\cdot)$ is the moment generating function for the distribution (Π). In this chapter, the logarithm of jump size is assumed to follow the normal distribution, and hence $g(x) = \exp\{\mu_J x + \frac{1}{2}x^2\sigma_J^2\}$, in which μ_J and σ_J are the average size and the standard deviation of normal distribution, respectively.

5.3 Numerical Studies

This section carries out a numerical investigation to highlight the important role of fanning effect played in reconciling the premium observed in the equity market with which implicit in the option market.

The experiment is designed as that in Liu et al. (2005). Three jump cases are considered. In each case, to yield the fixed 8% market premium, three scenarios of risk aversion correspond to different degrees of fanning effect. Results are presented in Table 5.1. As is shown, when the magnitude of risk aversion in each case is equal to 3.47, there exists no fanning effect, and therefore, the market premium is only measured by the risk aversion.

However, with the decrease of risk sensitivity, the risk aversion measure can not fully capture the total 8% market premium. Take Jump case 1 for instance, when the degree of risk aversion declines to 3.15, a jump risk premium of 0.19% is paid in accordance with the expected utility. However, this is much smaller than the 0.91% (8 − 7.09%) premium implicit in the market. In order to match the total 8% market premium, the fanning out preference captures the additional premium of 0.72%.

Table 5.1 Risk Premiums

	Jump case 1			Jump case 2			Jump case 3		
$1-\eta$	3.47	3.15	2.62	3.47	2.88	1.61	3.47	2.36	0.68
φ	0	–23	–32	0	–16	–23	0	–15	–18
π_D (%)	7.81	7.09	5.91	7.81	6.48	3.62	7.81	5.31	1.53
π_J (%)	0.19	0.19	0.15	0.19	0.15	0.08	0.19	0.12	0.03
π_F (%)	0	0.72	1.94	0	1.37	4.3	0	2.57	6.44
Total market premium is 8%									

Note This table reports the diffusive risk premium (π_D), the jump risk premium (π_J), and the fanning effect premium (π_F) to match the total 8% market premium, according to Eq. (2.15). Three jump cases are considered, case 1 represents a small jump with $\lambda = 1/3$ and $\mu_J = -1\%$, case 2 means a big jump with $\lambda = 1/25$ and $\mu_J = -10\%$, and case 3 denotes a rarely occurred crash with $\lambda = 1/100$ and $\mu_J = -20\%$. In each case, the representative agent's risk preference are measured by the risk aversion $(1-\eta)$ as well as the fanning out preference determined by φ

To examine the option pricing implication of our model, we plot the Black-Scholes implied volatilities for one-month options in Fig. 5.1. As is shown, the model incorporating fanning effect generates pronounced volatility smirks in three cases, comparing with the flat patterns depicted by the standard expected utility model.

Our results are comparable to findings of the literature. For example, when $\varphi = 0$ in the jump case 1, our model degenerates to that of Naik and Lee (1990), and it produces 15.2 and 15.6% implied volatilities for the ATM options and the 10% OTM put options, respectively. Clearly, the model fails to generate a pronounced volatility smirk consistent with the post-1987 evidence on S&P500 index options. When the fanning effect is incorporated and $\varphi = -32$, our model results in remarkably large implied volatilities of 15.9% for the ATM options and 18.3% for the 10% OTM put options. As a comparison, (Liu et al. 2005) report 15.5 and 17.2% (when $\phi = 20$ in their paper) for the ATM options and the 10% OTM put options, respectively. Du (2011) presents a 15.5% implied volatility for the ATM options and 17.2% for the 10% OTM put options.

The implied volatilities produced by the fanning model can be translated into a premium of 4.61% implicit in the one-month ATM options and a premium of 17.3% implicit in the 10% OTM put options. Therefore, a pronounced volatility smirk is produced as displayed in Fig. 5.1. This is in line with the findings of Jackwerth and Rubinstein (1996), Pan (2002) that typical options, including ATM options, are priced with premiums and the premiums implicit in the OTM puts are higher than those implicit in ATM options.

In our study, the pronounced volatility smirks are generated because of incorporating the fanning out preference. As is known, options with varying degrees of moneyness, especially the deep OTM put options, are sensitive to the rare event. In the presence of jump, however, the agent does not regard the financial assets including options as risky as dictated by the objective probability distribution. Consequently, the risk aversion only captures a small portion of the total premiums implicit in the option market. On the other hand, the fanning effect adjusts the probability

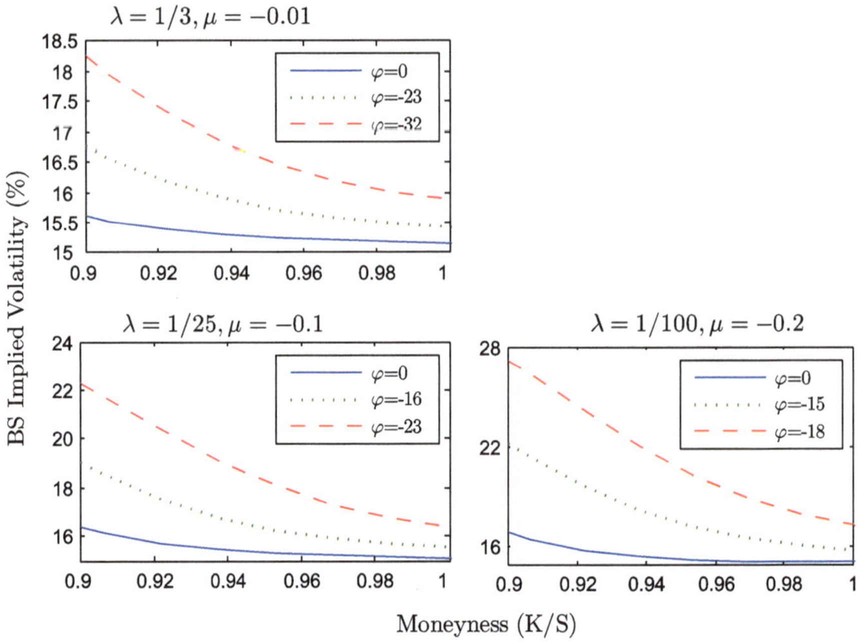

Fig. 5.1 Volatility smirks This figure plots the Black-Scholes implied volatilities against the moneyness, according to the results presented in Table 5.1. The moneyness is defined as the ratio of strike to spot prices (K/S) and varies from 0.9 (the 10% OTM put options) to 1 (the ATM options). Three panels correspond to three jump cases in Table 5.1, respectively. In each panel, we consider three scenarios of the risk aversion and corresponding fanning effects

distribution in accordance with the agent's subjective view, and as a result, produces pronounced smirked pattern consistent with the post-1987 evidences on S&P500 index options.

5.4 Empirical Analysis

This section empirically tests the model with fanning effect and it's reduced form with the expected utility. First, we provide the data and the methodology used in this chapter. Second, we estimate the option pricing models. Third, we study the option implied risk premiums. Finally, we investigate the model fit and the volatility smirk.

5.4.1 Data and Methodology

The option data used in this chapter is the European-style S&P500 index options traded on the Chicago Board Options Exchange (CBOE) for the period from January

2002 to December 2011 obtained from OptionMetrics. The risk-free interest rates are LIBOR rates and downloaded from CEIC. We match interest rates and options that share the same maturity. As the stocks within the S&P 500 index pay dividends, we use the discounted future dividends which are replaced by the realized dividends obtained from Bloomberg as a proxy.

Some standard filter rules are applied to exclude infrequently traded options. First, following the literature, we use the weekly frequent options in this chapter. Therefore, we collect only the data on Wednesday of each week. If Wednesday is not a trading day, we obtain prices from, in order of preference, Tuesday, Thursday, Monday, or Friday. Second, as this study focuses on the jump risk, we only employ the short term options with the time to maturity greater than 7 days but less than 90 days. Third, for each contract, we use the average of bid and ask prices as the value of option. We eliminate those with prices less than \$3/8, in order to mitigate microstructure problems. Fourth, to ensure that the used options are liquid enough, we exclude contracts with no trading volume and employ options with moneyness, defined as the ratio of K/S, between 0.9 and 1.1. Finally, we check for no-arbitrage violations in option prices.

In all, we have 53833 options including calls and puts over 518 trading days. Table 5.2 reports the summary statistics for our data sample. We divide all options into nine buckets according to the moneyness and the maturity: moneyness less than 0.95, between 0.95 and 1.05, and above 1.05; maturity less than 30 days, between 30 and 60 days, and greater than 60 days but less than 90 days. In each category, we present the numbers of options and the average implied volatilities.

The time series of the weekly S&P500 index returns and the Black-Scholes implied volatilities are plotted in Fig. 5.2. Clearly, the patterns for variations display three spikes over the period from 2002 through 2011. The first one occurs at the end of 2002, which coincides with the high macroeconomic uncertainty reported in the second semester of 2002 in US. The second peak, and also the most volatile time,

Table 5.2 Summary Statistics for S&P500 Index Options

Maturity				
Moneyness	$7 < T \leq 30$	$30 < T \leq 60$	$60 < T \leq 90$	Total
$K/S < 0.95$	3636 (29.52)	5123 (24.57)	1722 (23.85)	10481
$0.95 \leq K/S < 1.05$	13188 (20.44)	16575 (19.09)	6280 (19.88)	36043
$1.05 \leq K/S$	1630 (26.42)	3950 (19.76)	1729 (18.49)	7309
Total	18454	25648	9731	53833

Note This table presents a summary statistics for the option data used in our paper. According to the maturity and the moneyness defined as the ratio of strike to spot prices (K/S), we divide all options into nine buckets. In each category, we report the number of options including calls and puts, and the average Black-Scholes implied volatilities in the parentheses

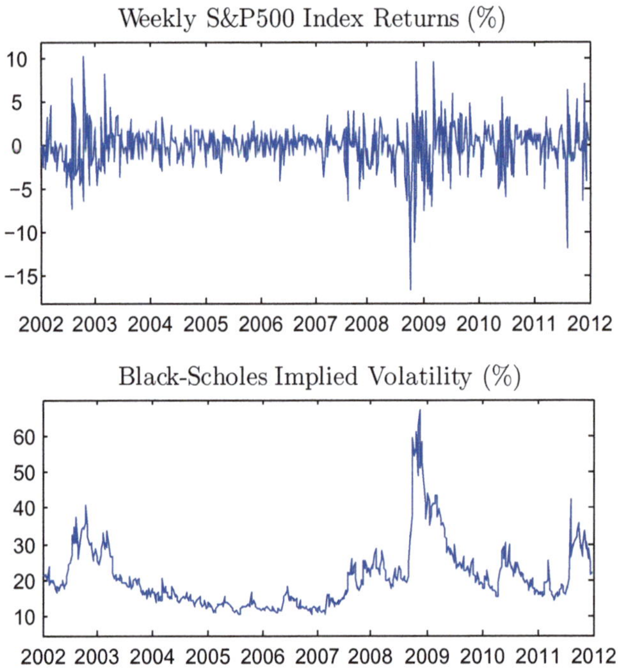

Fig. 5.2 Weekly S&P500 index returns and BS implied volatilities This figure plots the time series of the weekly S&P500 index returns and the Black-Scholes implied volatilities over the period extending from January 2002 through December 2012

is a result of the recent financial crisis from 2008 to 2009. The last spike is observed at the end of 2011, which corresponds to the episode of sovereign credit risk in US.

In this chapter, we estimate the models using the method of implied volatility mean squared error (IV-MSE). The loss function is defined as

$$\text{IV-MSE}_t(\vartheta) \equiv \frac{1}{N_t}\sum_{i=1}^{N_t}(\sigma_i(\vartheta) - \hat{\sigma}_i(\vartheta))^2 \tag{5.1}$$

where ϑ is the vector of unknown parameters, σ_i is the Black-Scholes implied volatilities corresponding to observed option prices on day t, $\hat{\sigma}_i$ is the implied volatilities corresponding to theoretical option prices determined by the option pricing models, and N_t is the total amount of option contracts on day t. Since the difference between σ_i and $\hat{\sigma}_i$ is a function of the parameter vector ϑ to be estimated, we can obtain the estimates of implied model parameters through minimizing the mean squared errors.

Table 5.3 Estimated Parameters

	λ	μ_J	σ_J	σ	η	φ	IV-MSE
Fanning model	0.380 (0.392)	−0.080 (0.031)	0.037 (0.023)	0.139 (0.055)	−2.264 (0.817)	−21.590 (3.141)	2.508
Naik-Lee model	0.515 (0.784)	−0.139 (0.051)	0.075 (0.069)	0.154 (0.059)	−2.138 (0.901)		6.571

Note This table presents the estimated results for our model incorporating the fanning out preference and the Naik and Lee (1990)'s expected utility model. We abbreviate them to the fanning model and the Naik-Lee model, respectively. For the estimate of each parameter, the standard error is reported in parentheses. The IV-MSE represents the implied volatility mean squared error.

5.4.2 *Estimation*

According to the loss function (5.1), we can estimate the structural parameters implied by the model incorporating the fanning out preference and it's reduced form with the expected utility function. Results are reported in Table 5.3. When $\varphi = 0$, our model degenerates to that of Naik and Lee (1990), and the fanning effect premium is not incorporated. As a result, to fit market observations, Naik-Lee model implies greater volatilities and more significant jumps of the underlying index than those estimated by the fanning model.

Our results for the estimate of jump component in Table 5.3 are comparable to some existing studies, e.g., Pan (2002), Santa-Clara and Yan (2010), Du (2011). First, our estimate of the average jump intensity is equal to 0.38 with a standard error of 0.392, which is very close to Pan (2002)'s 0.36 per year, but much higher than (Du 2011)'s 0.022. The large standard error indicates that the jump intensity varies over time. This insight is modeled by Santa-Clara and Yan (2010) who use a separate stochastic process to control the dynamics of jump intensity. Second, the average jump size implied by our model is −8%. As a comparison, (Pan 2002) estimate it to −0.3 and −18% under the physical and the risk-neutral measures, respectively; Santa-Clara and Yan (2010) present −9.8% for their SVSJ model and −7% for the SVJ model; Du (2011) reports it to −17.2%.

In addition, we estimate the risk aversion to 3.264. It is a reasonable and moderate estimate comparing to the literature. Reference Du (2011) argue that the degree of risk aversion reaches to 34, and Santa-Clara and Yan (2010) suggest 1.917 and 1.984 for the SVSJ and the SVJ models, respectively. Other related estimations include (Aït-Sahalia and Lo 2000)'s 12.7, Bliss and Panigirtzoglou (2004)'s 9.52 (5.38) for one (two) week forecasting horizon, and Bakshi and Madan (2006)'s approximate 17.3 (12.7) for 90 (200) day returns.

More importantly, we estimate the option implied fanning effect. The average magnitude is equal to −21.59 with a standard error of 3.141. This implies a fanning out preference implicit in the option market. In a related study, Epstein and Zin (2001) also estimate the fanning effect implied by returns on both the stock and the bond markets. They find an average fanning effect of −0.648 (−4.037) for nondurables (nondurables and services), using the value-weighted returns on stocks traded on the

NYSE and the return on a one-month Treasury bill. However, large standard errors for both data sets (presented in their Table 5.3) do not allow fanning in to be rejected. The difference for the estimate of fanning effect between these two papers are not unexpected, as different markets and sample periods are given.

5.4.3 Implied Risk Premiums

Next, according to Eq. (2.15) and the estimated parameters given in Table 5.3, we construct the time series of the total market premium, the diffusive risk premium, the jump risk premium, and the fanning effect premium, respectively, and plot them in Fig. 5.3. As is shown, the market premium varies substantially over time, from a low of 1.28% to a high of 216%, and the average is 25.3%. Three spikes in the variation of market premium are consistent with those observed in Fig. 5.2. During the first high volatile episode, the market premium exceeds 50%, which is in line with findings of Santa-Clara and Yan (2010) (see Fig. 5.5). On the second and third spikes, the market premium exceeds 200% and 100%, respectively.

We can see from Fig. 5.3 that, the moderate degree of risk aversion, which is estimated to 3.264 in our sample, results in a small amount of compensation demanded for bearing the jump risk. On average, it is equal to 1.4% and only accounts for 5.5%

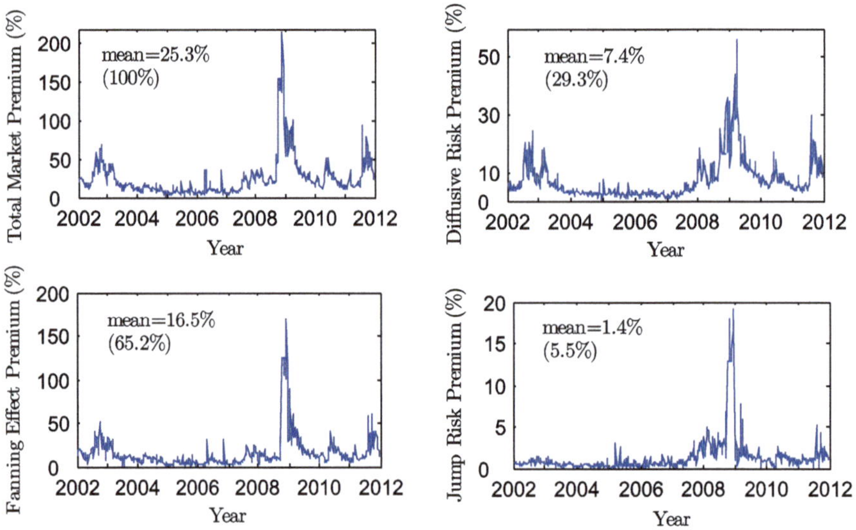

Fig. 5.3 Time series of the implied risk premiums According to Eq. (2.15) and the estimated parameters given in Table 5.3, we construct the time series of the market premium, the diffusive risk premium, the jump risk premium, and the fanning effect premium over the period from 2002 through 2011. We also report the average magnitude of each risk premium and the corresponding proportion accounting for the total market premium in parentheses

of the total market premium. This proportion is much smaller than the findings of existing studies. Pan (2002) presents an average jump-size risk premium of 3.5% that accounts for 38.9% of the total market premium, and Du (2011) reports an average jump-timing risk premium of 2.46% accounting for 41.8% of the market premium. Constructing a time varying premiums, Santa-Clara and Yan (2010) show that the jump risk premium ranges from 0 to 45.4% and accounts for more than half of the total market premium.

The difference between our result and the findings of prior papers is attributed to the fanning out preference. In our model, the jump risk premium is defined as that in Naik and Lee (1990) and it is measured by the risk aversion exclusively. According to Eq. (2.15), however, the agent's risk attitude is also driven by the fanning out preference. Therefore, the fanning effect captures a significant portion of the market premium. As is shown in Fig. 5.3, the average fanning effect premium is equal to 16.5% and accounts for 65.2% of the full market premium.

To further investigate the role of fanning effect played in the implied risk premium, we plot the total market premium and its three components implicit in the one-month ATM options across the market implied volatility in Fig. 5.4. As is shown, the market premium and the fanning effect premium respond to the market volatility more significantly than the other two premiums. Specifically, when the market volatility grows from 20–60%, both the market premium and the fanning effect premium raise sharply, whereas the diffusive premium and the jump premium increase only by small amounts.

The relatively flat pattern for the jump risk premium against the market volatility is inconsistent with (Pan 2002)'s finding (see Fig. 5.4), and indicates that the agent is

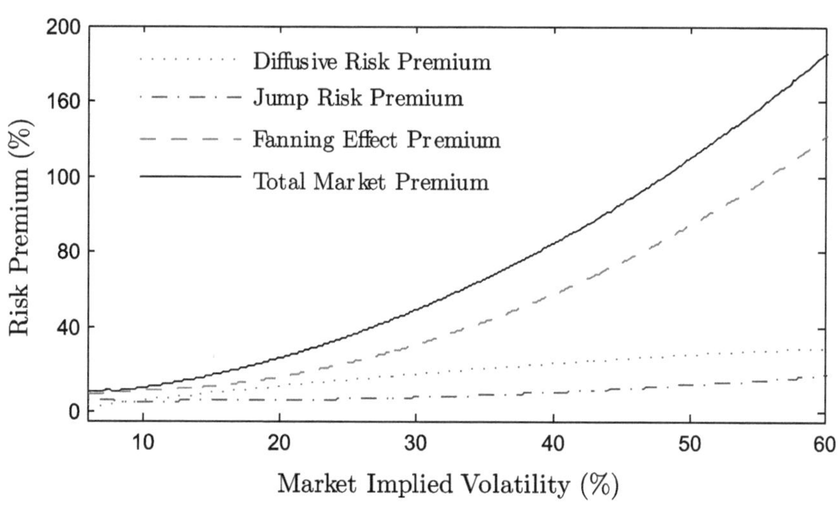

Fig. 5.4 Implied risk premiums against market volatility Using the one-month ATM options, we plot the responsiveness of the market premium, the diffusive risk premium, the jump risk premium, and the fanning effect premium to the market volatility, which increases from 5–60%

indifferent to the jump risk. Clearly, the risk aversion fails to capture the significant responsiveness of the market premium. However, the fanning out preference is able to do so. As is shown in Fig. 5.4, the fanning effect premium is sensitive to the market volatility and the extent of responsiveness is in line with that of the market premium.

5.4.4 Model Fit and Volatility Smirks

Finally, we examine the mode fit and the option implied volatility smirk. Clearly, in Table 5.3, the fanning model fits the in-sample data better than Naik-Lee model, as it has a smaller implied volatility mean squared error (IV-MSE) of 2.508 $(1/10^4)$. For the out-of-sample performance, we also calculate the IV-MSE between the one-week ahead forecasted option prices and the market observations. The error for the fanning model is 12.567 $(1/10^4)$ which is still smaller than Naik-Lee's 16.023 $(1/10^4)$.

Figure 5.5 depicts the market implied volatilities of the near one-month options across the moneyness, together with the fitted implied volatilities of the two alternative pricing models in four different dates of the sample. According to the time series

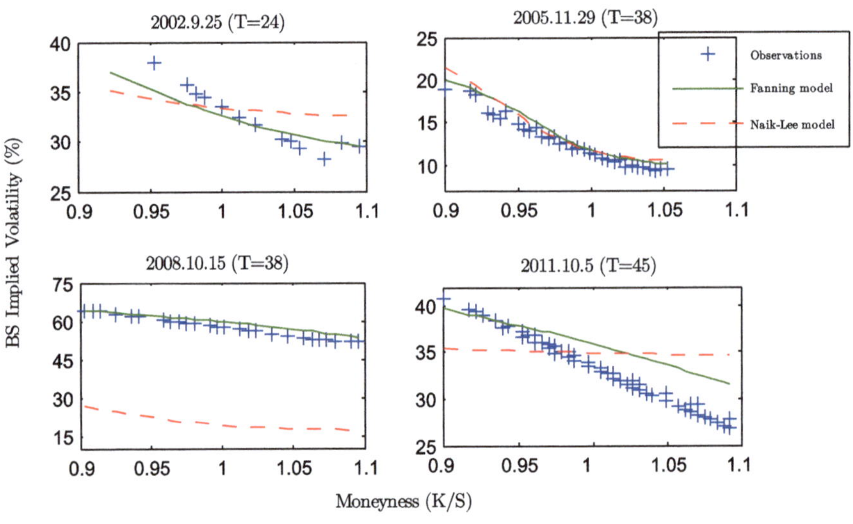

Fig. 5.5 Market and fitted implied volatilities This figure plots the Black-Scholes implied volatilities of the market observations and the fitted implied volatilities calculated by the pricing models. The fanning model and the Naik-Lee model denote the model incorporating the fanning out preference and the expected utility model of Naik and Lee (1990), respectively. Four specific days are selected to represent different episodes of the market, which coincides with the variations of S&P500 index returns and implied volatilities exhibited in Fig. 5.2. October 15th, 2008 represents the most volatile time, November 29th, 2005 means a low volatile day, and September 25th, 2002 and October 5th, 2011 denote high volatile episodes. In each day, options with near one-month to expiration are used to calculate the implied volatilities

of the S&P500 index returns and the Black-Scholes implied volatility exhibited in Fig. 5.2, October 15th, 2008 represents a most volatile day, September 25th, 2009 and October 5th, 2011 denote high volatile days, and November 29th, 2005 means a low volatile time.

As is shown in Fig. 5.5, on the low volatile day, both pricing models predict options very well. But they perform differently on the high volatile days. More specifically, the Naik-Lee model generates relatively flat patterns for the plots of implied volatilities against the moneyness. In contrast, the fanning model produces downward sloping volatility smirks close to the market observations. During the episode of recent financial crisis, the fanning model nearly fits all cross-sectional index options with varying degrees of moneyness, especially the deep OTM puts. While the Naik-Lee model severely underprices those data and the fitted implied volatilities are even smaller than the half of market volatilities.

5.5 Concluding Remarks

This chapter proposes a preference-based general equilibrium model that can explain the pricing of S&P500 index options since the 1987 market crash. Motivated by the Allais Paradox and the evidences for the violation of expected utility model in the option market, we use a non-expected recursive utility function, in which the certainty equivalent satisfies the weighted utility's form and displays a fanning out preference. This setting is able to explain the Allais Paradox and puzzles in the option market, as the probabilities of uncertain economic states are adjusted by the fanning effect in accordance with the agent's subjective probabilities. Therefore, in equilibrium, our model decomposes the total market premium into three components: the diffusive risk premium, the jump risk premium defined as in Naik and Lee (1990), and the fanning effect premium.

To examine the role of fanning out preference played in pricing options, we carry out numerical and empirical tests. Results show that the fanning out preference captures a significant portion of the total market premium, and it is also able to reconcile the moderate degree of risk aversion with the true premium implicit in the option market. Incorporating the fanning out preference, our model generates pronounced volatility smirks consistent with the post-1987 evidences on S&P500 index options, and fit the market observations better than the conventional expected utility model.

Chapter 6
Jump Size Distributions and Option Pricing

6.1 Introduction

Growing evidences suggest two violations of Black and Scholes (1973) model: the downwards sloping volatility smile across moneyness and the heavy-tailed asset return distribution implied by option prices. Both abnormalities are caused by the existence of rare disasters or tail events in asset returns. Rubinstein (1994) find that the implied volatility across moneyness becomes skewed since October 1987. This feature is often referred to as "volatility smirk". On the other hand, Jackwerth and Rubinstein (1996) show that the option implied probability distribution is more left-skewed and changes from platykurtic to leptokurtic after the market crash in 1987.

Therefore, a vast literature suggests more general models incorporating the discontinuous jump into the underlying return dynamics, for example, Merton (1976), Bates (1991, 1996, 2000), Bakshi et al. (1997), Pan (2002), Huang and Wu (2004), Carr and Wu (2004), Santa-Clara and Yan (2010), Yun (2011), among many others. These previous papers, however, price options under a partial equilibrium framework and assume an underlying return dynamics given exogenously. Alternatively, Naik and Lee (1990) propose a general equilibrium model based on the pure exchange economy of Lucas (1978). The equilibrium price of European-style option is obtained when representative agent maximizes his/her expected utility of lifetime consumption. Allowing a more flexibility of pricing the jump risk and the diffusive risk separately, many papers use the non-expected utility models in the general equilibrium framework, for example, Liu et al. (2005), Bates (2008), Du (2011), Benzoni et al. (2011), and Chen and Ma (2013).

All these studies follow Merton (1976)'s assumption of lognormal distribution for jump sizes. In a jump-diffusion model of Merton (1976), the price of underlying stock (S_t) at time t is determined by

$$S_t = S_0 \exp\left\{(\alpha - \frac{1}{2}\sigma^2)\,t + \sigma B_t\right\} \prod_{i=1}^{N_t} u_i \ ,$$

J. Chen, *General Equilibrium Option Pricing Method: Theoretical and Empirical Study*, https://doi.org/10.1007/978-981-10-7428-8_6

where α is the expected return of stock, σ is the constant volatility of Brownian motion denoted by B_t, N_t is a Poisson process, and u is the jump size. Clearly, the pattern of jump size distribution is inherited by that of stock return distribution. In other words, if the log return of stock follows a normal distribution, the logarithm of jump size will be normally distributed as well. However, empirical findings show that the log return distribution for stock displays a high peak and asymmetric heavy tails. Consequently, the distribution for logarithm of jump size could also exhibit such an leptokurtic feature.

Motivated by this insight, Kou (2002) and Kou and Wang (2004) consider a double-exponential jump size distribution. Recently, this model is further developed to a more general form of mixed-exponential distribution proposed by Cai and Kou (2011). They find that the leptokurtic feature of jump size distribution is helpful to produce analytical solutions for a variety of option-pricing problems, including call and put options, interest rate derivatives, and path-dependent options.

The jump size plays an important role not only in pricing options, but also in predicting the expected stock returns. Yan (2011) argue that the expected stock return is a function of the average jump size, which can be proxied by the slope of option implied volatility smile.

Related to prior studies, this chapter aims to investigate the effect of jump size distribution on the volatility smirk and the leptokurtic feature of option implied probability distribution. Bakshi et al. (2003) suggest that the slope of implied volatility is determined by the skewness and kurtosis of stock return distribution. However, it still remains unclear how the jump size affects this relationship between volatility smirk and return distribution. Our model shows that the skewness (kurtosis) of stock return distribution is proportional to the counterpart of jump size distribution. As it is difficult to extract the jump size distribution from actual trading data, we only consider two specific examples: Laplace distribution and normal distribution, in this chapter. The Laplace distribution is a special case of the double-exponential model of Kou (2002) and Kou and Wang (2004)[1] and displays heavy tails in comparison to the conventional normal distribution.

Different from studies of Kou (2002) and Kou and Wang (2004), our analysis is built upon a pure exchange economy, in which the representative agent's risk preference shows a fanning out characteristic. A growing literature finds the behavioral bias of investors in financial market, especially in the derivative market. As a result, a non-expected utility is used to explain the violations of additive expected utility (see Chen and Ma 2013 and the references therein).

Our investigation is carried out in two aspects. First, we examine which assumption of jump size distribution is better to explain the phenomena of volatility smirk consistent with the post-1987 evidence on S&P500 index options. Second, which model is able to generate the left-skewed and heavy-tailed feature of option implied probability distribution as shown in the literature.

---

[1] For the purpose of mathematic simplicity, we only examine a special case of the double exponential model of Kou (2002) and Kou and Wang (2004), i.e., the Laplace model, in this chapter.

To address these two questions, we carry out a numerical test. Results show that, when fanning effect is zero, our model reduces to the expected utility model, and prices jump risk similarly for both jump size distributions. However, when fanning effect is present, Laplace model is able to capture more jump risk premium implicit in options than that of normal model. This larger portion of jump risk premium captured by Laplace model eventually results in more pronounced volatility smirks relative to those of normal model.

These results are further confirmed through an empirical investigation. We fit both Laplace and normal models to S&P500 index options over the period from January 2002 through December 2011. We find that Laplace model captures less diffusive risk premium but larger jump risk premium than those of normal model. This is in line with our numerical findings. Specifically, for Laplace model, the jump risk premium is 17.29% and accounts for 79.08% of the total market risk premium, in which the premium determined by fanning effect is 14.86% accounting for 72.14% of the market premium. In comparison, normal model only captures 10.57% jump risk premium accounting for 68.17% of total equity premium. The difference between two models in pricing jump risk results in different performance in fitting market implied volatilities. Unsurprisingly, Laplace model outperforms normal model, although both of them can generate downward sloping volatility smirks on highly volatile days.

On the other hand, we find that Laplace model is able to produce more remarkable heavy-tailed and left-skewed pattern of risk-neutral distribution than that of normal model. This is closely related to their different performances in generating volatility smirks. Bakshi et al. (2003) and Yan (2011) suggest that the slope of implied volatility is determined by the skewness and kurtosis of underlying return distribution. Empirical results show that the average risk-neutral skewness and kurtosis implied by Laplace model are -1.86 and 10.31, respectively, consistent with findings of Polkovnichenko and Zhao (2013). While normal model suggest the skewness and kurtosis to -0.98 and 4.93, respectively, which are moderate estimates in comparison with Polkovnichenko and Zhao (2013)'s results.

The rest of this chapter is organized as follows. Section 6.2 provides the models. Section 6.3 fits models to the S&P500 index options and provides empirical results. Section 6.4 concludes this chapter.

6.2 Model Setup

$\Theta(\cdot)$ in Eq. (2.29) is the characteristic function for the instantaneous risk-neutral growth rate $\frac{1}{T}\left(\ln\,\widehat{S}_T - \ln\,S_0\right)$, we may refer it to be the risk-neutral moment generating function for the distribution of aggregate equity returns at the maturity. Note, in Eq. (2.29), the assumption for jump size distribution is general and we can impose any forms of distribution on jump sizes. In the literature, Zhang et al. (2012) also consider a general setting on the jump size, which is a special case of our models (2.28) and (2.29) in the absence of fanning effect.

According to Eq. (2.29), we can obtain the risk-neutral skewness ($skew$) and kurtosis ($kurt$) of aggregate equity return distribution at the maturity, as follows

$$\begin{aligned} skew &= \frac{\mathrm{E}[\widehat{S}_T - \mathrm{E}(\widehat{S}_T)]^3}{\{\mathrm{E}[\widehat{S}_T - \mathrm{E}(\widehat{S}_T)]^2\}^{3/2}} = \frac{\mathrm{E}(\widehat{S}_T^3) - 3\mathrm{E}(\widehat{S}_T)\,\mathrm{E}(\widehat{S}_T^2) + 2[\mathrm{E}(\widehat{S}_T)]^3}{\{\mathrm{E}(\widehat{S}_T^2) - [\mathrm{E}(\widehat{S}_T)]^2\}^{3/2}} \\ &= \frac{\Theta(-3) - 3\Theta(-1)\,\Theta(-2) + 2[\Theta(-1)]^3}{\{\Theta(-2) - [\Theta(-1)]^2\}^{3/2}} \\ kurt &= \frac{\mathrm{E}[\widehat{S}_T - \mathrm{E}(\widehat{S}_T)]^4}{\{\mathrm{E}[\widehat{S}_T - \mathrm{E}(\widehat{S}_T)]^2\}^2} \\ &= \frac{\mathrm{E}(\widehat{S}_T^4) - 4\mathrm{E}(\widehat{S}_T)\,\mathrm{E}(\widehat{S}_T^3) + 6[\mathrm{E}(\widehat{S}_T)]^2\,\mathrm{E}(\widehat{S}_T^2) - 3[\mathrm{E}(\widehat{S}_T)]^4}{\{\mathrm{E}(\widehat{S}_T^2) - [\mathrm{E}(\widehat{S}_T)]^2\}^2} \\ &= \frac{\Theta(-4) - 4\Theta(-1)\,\Theta(-3) + 6[\Theta(-1)]^2\,\Theta(-2) - 3[\Theta(-1)]^4}{\{\Theta(-2) - [\Theta(-1)]^2\}^2}\,. \end{aligned}$$

The risk-neutral skewness and kurtosis of log return distribution for aggregate equity are proportional to the counterpart of jump size distribution. According to Eqs. (2.31) and (2.32), the risk-neutral skewness ($skew^*$) and kurtosis ($kurt^*$) of log return distribution are given by

$$skew^* = \Psi\, skew_u + \Lambda\,, \qquad kurt^* = \Upsilon\, kurt_u + \Gamma\,,$$

where $skew_u$ and $kurt_u$ are risk-neutral skewness and kurtosis of jump size distribution, respectively, Ψ and Υ are the coefficients, and Λ and Γ, respectively, represent all remaining terms that affect the skewness and kurtosis of stock return distribution.

Bakshi et al. (2003) find that the slope of implied volatility is determined by the skewness and kurtosis of stock return distribution. Therefore, the jump size distribution also plays an important role on the volatility smirk.

6.3 Empirical Investigation

In this section, we empirically compare Laplace model with normal model in the aspect of pricing S&P500 index options.

6.3.1 *Data and Methodology*

The option data used in this chapter is the European-style S&P500 index option traded on the Chicago Board Options Exchange (CBOE) for the period from January

Table 6.1 Summary statistics for S&P500 index options

	Maturity			
Moneyness	$7 < T \leq 30$	$30 < T \leq 60$	$60 < T \leq 90$	Total
$X/S < 0.95$	3636 (29.52)	5123 (24.57)	1722 (23.85)	10481
$0.95 \leq X/S < 1.05$	13188 (20.44)	16575 (19.09)	6280 (19.88)	36043
$1.05 \leq X/S$	1630 (26.42)	3950 (19.76)	1729 (18.49)	7309
Total	18454	25648	9731	53833

Note This table presents a summary statistics for the option data used in our paper. According to the maturity and the moneyness defined as the ratio of strike to spot prices (X/S), we divide all options into nine buckets. In each category, we report the number of options including calls and puts, and the average Black–Scholes implied volatilities in the parentheses

2002 to December 2011 and obtained from OptionMetrics. The risk-free interest rates are LIBOR rates and downloaded from CEIC. We match interest rates and options that share the same maturity. As the stocks within the S&P 500 index pay dividends, we use the discounted future dividends which are replaced by the realized dividends obtained from Bloomberg as a proxy.[2]

Some standard filter rules are applied to exclude infrequently traded options. First, following the literature, we use the weekly frequent options in this chapter. Therefore, we collect only the data on Wednesday of each week. If Wednesday is not a trading day, we obtain prices from, in order of preference, Tuesday, Thursday, Monday, or Friday. Second, as this study focuses on the jump risk, we only employ the short term options with the time to maturity greater than 7 days but less than 90 days. Third, for each contract, we use the average of bid and ask prices as the value of option. We eliminate those with prices less than $3/8, in order to mitigate microstructure problems. Fourth, to ensure that the used options are liquid enough, we exclude contracts with no trading volume and employ options with moneyness, defined as the ratio of X/S, between 0.9 and 1.1. Finally, we check for no-arbitrage violations in option prices.

In all, we have 53,833 options including calls and puts over 518 trading days. Table 6.1 reports the summary statistics for our data sample. We divide all options into nine buckets according to the moneyness and the maturity: moneyness less than 0.95, between 0.95 and 1.05, and above 1.05; maturity less than 30 days, between 30 and 60 days, and greater than 60 days but less than 90 days. In each category, we present the numbers of options and the average implied volatilities.

The time series of the weekly S&P500 index returns and the Black–Scholes implied volatilities are plotted in Fig. 6.1. Clearly, the patterns for variations display three spikes over the period from 2002 through 2011. The first one occurs at the

[2]In this study, the inputs of equilibrium interest rate and dividend yield are from the real market observations. According to Liu et al. (2005), this is without much loss of generality.

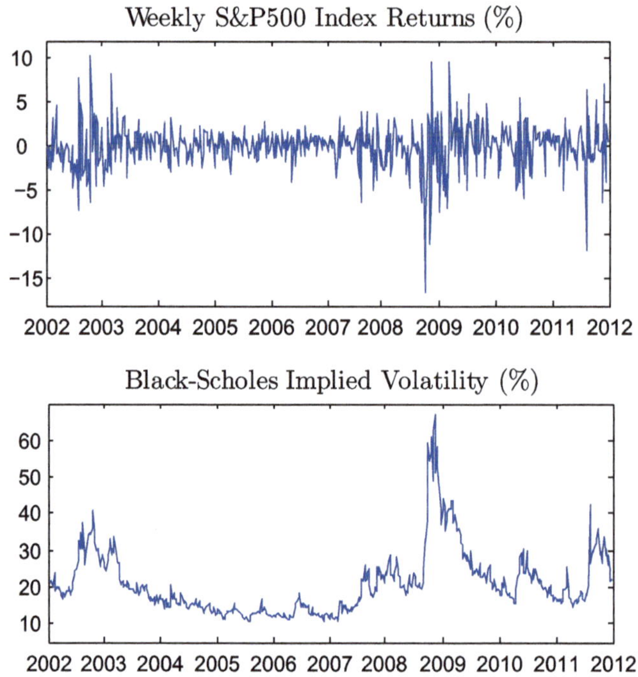

Fig. 6.1 Weekly S&P500 index returns and BS implied
This figure plots the time series of weekly S&P500 index returns and Black–Scholes implied volatilities over the period extending from January 2002 through December 2011

end of 2002, which coincides with the high macroeconomic uncertainty reported in the second semester of 2002 in US. The second peak, and also the most volatile time, is a result of the recent financial crisis from 2008 to 2009. The last spike is observed at the end of 2011, which corresponds to the episode of sovereign credit risk in US.

In this chapter, we estimate models using the method of implied volatility mean squared error (IV-MSE). The loss function is defined as

$$\text{IV-MSE}_t(\vartheta) \equiv \frac{1}{N_t}\sum_{i=1}^{N_t}(\sigma_i(\vartheta) - \hat{\sigma}_i(\vartheta))^2 \tag{6.1}$$

where ϑ is the vector of unknown parameters, σ_i is the Black–Scholes implied volatilities corresponding to observed option prices on day t, $\hat{\sigma}_i$ is the implied volatilities corresponding to theoretical option prices determined by the option pricing models, and N_t is the total amount of option contracts on day t. Since the difference between σ_i and $\hat{\sigma}_i$ is a function of the parameter vector ϑ to be estimated, we can obtain the estimates of implied model parameters by minimizing the mean squared errors.

Table 6.2 Estimation and model fit

Panel A: Estimation

	λ	μ_J	σ_J	a (%)	η	φ
Laplace model	1.808 (2.241)	−0.077 (0.036)	0.040 (0.010)	13.35 (0.041)	−1.434 (1.337)	−16.917 (5.022)
Normal model	0.335 (0.293)	−0.075 (0.025)	0.035 (0.018)	12.24 (0.039)	−2.295 (0.785)	−21.556 (2.924)

Panel B: Option pricing errors

	In-sample fit	Out-of-sample forecast
Laplace model	0.958 (10^{-4})	1.076 (10^{-4})
Normal model	1.043 (10^{-4})	1.288 (10^{-4})

Note This table exhibits results of estimation and model fit for Laplace model and normal model, respectively. Panel A reports estimated parameters for both models and corresponding standard errors in parentheses. Here, we translate the standard deviation of Laplace jump size distribution into the corresponding standard deviation of normal distribution, according to $2\chi^2 = \sigma_J^2$. Panel B presents the average in-sample and out-of-sample pricing errors using the IV-MSE method

6.3.2 Empirical Results

Estimated parameters are reported in panel A of Table 6.2. We can see that both Laplace model and normal model imply similar jump size mean and standard deviation. That is to say, both models are able to capture the market implied jump sizes of underlying index. However, to price jump risk implicit in options, less degrees of risk aversion and fanning effect are estimated for Laplace model than those of normal model. We also present the average in-sample and out-of-sample pricing errors in panel B. Clearly, Laplace model outperforms normal model, due to smaller in-sample error of 0.958 and out-of-sample error of 1.076 in comparison to normal model's 1.043 and 1.288.

This can be seen from Table 6.3 as well. Table 6.3 reports the average out-of-sample pricing errors separated into nine categories according to the moneyness and the maturity. In line with results exhibited in Table 6.2, Laplace model provides a substantial better pricing performance than normal model across all moneyness and maturity categories.

To further see the ability of both models to fit the market implied volatilities across moneyness, we depict the BS implied volatilities of near one-month options predicted by two alternative pricing models and Naik and Lee (1990)'s model as a benchmark in Fig. 6.2. Four days in our data sample are selected to represent different volatile scenarios. According to the time series of the S&P500 index returns and the Black–Scholes implied volatility exhibited in Fig. 6.1, October 15th, 2008 is the most volatile day, September 25th, 2002 and October 5th, 2011 are two high volatile days, and November 29th, 2005 is a low volatile time.

As exhibited in Fig. 6.2, on the low volatile day, all pricing models predict options well. But they perform differently on high volatile days. More specifically, Naik-Lee model generates relatively flat patterns for the plots of implied volatilities against

Table 6.3 Out-of-sample errors by moneyness-maturity categories

Moneyness	Models	Maturity		
		$7 < T \leq 30$	$30 < T \leq 60$	$60 < T \leq 90$
$X/S < 0.95$	Laplace	1.348	1.088	1.371
	Normal	1.629	1.278	1.603
$0.95 \leq X/S < 1.05$	Laplace	1.138	0.999	0.973
	Normal	1.365	1.190	1.229
$1.05 \leq X/S$	Laplace	1.180	1.161	1.122
	Normal	1.431	1.328	1.331

Note This table shows the average out-of-sample pricing errors for Laplace model and normal model across moneyness and maturity. The errors are separated into nine moneyness-maturity categories

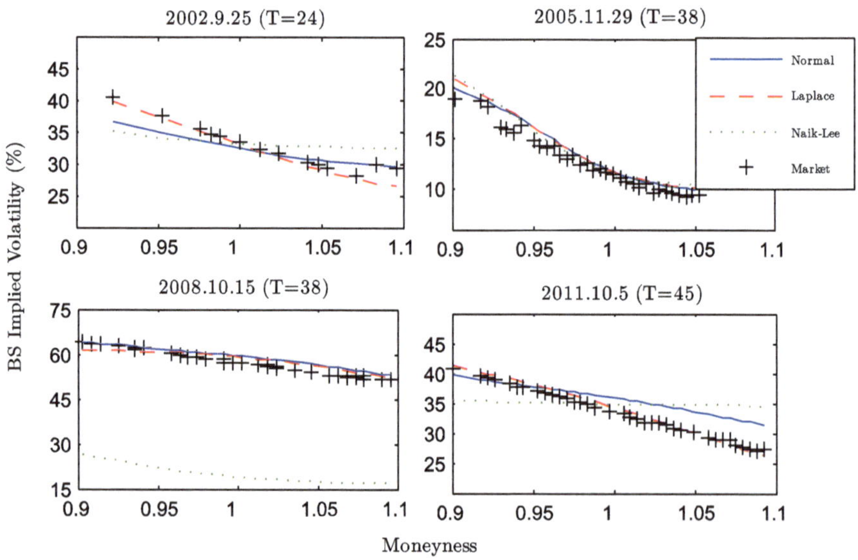

Fig. 6.2 Market and fitted implied volatilities
This figure plots Black–Scholes implied volatilities of the market observations and fitted implied volatilities calculated by pricing models based on Laplace jump size distribution and normal jump size distribution, respectively. Four specific days are selected to represent different episodes of the market, which coincides with the variations of S&P500 index returns and BS implied volatilities exhibited in Fig. 6.1 October 15th, 2008 is the most volatile time, November 29th, 2005 is a low volatile day, and September 25th, 2002 and October 5th, 2011 are two high volatile days. In each day, options with near one-month to expiration are used to calculate the implied volatilities

the moneyness. In contrast, both Laplace model and normal model can produce downward sloping volatility smirks. But evidently, Laplace model fits market implied volatilities better than normal model. During the period of recent financial crisis, both Laplace and normal models price the cross-sectional index options well, whereas Naik-Lee model severely underprices these data.

Table 6.4 Risk premium and risk-neutral distribution

Panel A: Average percentage jump size			
	K (%)	$\widehat{K}$ (%)	
		$\varphi = 0$	$\varphi \neq 0$
Laplace model	−7.34	−7.70	−10.35
Normal model	−7.17	−7.54	−9.53
Panel B: Risk premium			
	π_D (%)	π_J (%)	π_F (%)
Laplace model	4.31 (20.92%)	1.43 (6.94%)	14.86 (72.14%)
Normal model	4.94 (31.83%)	0.86 (5.52%)	9.71 (62.65%)
Panel C: Risk-neutral skewness and kurtosis			
	Skewness		Kurtosis
Laplace model	−1.86		10.31
Normal model	−0.98		4.93

Note This table displays empirical results of average percentage jump size, jump risk premium, and risk-neutral skewness and kurtosis implied by Laplace model and normal model, respectively. Panel A shows the average percentage jump size (K) and the risk-neutral counterpart ($\widehat{K}$) for both models. φ denotes the fanning effect. Panel B reports risk premiums implied by both models and the proportion of each premium accounting for the total market risk premium is given in parentheses. Panel C presents the risk-neutral skewness and kurtosis of stock return distribution implied by options

With estimated parameters of Laplace model and normal model exhibited in Table 6.1, we calculate the average percentage jump size and jump risk premium according to Eqs. (2.15) and (2.19). Results are presented in panel A and panel B of Table 6.4, respectively. Consistent with our numerical findings, when fanning effect is zero, Laplace model produces a little bit larger mean percentage jump size than that of normal model under both physical and risk-neutral probability measures. However, when the estimated fanning effect is incorporated, the difference between two models becomes conspicuous. Moreover, when fanning effect is present, premiums for jump size risk remarkably increase. Therefore, we next examine the jump risk premium implicit in options for both Laplace model and normal model.

Comparing results of both models, we can see that Laplace model captures less diffusive risk premium but larger jump risk premium than normal model. More specifically, the diffusive risk premium is 4.31% and accounts for 20.92% of the total market risk premium for Laplace model, while the corresponding diffusive premium for normal model is 4.94%, accounting for 31.83% of equity premium.

In pricing the jump risk implicit in options, Laplace model captures a premium of 1.43% that is a little bit higher than normal model's 0.86% when fanning effect is absent. That is to say, both models price jump risk similarly in the absence of fanning effect. However, when fanning effect is incorporated, an extra large amount of jump risk premium is produced. For Laplace model, it is 14.86% and accounts for 72.14%

of total equity risk premium, which are much larger than normal model's 9.71% and corresponding proportion of 62.65%. Our results are reasonable and comparable to findings of literature. For example, Pan (2002) find a jump size risk premium of 3.5% which accounts for 38.9% of the total market risk premium, Du (2011) reports 2.46% jump risk premium accounting for 41.8% of the total market risk premium, and Santa-Clara and Yan (2010) suggest time varying jump risk premiums that exceeds 50% of the total market risk premium.

Finally, according to Eqs. (2.31) and (2.32), we calculate the risk-neutral skewness and kurtosis of underlying index return distribution implied by option prices. Results are displayed in panel C of Table 6.4. Clearly, both models generate left-skewed and leptokurtic distribution of underlying stock returns. However, the nonnormal pattern produced by Laplace model is more remarkable than that of normal model. More specifically, the skewness and kurtosis for Laplace model are estimated to −1.86 and 10.31, respectively, in comparison with normal model's −0.98 and 4.93.

Our results are comparable with those of Polkovnichenko and Zhao (2013). Using a non-parametric method, Polkovnichenko and Zhao (2013) estimate the risk-neutral probability distribution over the period from 1996 through 2008. They provide time-varying skewness and kurtosis under both risk-neutral and physical measures (see their Figs. 3, 4 and 5). According to their findings, the risk-neutral skewness exceeds −1 overtime and reaches −2.5 approximately in some spikes, e.g., the period of recent financial crisis. They also show that most risk-neutral kurtosis exceed 5 during their data sample and some are even greater than 10. Particularly, it is more evident for shot-term options. Comparing our results with Polkovnichenko and Zhao (2013)'s empirical findings, we can see that the degree of risk-neutral skewness and kurtosis implied by normal model is moderate, even though our data sample covers the recent financial crisis. In contrast, Laplace model implies consistent risk-neutral distributions with those of Polkovnichenko and Zhao (2013).

6.4 Concluding Remarks

As is well known, the volatility smirk and the nonnormal asset return distribution implied by option prices are two violations of Black–Scholes model. This chapter investigates the effect of jump size distribution on option smirk and risk-neutral stock return distribution. As suggested in Kou (2002) and Kou and Wang (2004) that the jump sized distribution could also exhibit a leptokurtic feature similar as the stock return distribution, we consider a jump-diffusion model with Laplace jump size distribution in comparison with the conventional normal model. In addition, our analysis is built upon a general equilibrium framework, in which the representative agent's risk preference shows a fanning out characteristic.

Results show that, when fanning effect is zero, both Laplace model and normal model price jump risk similarly, and generate relatively flat volatility smirks. Also, both models produce similar patterns of risk-neutral probability distribution. However, when fanning effect is present, Laplace model captures larger jump risk premium implicit in options than that of normal model. As a result, it generates more pronounced volatility smirks relative to normal model. On the other hand, imposing the Laplace distribution on jump sizes results in more remarkable left-skewed and heavy-tailed pattern of the risk-neutral distribution, in comparison with those generated by normal model.

Part IV
Variance Risk Premium

Chapter 7
Risk Aversion Estimated from Volatility Spread

7.1 Introduction

In the recent finance literatures, the model-free volatility measures feature prominently in analyzing the properties of equity market volatility. One strand focuses on the model-free realized volatility calculated by summing intraday high-frequency returns over short time intervals. The volatility constructed in this way is an unbiased and highly efficient estimator. This approach has been popularized by Andersen et al. (2001a, b, c, 2003a, b), Areal and Taylor (2002), Barndorff-Nielsen and Shephard (2002), Barndorff-Nielsen and Shephard (2004a), and Ebens (1999). In parallel to the realized volatility measure, another strand of literature looks at the model-free implied volatility from option prices proposed by Britten-Jones and Neuberger (2000), Jiang and Tian (2005), and Lynch and Panigirtzoglou (2003), which provides a risk-neutral expectation of future volatilities. Contrary to the option implied volatility based on the Black-Scholes model, the model-free implied volatility computed from option prices does not rely on any particular option pricing models.

Relating the risk-neutral volatility to the physical volatility in a unified framework, Bakshi and Madan (2006) formalize the difference between the risk-neutral and the physical volatilities, termed the volatility spreads. They demonstrate that the positive volatility spreads are primarily due to the existence of risk aversion and the heavy left tail of the physical asset distribution. In addition, Bollerslev et al. (2009, 2011) establish a direct link between the model-free implied volatility and the realized volatility in conjunction with moment restrictions. They parameterize the volatility risk premium and suggest that the premium responds to economic state variables.

This chapter first follows the two model-free measures to construct time series of the risk-neutral and the physical volatilities. In particular, the realized volatility is calculated by summing the FTSE-100 index returns and the risk-neutral volatility is obtained by applying the discrete model-free approach of Jiang and Tian (2005) to FTSE-100 index options. Monthly non-overlapping sample is used in this chapter to avoid the telescoping overlap problem described in Christensen et al. (2001). We then carry out the GMM to evaluate the volatility risk aversion. Consistent with prior

J. Chen, *General Equilibrium Option Pricing Method: Theoretical and Empirical Study*, https://doi.org/10.1007/978-981-10-7428-8_7

findings, empirical result shows that the distribution of index returns in our sample is left-skewed. However, the annualized excess kurtosis is negative and we obtain a much smaller estimate of the volatility risk aversion than that in Bakshi and Madan (2006).

The rest of this chapter proceeds as follows. Section 7.2 describes the theoretical relationship between the realized volatility, the model-free implied volatility, and the volatility spread. Data and empirical results are discussed in Sect. 7.3. Finally, Sect. 7.4 concludes.

7.2 Methodology

7.2.1 Realized Volatility

The daily realized volatility (RV), denoted by $\sigma_{RV}(t)$, is calculated by summing the squared intraday returns $r(t, j)$ as follows,

$$\sigma_{RV}^2(t) = \sum_{j=1}^{N} r^2(t, j) \tag{7.1}$$

where t represents day t in the sample and it can be further divided into N intraday periods $j = 1, \ldots, N$. Many studies select the five-minute frequency, including Andersen et al. (2001a, b), and Areal and Taylor (2002) whereby the daily volatilities are calculated by summing 79 squared five-minute intraday returns. In this case, the impact of mean-adjustment is negligible. Some other studies use 48 half-hours, including Andersen et al. (2001c) and Andersen et al. (2003b).

In this chapter, the daily frequency is used and the rolling mean during the time period is taken into account. The monthly realized volatility is given by

$$\sigma_{RV}^2(t) = \sum_{\ell=1}^{N} (r(t, \ell) - \bar{r})^2 \tag{7.2}$$

where t presents tth month in the sample; $\ell = 1, \ldots, N$ represents day ℓ in month t and N is equal to 28; $r(t, \ell)$ is the daily return, and $\bar{r}$ is the rolling mean of month t. It is important to note that the above representation holds only when there is no jump in the price process. Otherwise an alternative estimate of the realized volatility, the realized bipower, has to be used. In the presence of jumps, the realized volatility and the realized bipower converge to different limits. For simplification, we assume the absence of jumps in this chapter.

7.2.2 Model-Free Implied Volatility

According to Carr and Madan (1998) and Britten-Jones and Neuberger (2000), the true risk-neutral expectation of the integrated volatility is equal to the model-free volatility implied by a complete set of call option prices,

$$\sigma_{MF}^2(T_1, T_2) = E^Q\left[\int_{T_1}^{T_2} \sigma_t^2\,\mathrm{d}t\right] = 2\int_0^{\infty} \frac{c(T_2, K) - c(T_1, K)}{K^2}\mathrm{d}K \qquad (7.3)$$

where $\sigma_{MF}(T_1, T_2)$ is the model-free volatility over the period between T_1 and T_2; $c(T_1, K)$ and $c(T_2, K)$ are the prices of European call options that expire at T_1 and T_2, respectively, with the same strike price K; $E^Q(\cdot)$ denotes the risk-neutral expectation. Assume no dividend and zero interest rate, formula (7.3) implies that the model-free volatility between two arbitrary dates T_1 and T_2 is completely determined by a set of call options that expire on these two dates. Because we make no assumption of the underlying process or specific option pricing model for the call prices, the measure is model-free.

Following Taylor (2005) when we relax the restriction of zero interest rate, the model-free implied volatility is given by

$$\sigma_{MF}^2(0, T) = E^Q\left[\int_0^{T} \sigma_t^2\,\mathrm{d}t\right] = 2\mathrm{e}^{rT}\left[\int_0^{F_0} \frac{p(T, K)}{K^2}\mathrm{d}K + \int_{F_0}^{\infty} \frac{c(T, K)}{K^2}\mathrm{d}K\right] \qquad (7.4)$$

where F_0 is the current future price, $p(T, K)$ and $c(T, K)$ are the prices of European put and call option that mature at time T with strike price K, and r is the risk-free interest rate. Applying the put-call parity to Eq. (7.4) we have,

$$\sigma_{MF}^2(0, T) = E^Q\left[\int_0^{T} \sigma_t^2\,\mathrm{d}t\right] = 2\int_0^{\infty} \frac{\mathrm{e}^{rT}c(T, K) - (F_0 - K)^+}{K^2}\mathrm{d}K \qquad (7.5)$$

Equation (7.5) can be derived from Eq. (7.3) as follows,

- the call option valuation $c_0 = E^Q[\max(S_T - K, 0)]$ Eq. (7.3) based on can be rewritten as
$$c_0 = \mathrm{e}^{rT}\left(\mathrm{e}^{-rT}E^Q[\max(S_T - K, 0)]\right),$$
when a positive interest rate is assumed;
- replace the underlying asset price S_T by the forward price F_T so that
$$\mathrm{e}^{-rT}E^Q[\max(S_T - K, 0)] = \mathrm{e}^{-rT}E^Q[\max(F_T - K, 0)].$$

This can be seen as the price of a call option $c_0^{'}$ written on the forward contract F_t with strike price K. Clearly, $c_0 = e^{rT} c_0^{'}$ and

$$\begin{aligned}\sigma_{MF}^2(T_1, T_2) &= E^Q\left[\int_{T_1}^{T_2} \sigma_t^2 \, dt\right] \\ &= 2\int_0^\infty \frac{c(T_2, K) - c(T_1, K)}{K^2} dK \\ &= 2\int_0^\infty \frac{e^{rT} c^{'}(T_2, K) - e^{rT} c^{'}(T_1, K)}{K^2} dK\end{aligned}$$

- consider T_1 as the present time and T_2 as a time in the future,

$$\sigma_{MF}^2(0, T) = E^Q\left[\int_0^T \sigma_t^2 \, dt\right] = 2\int_0^\infty \frac{e^{rT} c^{'}(T, K) - (F_0 - K)^+}{K^2} dK.$$

After substituting the notation of $c(T, K)$ for $c^{'}(T, K)$, we have Eq. (7.5).

Due to the discrete nature of observed options and strike prices, a discretized version of Eq. (7.5) is given by Jiang and Tian (2005) as follows,

$$\sigma_{MF}^2(0, T) = \left(u - \frac{1}{u}\right) \sum_{i=-m}^{m} \frac{e^{rT} c(T, K_i) - (F_0 - K_i)^+}{K_i} \tag{7.6}$$

where

$$K_i = F_0 u^i, \quad i = 0, \pm 1, \pm 2, \cdots, \pm m,$$
$$u = (1 + k)^{\frac{1}{m}}.$$

Here k and m are positive constant and integer respectively, and they need to be sufficiently large to avoid approximation error. The values of strike prices range from $S_0/(1 + k)$ to $S_0(1 + k)$.

7.2.3 Volatility Spread

As defined in Bakshi and Madan (2006), the volatility spreads are equal to the difference between the risk-neutral and the physical variances divided by the physical variances,

$$\frac{\sigma_Q^2(t) - \sigma_P^2(t)}{\sigma_P^2(t)}$$

where Q and P denote the risk-neutral and the physical measure, respectively. Assuming a pricing kernel with the power utility function (Dybvig 1981),

$$m(R) = \exp(-\gamma R)$$

where γ is the risk aversion parameter and R is the market index returns, Bakshi and Madan (2006) show that volatility spreads can be written as

$$\frac{\sigma_Q^2(t) - \sigma_P^2(t)}{\sigma_P^2(t)} \approx -\gamma\,(\sigma_P^2(t))^{\frac{1}{2}}\,\theta_P(t) + \frac{\gamma^2}{2}\,\sigma_P^2(t)\,(\kappa_P(t) - 3) \tag{7.7}$$

where $\theta_P(t)$ and $\kappa_P(t)$ represent skewness and kurtosis of the physical distribution of market index returns. Equation (7.7) shows that the tail asymmetry and tail size of physical index distribution simultaneously determine the volatility spreads. In particular, the physical skewness and the excess kurtosis have a weight of $-\gamma(\sigma_P^2(t))^{\frac{1}{2}}$ and $(\gamma^2/2)\sigma_P^2(t)$, respectively.

7.3 Data and Empirical Results

The FTSE-100 option contracts used in this study are European options written on the FTSE-100 index traded on the London International Financial Futures and Options Exchange (LIFFE). Both the FTSE-100 options and futures expire at the same time on the third Friday of the maturity month. Therefore the future price is equal to the spot price when the options expire and the European-style FTSE-100 options can then be viewed as if they are written on the futures. Hence the spot index is not needed.

Our sample period is from April 1992 to March 2005. Conventional exclusion rules are applied. First, the time to maturity is between 7 and 365 days. Second, options prices must be greater than 0.5. Third, in-the-money options are removed as they contain less information due to infrequent trading.

The risk-free interest rates used in this study are the London Interbank Offer Rate (LIBOR) obtained from the DataStream. On each trading day, we match the interest rate with options having the same time to maturity.

Summary statistics for the daily FTSE-100 index returns are reported in Table 7.1, along with those reported in a few existing studies. The daily index returns in this chapter are clearly fat-tailed and mildly left-skewed. This is also evident from Fig. 7.1a which plots the index return distributions against the normal distribution with the same mean and standard deviation. As a matter of fact, all previous studies tabulated in Table 7.1 show a positive excess kurtosis regardless of the sample period or the asset under investigation. However, for skewness Areal and Taylor (2002),

Table 7.1 Summary statistics for daily returns

Studies	Sample period	Underlying asset	Daily returns			
			Mean	Stdev	Skew	Kurt
Current study	1992–2005	FTSE-100 index	0.0002	0.0107	−0.1016	6.0656
Areal and Taylor (2002)	1990–1998	FTSE-100 index	0.0005	0.0098	0.1614	4.8084
ABDE (2001)	1993–1998	DJIA	0.036	1.438	0.172	5.908
ABDL (2003)	1986–1996	DM/$	−0.007	0.700	0.003	5.28
ABDL (2003)	1986–1996	¥/$	−0.01	0.692	−0.129	6.64
Engle (2004)	1963–2003	S&P 500	0.0003	0.0094	−1.44	41.45
Engle (2004)	1990–2003	S&P 500	0.0003	0.0104	−0.10	6.78
Brock et al. (1992)	1897–1986	DJIA	0.00017	0.0108	−0.1047	16.00

Note this table reports the distribution of daily FTSE-100 index returns over the period from April 1992 to March 2005. Also presented are the summary statistics in a number of existing studies. ABDE (2001) refers to Andersen et al. (2001a), ABDL (2003) refers to Andersen et al. (2003b), and Brock et al. (1992) refers to Brock et al. (1992)

Andersen et al. (2001a), and Andersen et al. (2003b) report a fat right tail while others find a left tail.[1]

The monthly realized volatilities $\sigma_{RV}(t)$ are calculated according to Eq. (7.2) and plotted in Fig. 7.1b. The distribution of $\sigma_{RV}(t)$ is strongly right-skewed and leptokurtic with a skewness of 1.88 and a kurtosis of 7.572. The values are similar to those in most of the existing studies. For example, Areal and Taylor (2002) show that the estimate of skewness is 2.47 and kurtosis is 18.51 for the FTSE-100 index; Andersen et al. (2003b) find that the estimate of skewness is 1.99 and kurtosis is 10.49 for DM/$, and for ¥/$ the skewness is 2.20 and kurtosis is 12.94. In contrast, the logarithm of realized volatilities $\ln(\sigma_{RV}(t))$ are much closer to normal distribution as plotted in Fig. 7.1c. The logarithm transform reduces the skewness estimate to 0.5752 and kurtosis to 2.9997.

To obtain the model-free implied volatilities $\sigma_{MF}(t)$ as defined in Eq. (7.6), we need to construct an implied volatility surface to extract the unobserved prices as a result of the limited number of strikes traded in the market. Following the method in Jiang and Tian (2005), we first use the Black-Scholes model to back out implied volatilities from traded options. We then apply the curve-fitting approach to the

[1] Andersen et al. (2003b) show a positive skewness only when they consider DM/$ as the underlying asset.

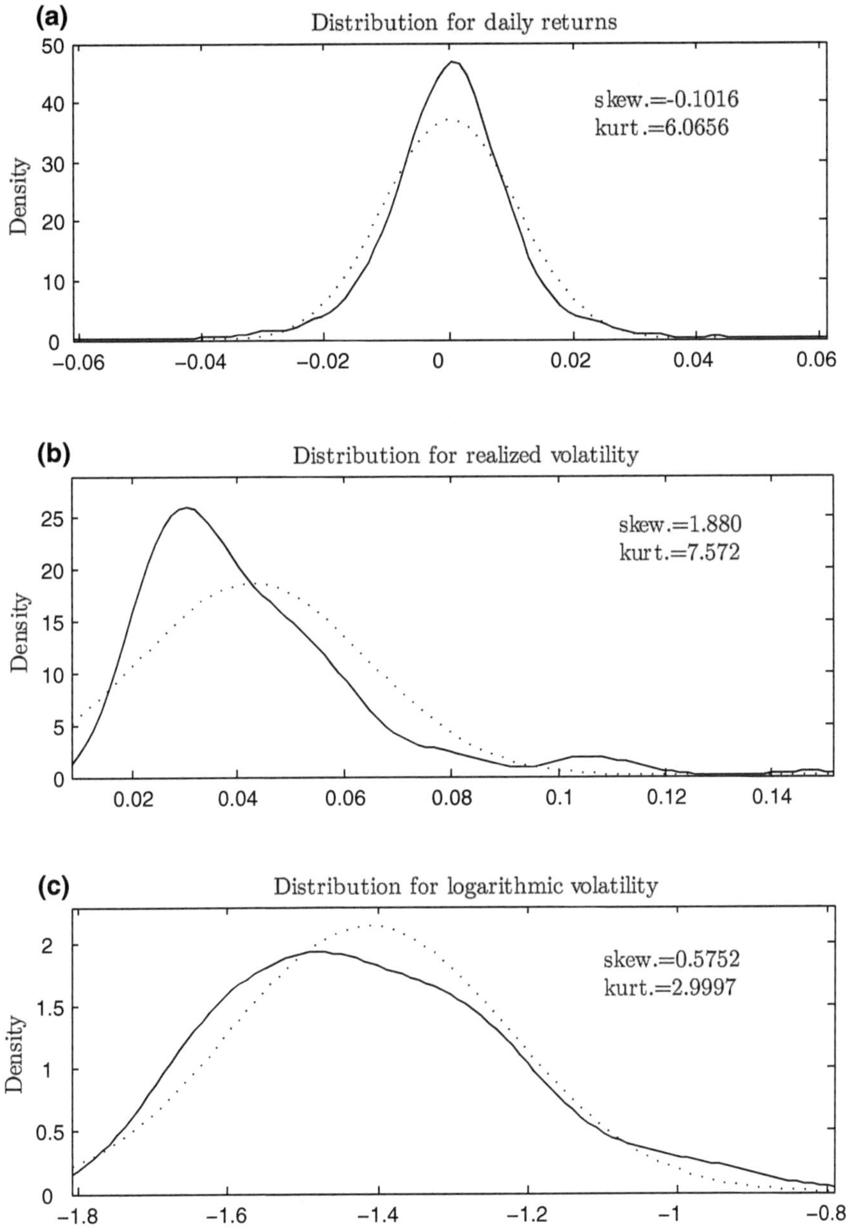

Fig. 7.1 Distributions of daily returns and monthly volatilities
Distributions for the FTSE-100 index daily returns, the monthly realized volatilities, and the logarithm of monthly volatilities are plotted in solid line. The skewness and kurtosis for each distribution are shown in the top-right corner. The normal distribution with the same mean and standard deviation is plotted in dotted line

Table 7.2 Summary statistics

	$\sigma_{RV}(t)$	$\ln(\sigma_{RV}(t))$	$\sigma_{MF}(t)$	$\ln(\sigma_{MF}(t))$
Mean	0.0428	−1.4110	0.05	−1.3131
Stdev	0.0214	0.1859	0.012	0.1047
Skewness	1.880	0.5752	0.7419	0.2998
Kurtosis	7.572	2.9997	2.8619	2.3260
Minimum	0.0175	−1.7696	0.0265	−1.3132
Maximum	0.1472	−0.8321	0.0887	−1.0521

Note Summary statistics for the monthly realized volatilities $\sigma_{RV}(t)$, the monthly model-free volatilities $\sigma_{MF}(t)$ and the logarithm of both are reported for the sample period from April 1992 to March 2005

options with the same maturity. We define the option moneyness as the ratio of strike price over futures level (K/F) and divide the moneyness dimension from 0 to infinity into a large quantity of intervals with an equal width of 0.01, called moneyness bin. Some bins may have more than one option while others none. An average value is taken for the bins with multiple options while the bins with no options are removed. The cubic spline is fitted to produce a continuum of implied volatilities and this is carried out for all maturities. Outside the range of moneyness the fitted curve is assumed to be flat. Finally, the Black-Scholes model is used again to transform all implied volatilities back into call option prices. Note that the curve fitting approach is applied to the implied volatilities, not directly to option prices due to the non-linear relationship between the option prices and the strike prices. In addition, the Black-Scholes model is used only as a mapping tool between the option prices and the implied volatilities.

The extracted call prices have a common maturity of 28 calendar days to avoid the telescoping overlap problem discussed in Christensen et al. (2001). The monthly model-free volatilities are then obtained using Eq. (7.6) where the discretization and truncation parameters m and k are set to be 40 and 0.4, respectively, in order to minimize the approximation errors.[2]

As reported in Table 7.2, the model-free volatilities are right-skewed and leptokurtic, similar to the realized volatilities, and the logarithm transform reduces both skewness and kurtosis. Moreover, the model-free volatilities are less volatile with a standard deviation of 0.012 than the realized counterpart which has a standard deviation of 0.0214. This is different from the findings in Jiang and Tian (2005).

In Fig. 7.2, the model-free volatilities fluctuate mildly above the time series of the realized volatilities. The model-free volatilities are substantially higher than the realized volatilities with positive spreads or risk premium, which is consistent with previous findings in Jiang and Tian (2005), Bakshi and Madan (2006), and Bollerslev et al. (2011).

[2] In the numerical experiment in Jiang and Tian (2005), the approximation errors due to discretization and truncation are negligible when m and k increase to 40 and 0.4, respectively.

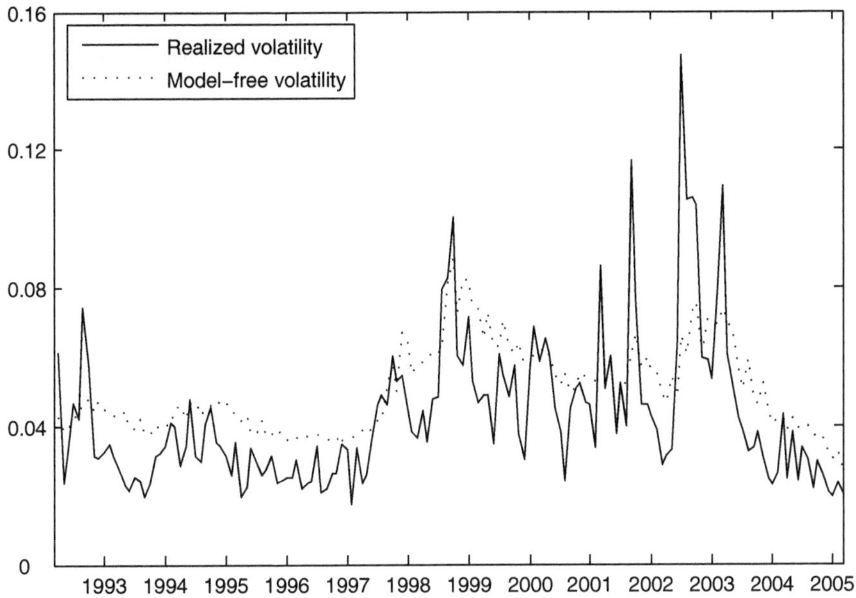

Fig. 7.2 Difference between realized volatilities and model-free implied volatilities
This figure plots the difference between the monthly realized volatilities defined in Eq. (7.2) and the monthly model-free implied volatilities defined in Eq. (7.6) for the sample period from April 1992 to March 2005

In Table 7.3, the realized volatilities, the model-free volatilities, and the volatility spread for each year in the sample are tabulated. We can see that with the monthly estimates, the volatility spreads are systematically and substantially positive.

7.3.1 Risk Aversion Estimate

The volatility spreads defined in Eq. (7.7) can be estimated using the Generalized Method of Moments (GMM). According to Eq. (7.7), the error term $\varepsilon(t+1)$ is given by

$$\varepsilon(t+1) = \frac{\sigma_Q^2(t+1) - \sigma_P^2(t+1)}{\sigma_P^2(t+1)} + \gamma\,(\sigma_P^2(t+1))^{\frac{1}{2}}\,\theta_P(t+1)$$
$$-\frac{\gamma^2}{2}\,\sigma_P^2(t+1)\,(\kappa_P(t+1) - 3) \tag{7.8}$$

where $\theta_P(t+1)$ and $\kappa_P(t+1)$ are the conditional skewness and kurtosis of the physical underlying distribution at time $t+1$ and γ is the risk aversion parameter.

Table 7.3 Empirical Estimates of the Volatility Spreads

	Realized volatility	Model-free volatility	Volatility spread
	σ_{RV} (%)	σ_{MF} (%)	$(\sigma_Q^2 - \sigma_P^2)/\sigma_P^2$
1992:04–1993:03	14.38	15.16	0.1113
1993:04–1994:03	9.88	14.09	1.0357
1994:04–1995:03	12.09	15.74	0.6939
1995:04–1996:03	9.15	13.35	1.1268
1996:04–1997:03	9.22	12.74	0.9098
1997:04–1998:03	14.83	17.39	0.3761
1998:04–1999:03	21.01	24.79	0.3924
1999:04–2000:03	17.50	21.96	0.5756
2000:04–2001:03	17.15	18.78	0.1992
2001:04–2002:03	18.37	19.04	0.0743
2002:04–2003:03	27.48	22.22	−0.3461
2003:04–2004:03	12.85	17.83	0.9268
2004:04–2005:03	8.99	12.41	0.9071

Note This table reports the annualized estimate of realized volatilities σ_{RV}, the model-free volatilities σ_{MF}, and the volatility spreads $(\sigma_Q^2 - \sigma_P^2)/\sigma_P^2$ for the period from April 1992 to March 2005, with σ_Q being equivalent to σ_{MF} and σ_P to σ_{RV}

We follow the approach in Bakshi and Madan (2006) and estimate γ via the GMM by minimizing the function,

$$J_T \equiv \arg\min_{\gamma} g_T^{'} W_T \, g_T \tag{7.9}$$

where W_T is a symmetric weighting matrix, and $g_T(\gamma) \equiv \frac{1}{T}\sum_{t=1}^{T} \varepsilon(t+1) \otimes Z(t)$, in which $Z(t)$ is a time-t information variable. Three sets of instrumental variables are employed here. Set 1 contains a constant and $\sigma_Q^2(t)$; Set 2 contains a constant, $\sigma_Q^2(t)$, and $\sigma_Q^2(t-1)$; Set 3 contains a constant, $\sigma_Q^2(t)$, $\sigma_Q^2(t-1)$, and $\sigma_Q^2(t-2)$. As discussed in Hansen (1982), the test statistic for the over-identifying restriction follows the χ^2 distribution asymptotically with degrees of freedom determined by the difference between the number of moment conditions and the number of estimated parameters.

Jackwerth and Rubinstein (1996) argue that the skewness and the kurtosis might be underestimated when a relatively short window, say 30 days, is selected to estimate the higher moments. Hence in this chapter the physical skewness (θ_P) and kurtosis (κ_P) are calculated using the FTSE-100 index returns of either 120 or 270 days, respectively. We also calculate the quarterly skewness and kurtosis, and then annualize the average.[3]

[3]Under the i.i.d assumption, the annualized skewness and excess kurtosis can be obtained by dividing the quarterly skewness and excess kurtosis by $\sqrt{4}$ and 4, respectively.

Table 7.4 Risk aversion parameter estimation

	df	γ	t-ratio	J_T	p-value
Panel A. 120-day window					
Set 1	1	3.37	7.11	4.68	0.031
Set 2	2	3.4	7.22	3.38	0.185
Set 3	3	3.46	7.53	3.25	0.355
Panel B. 270-day window					
Set 1	1	2.05	9.31	4.42	0.036
Set 2	2	2.13	3.49	3.38	0.185
Set 3	3	2.17	4.09	3.51	0.319

Note The risk aversion parameter γ is estimated using Eq. (4.9) via the GMM. The degrees of freedom, df, are the difference between the numbers of instrument and unknown parameters. In Panel A the skewness and kurtosis are calculated from returns of a 120-day window. In Panel B the skewness and kurtosis are calculated from returns of a 270-day window

Parameter estimates for the risk aversion factor γ are reported in Table 7.4. With the first set of instrumental variables and 1 degree of freedom, the model is rejected for both estimate windows of 120 and 270 days. With the other two sets of instrumental variables, the model is accepted with higher p-values for the over-identifying test. In addition, the estimates of γ are all statistically significant and stable across different sets of instrumental variables.

When the estimate window for the physical skewness and kurtosis extends from 120 days to 270 days, the estimate of the risk aversion decreases to 2. Using the FTSE-100 index options and power utility, Bliss and Panigirtzoglou (2004) reports comparable findings for γ at 7.91 for the one-week forecasting horizon and 4.44 for the two-week forecasting horizon. Using the S&P100 index options and the power utility, Bakshi and Madan (2006) provide an estimate of γ at 17 and 12 when the physical skewness and kurtosis are extracted from 90 and 200 days returns, respectively. In their analysis, the volatility spreads are greatest when the physical index distribution is negatively-skewed and fat-tailed. Specifically, the annualized estimates for the skewness θ_P and the kurtosis κ_P are -0.0142 and 3.0065, respectively, for 90 days returns. On the other hand, with 200 days history, θ_P is -0.0267 and κ_P is 3.0144.

Our findings differ from those reported in Bakshi and Madan (2006) as we have a left-skewed and heavy-tailed index distribution. Particularly, the average annualized skewness and kurtosis in our sample period are -0.0049 and 2.8909 for 120-day horizon and -0.0144 and 2.8804 for 270-day horizon. It implies that although the volatility spreads can be decomposed into two parts that represent the tail asymmetry and the tail size of the physical index distribution, positive skewness and negative excess kurtosis jointly determine the evolution of the volatility spreads. This is the reason why the estimates of γ in this chapter is much smaller than those in Bakshi and Madan (2006).

7.4 Conclusions

Utilizing the relationship between the risk-neutral and the physical volatilities proposed by Bakshi and Madan (2006), this chapter constructs time series of the model-free and the realized volatilities and estimates the volatility spreads and the volatility risk aversion embedded in these time series.

Our empirical evidence shows that the risk-neutral volatilities calculated by a complete set of call options traded on the FTSE-100 index exceed their physical counterparts. Positive volatility spreads are thus constructed and they are found to be related to the tail size and the tail asymmetry. Contrary to the evidence in Bakshi and Madan (2006), we find that the annualized excess kurtosis is less than zero and the annual distributions for index returns are heavily right-tailed. As the higher moments jointly determine the volatility spreads, the estimates of risk aversion we obtained via the GMM is much smaller than that obtained by Bakshi and Madan (2006).

Chapter 8
Predictability of VRP: Hongkong Evidence

8.1 Introduction

Volatility modeling is one of the central issues for theoretical studies and practical applications. In the literature, the conditional volatility model family, i.e. GARCH type model proposed by Engle (1982) and Bollerslev (1986) is used to model the fat-tail and the volatility clustering of stock return. On the other hand, the stochastic volatility model (Heston 1993 and Shephard and Andersen 2009) provides an alternative approach to model the time-varying behavior of volatility as a latent state variable. Despite the success of previous models, their predictions of volatility crucially rely on the specification of models used. Therefore, once there exists model misspecification error, the estimates would become inconsistent. Partially inspired by above issues, the model-free volatility approach, including realized volatility and model-free implied volatility, attracts a lot of research attention.

The realized volatility based on high frequency intraday transaction data (Andersen et al. 2001a, b, c, 2003b; Areal and Taylor 2002, Barndorff-Nielsen and Shephard 2004a, b) is more and more popular due to development of information technology and availability of high frequency or even tick-by-tick transaction data. Andersen et al. (2003b) prove that in the absence of microstructure market noise and jumps, realized variance is a consistent estimator of underlying integrated variance. Barndorff-Nielsen and Shephard (2004a, b) further propose to use the realized bipower variation as a consistent measure of integrated variance in presence of jumps. Although sampling at higher frequency would reduce the error introduced by discretization, errors caused by microstructure noise would increase due to the well known bias-variance tradeoff.

In addition to the realized method which utilizes high frequency stock transaction data to recover the volatility in physical measure, (Jiang and Tian 2005) extend the (Britten-Jones and Neuberger 2000) result to calculate the model-free implied volatility from option prices under risk neutral measure. Britten-Jones and Neuberger (2000) assume that the no-arbitrage condition holds and the stock price follows diffusion process. Jiang and Tian (2005) relax the assumption by considering

J. Chen, *General Equilibrium Option Pricing Method: Theoretical and Empirical Study*, https://doi.org/10.1007/978-981-10-7428-8_8

jump-diffusion process and further point out that compared with past realized volatility and B-S implied volatility, model-free implied volatility contains more information and performs better in predicting future realized volatility. This approach does not depend on a specific option pricing model and aggregates the information contained in option prices.

It is worth mentioning that the model-free implied variance is the expectation of future return variance under risk neutral measure while the realized variance is under real or physical measure. The difference is called variance risk premium. Carr and Wu (2009) document that this premium is statistically significant for indexes and most individual stocks chosen in U.S. market. They argue that this premium is among the predictors of stock return and can not be explained by conventional predictors. Bollerslev et al. (2009) use the variance risk premium as stock return predictors and contend that it is a proxy of overall market degree of risk aversion. Bollerslev et al. (2011) employ the GMM method to estimate time-varying risk aversion and risk premium parameters and relate these with macroeconomic state variables. Zhou (2010) points out that variance risk premium could predict future stock return, bond yield and credit spread. Bakshi and Madan (2006) study the volatility spread, which is defined as the ratio of variance risk premium and realized variance, and argue that this positive volatility spread is caused by investors risk aversion and fat tail of asset return. Taylor (2005) and Chen and Liu (2010) study realized volatility of FTSE-100 future prices and the volatility spread of FTSE-100 index options, respectively.

Since previous studies focus on U.S. or European markets, this chapter study the Hong Kong market using model-free volatility method. More specifically, this chapter use variance risk premium as a predictor of stock return. We find that, in addition to conventional predictors such as dividend yield, short term interest rate and P/E ratio, variance risk premium still exhibits extra prediction power, especially in financial crisis period.

The paper is organized as follows. Section 8.2 describes the theoretical relationship between realized volatility, the model-free implied volatility and variance risk premium. Data and empirical results are discussed in Sect. 8.3. Finally, Sect. 8.4 concludes.

8.2 Model

8.2.1 Realized Volatility

The daily realized volatility, RV or $\sigma_{RV}(t)$ is defined as summation of intraday squared returns:

$$\sigma_{RV}^2(t) = \sum_{j=1}^{N} r^2(t,j)$$

where t is the tth day, which is divided into N subperiods, and $r(t, j)$ denotes the jth intraday return in day t. In application, Andersen et al. (2001c), Andersen et al. (2001a), and Taylor (2005) use the summation of 79 five-minute squared intraday returns to calculate realized volatility while Andersen et al. (2003b) use 30 min data.

In this chapter, we define the monthly realized variance as:

$$\sigma_{RV}^2 = \sum_{k=1}^{N} (r(t,k) - \bar{r})^2$$

where t, k denote the tth month in the sample and the kth day within in a given month. The total number of days given month t is N and $r(t, k)$, $\bar{r}$ is daily return and mean of the daily returns in month t, respectively. It is noted that we use mean adjustment in the formula and assume there is no jump component in stock price for simplicity.

8.2.2 Model-Free Implied Volatility

According to Carr and Madan (1998) and Britten-Jones and Neuberger (2000), the expectation of integrated variance under risk neutral measure could be calculated from a complete set of call option prices:

$$\sigma_{MF}^2(T_1, T_2) = E^Q\left[\int_{T_1}^{T_2} \sigma_t^2 \mathrm{d}t\right] = 2\int_0^{\infty} \frac{c(T_2, K) - c(T_1, K)}{K^2} \mathrm{d}K$$

where σ_{MF} is model-free implied volatility measure from T_1 to T_2; $c(T_1, K)$ and $c(T_2, K)$ are the European type option prices with strike price K and time to maturity T_1 and T_2; $E^Q(\cdot)$ denotes the expectation operator under risk neutral measure. Under the assumption of zero dividend yield and interest rate, it implies that the model-free implied volatility measure from T_1 to T_2 is determined by a series of option prices with time to maturity in these two days. Because we make no assumption of underlying process or specific option pricing model for the call prices, the measure is model-free.

Following Taylor (2005) by relaxing the assumption of zero interest rate, the model-free impled volatility from 0 to T could be expressed as

$$\sigma_{MF}^2(0, T) = E^Q\left[\int_0^{T} \sigma_t^2 \,\mathrm{d}t\right] = 2\mathrm{e}^{rT}\left(\int_0^{F_0} \frac{p(T, K)}{K^2} \,\mathrm{d}K + \int_{F_0}^{\infty} \frac{c(T, K)}{K^2} \,\mathrm{d}K\right)$$

where F_0 is the current future price, $p(T, K)$ and $c(T, K)$ are the European put and call options with time to maturity T and strike price K and r is the risk free interest rate. Applying the put-call parity to above equation, we obtain:

$$\sigma^2_{MF}(0,T) = E^Q\left[\int_0^T \sigma_t^2\,\mathrm{d}t\right] = 2\int_0^\infty \frac{\mathrm{e}^{rT}c(T,K) - (F_0 - K)^+}{K^2}\,\mathrm{d}K$$

with its discrete version as:

$$\sigma^2_{MF}(0,T) = E^Q\left[\int_0^T \sigma_t^2 \mathrm{d}t\right] \approx 2\sum_{i=1}^{m} \frac{\mathrm{e}^{rT}c(T,K_i) - (S_0\mathrm{e}^{rT} - K)^+}{K_i^2}\Delta K_i$$

where r is risk free interest rate, $\Delta K_i = (K_{max} - K_{min})/m$, $K_i = K_{min} + i\Delta K$, $(0 \leq i \leq m)$.

In the above formula, first, the dicretization error is introduced by replacing integration with summation. Second, in practice, the strike prices of options are within a certain range whereas the above formula requires an integration from zero to infinity, thus introducing truncation error. Jiang and Tian (2005) discuss the above two errors and conclude that under certain conditions, both types of errors could be controlled satisfactorily.

8.2.3 Variance Risk Premium

Following Bakshi and Madan (2006), Bollerslev et al. (2009), Zhou (2010), we define the variance risk premium as the difference of expectation of future returns under risk neutral measure and physical measure:

$$VRP_t = E_t^Q(Var_{t,t+1}) - E_t^P(Var_{t,t+1})$$

Of course, both terms are unobservable and we use the model-free implied volatility and ex post realized volatility as their empirical counterparts. The variance risk premium is considered as proxy of degree of risk aversion of representative agent (Rosenberg and Engle 2002; Bakshi and Madan 2006; Bollerslev et al. 2009). Bollerslev et al. (2009) and Drechsler and Yaron (2011) show that this premium is induced by uncertainty of consumption related to macroeconomic uncertainty through a recursive utility framework.

8.2.4 Predictability of Stock Return

The predictability of stock return refers to the phenomenon that in the long-run, if we regress stock return on certain traditional predictors, the coefficients in front of them are statistically significant and the stock return could be partially explained by those predictors. In traditional dividend growth model, price-dividend ratio is the discounted value of future stock returns. Campbell (1991) and Cochrane (1992) point out that dividend yield can predict excess returns. Campbell and Yogo (2006) use the logarithm of dividend price ratio, logarithm of earning price ratio, short term interest rate and term spread as predictors. In this chapter, we consider dividend yield, logarithm of P/E ratio and short term interest rate.

8.3 Data and Empirical Results

8.3.1 Data

We choose the Heng Seng stock index options in our empirical analysis, which have the longest history and largest trading volume in Hong Kong option markets. According to the contract rules of HSI(Heng Seng Index) options, HSI option is an European type option with time to maturity as the second last business day within the last trading month. The sample spans from January 2000 to September 2009. The original option data is obtained from Bloomburg and the Heng Seng stock index and HIBOR (Hong Kong Interbank Offering Rate) rate are from CEIC daily database. When constructing the option implied volatility, we choose the risk free interest rate from the HIBIOR rate with most close time to maturity. Conventional exclusion rules are applied. First, we delete the option data with prices less than minimum trading tick and zero trading volume; Second, we eliminate the option with time to maturity smaller than 7 days or larger than 365 calendar days; Third, we rule out the option data violating boundary conditions and put-call parity. We also use VIX index downloaded from the website of CBOE (Chicago Board of Options Exchange).Actually, CBOE replaces its original way calculating VIX from Black-Scholes model implied volatility based on S&P 100 index options with model-free implied volatility approach based on S&P 500 index options since September, 2003.

When constructing the model-free implied volatility, since the strike prices for options are within a certain range, we have to construct the implied volatility surface to extract option prices with other strike prices. Following Jiang and Tian (2005), first, we back out the Black-Scholes implied volatility from option prices observed from the market. Second, we apply the cubic spline to fit and interpolate the implied volatility curve for options with the same time to maturity. More specifically, we define the moneyness of option as the ratio of strike price divided by current stock price (K/S) and divided into many small intervals with length equals to 0.01, called moneyness bin. Some bins may have more than one option while others none. An average value is taken for the bins with multiple options while the bins with no options are removed. After that, cubic spline is used to interpolate and produce a continuum of implied volatility as curves and repeat it for all time to maturity days. The curve is flat outside the moneyness region implied from option prices. Finally, we back up option prices from implied volatility using Black-Scholes models. Considering that the relationship between option price and strike price is nonlinear, we interpolate the implied volatility rather than option prices. Note that we only use Black-Scholes as a one-to-one mapping tool from implied volatility to option prices and do not assume that option prices obey Black-Scholes models. Jiang and Tian (2005) discuss the discretization error and truncation error and make this method applicable in practice.

In the empirical result part, when calculating the model-free implied volatility for U.S. market, we follow Zhou (2010) to use VIX index published by CBOE directly. According to the white papers published by CBOE, VIX index is neutral expectation of future 30 days return variance inferred from every day option trading data. We use the VIX index at the last trading day of every trading month as expectation of next month so that we could obtain a non-overlapping sample. Jiang and Tian (2007) point out that there exists approximation error for VIX index. However, as Bollerslev et al. (2009) point out, VIX becomes the standard practice in industry with intense attention. In order to be comparable with other researches, we use VIX index as measure of model-free implied volatility in U.S. market and the realized volatility is obtained from S&P 500 index. We extract the implied volatility for HSI index from the HSI index option data, while the realized volatility is constructed from HSI index. As a comparison, we calculate the realized volatility from Shanghai Composite Stock Index as a measure for mainland, China market.

8.3.2 *Summary Statistics of Volatility Measures*

From the summary statistics reported in Table 8.1, we could conclude that: First, the realized volatility in mainland market is much higher than that of Hong Kong and U.S. market, which is consistent with the speculative atmosphere in mainland market. Moreover, it is in accordance with the abrupt market change from the bull market after 2006 to bear market in 2008 due to financial crisis. On the other hand, the realized volatility in Hong Kong and U.S. market follows similar trends, especially after 2008, when both of them reach historically high level with overall correlation greater than 0.8. However, the correlation between Hong Kong market, U.S. market and mainland market are 0.4 and 0.3, respectively, which is consistent with the

Table 8.1 Summary statistics and correlation matrix

	Summary statistic							Correlation			
	Mean	Median	Max.	Min.	Std.	Skew.	Kurt.	HRV	UMF	URV	SRV
HMF	0.28	0.25	0.55	0.16	0.09	0.83	2.95	0.73	0.69	0.62	0.38
HRV	0.23	0.20	1.09	0.07	0.14	2.72	15.32		0.74	0.87	0.41
UMF	0.22	0.21	0.60	0.10	0.09	1.44	5.85			0.91	0.27
URV	0.19	0.16	0.80	0.07	0.12	2.38	10.79				0.29
SRV	0.25	0.22	0.58	0.09	0.12	0.91	3.03				

Note HMF, UMF denote the model-free implied volatility from Hong Kong and U.S markets, respectively; HRV, URV, SRV denote the realized volatility from Hong Kong, U.S. and mainland, China markets, respectively

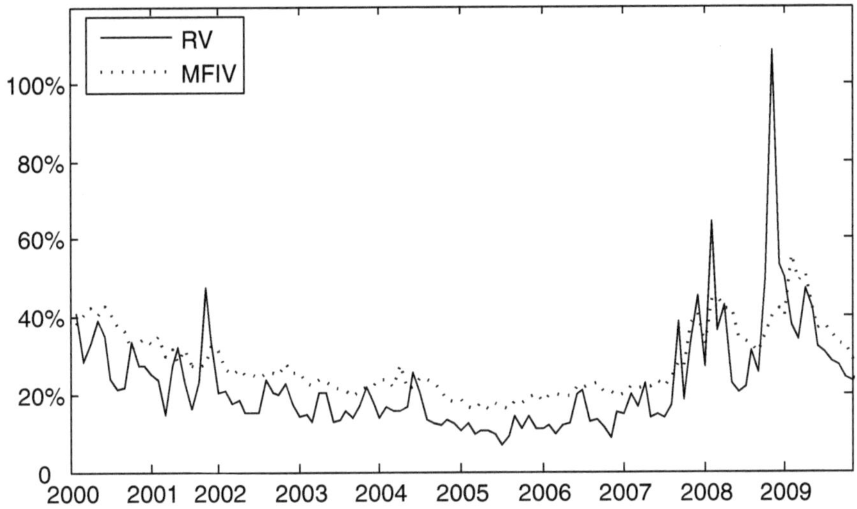

Fig. 8.1 Realized volatility and model-free implied volatility for the Hong Kong market
This figure plots the realized volatility (RV HK) and model-free implied volatility (MFIV HK) for the Hong Kong market over the sample from January 2000 to September 2009

deviation of mainland market from world market as a whole at the beginning of financial crisis. Due to this deviation, we mainly focus on the relationship between Hong Kong market and U.S. market in later discussion.

Second, the model-free implied volatility in Hong Kong market is generally greater than that of U.S. market. For the Hong Kong market and U.S. market individually, from Figs. 8.1 and 8.2 we can observe that in the long run, model-free implied volatility and realized volatility follow similar trends; model-free volatility is generally higher than realized volatility. Exception occurs during volatile market period when the realized volatility will temporarily be above model-free implied volatility, which is similar to previous studies such as Zhou (2010). The difference of model-free implied volatility and realized volatility are statistically significantly positive with mean difference at 0.0498, t-statistic at 5.72 for Hong Kong market and mean difference at 0.0308, t-statistic at 6.43 for U.S. market, respectively (Fig. 8.3).

8.3.3 Variance Risk Premium

Figure 8.4 shows the variance risk premium for the Hong Kong market and U.S. market, respectively. We can observe that both premiums share similar trends with correlation at 0.74. Moreover, the variance risk premium in Hong Kong market is greater than U.S. market, which is a reflection of more degree of risk aversion and Hong Kong's vulnerability to outer influence as a small open economy.

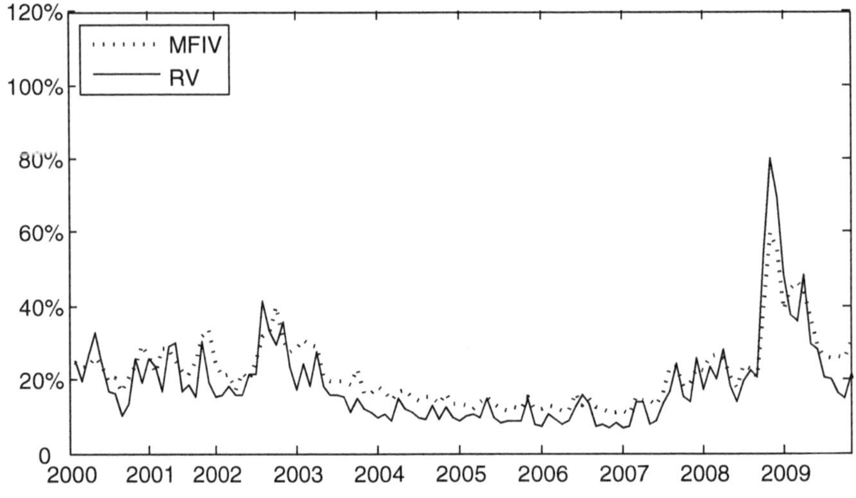

Fig. 8.2 Realized volatility and model-free implied volatility for the U.S. market
This figure plots the realized volatility (RV US) and model-free implied volatility (MFIV US) for the Hong Kong market over the sample from January 2000 to September 2009

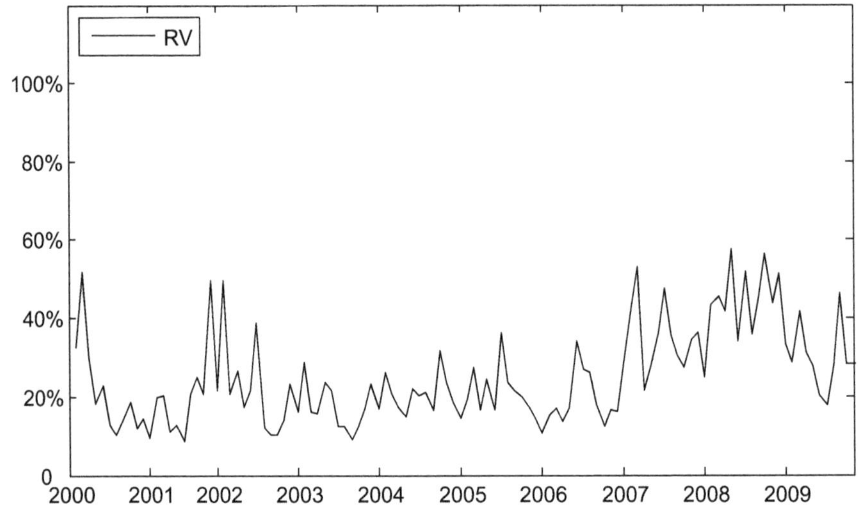

Fig. 8.3 Realized volatility in Mainland China market
This figure plots the realized volatility (RV Shanghai) for the mainland China market over the sample from January 2000 to September 2009

8.3.4 Predictability of Stock Return

We choose the difference between monthly return of Heng Seng index and one month HIBOR rate as excess return. Among conventional stock return predictors, short

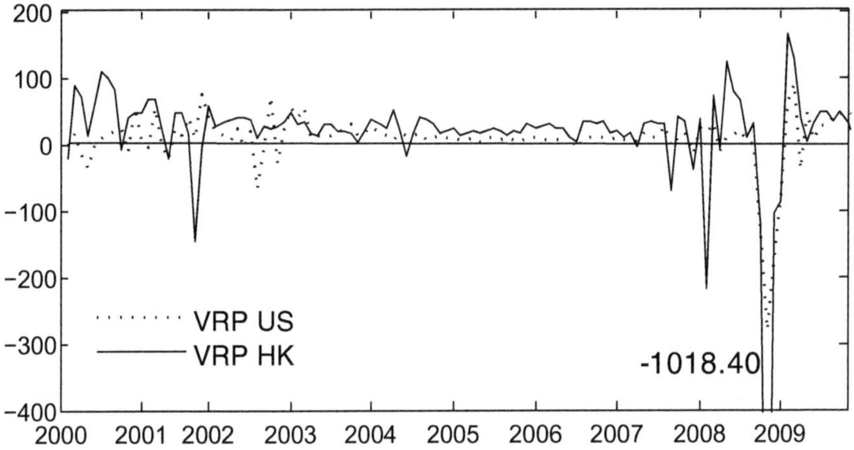

Fig. 8.4 Variance risk premiums for the Hong Kong and U.S. Markets
This figure plots the variance risk premium for the Hong Kong market (VRP HK) and U.S. market (VRP US), respectively, over the sample from January 2000 to September 2009

Table 8.2 Summary statistics

	Summary statistics							
	Mean	Median	Max.	Min.	Std.	Skew.	Kurt.	AR(1)
EXRET	–2.50	–2.31	6.72	–13.03	3.71	–0.39	3.32	0.45
HVRP	14.27	27.16	164.65	–1018.40	106.88	–7.90	76.14	0.22
Log(P/E)	2.73	2.74	3.27	2.03	0.22	–0.70	4.41	0.82
DY	3.09	3.08	5.48	1.71	0.75	0.85	4.54	0.93
MMR	2.47	2.00	7.13	0.07	1.99	0.37	1.93	0.94
UVRP	7.05	9.99	89.07	–280.52	41.57	–3.84	24.85	0.55

Note EXRET, HVRP, log(P/E), DY, MMR, UVRP denote the monthly excess return of Heng Seng index, variance risk premium for Hong Kong market, logarithm value of P/E ratio, dividend yield, Hong Kong money market rate and the variance risk premium for U.S. market, respectively

term interest rate is money market rate in Hong Kong market, logarithm of P/E ratio, dividend yield and the variance risk premium. The conventional predictors, such as P/E ratio, dividend yield and short term interest rate are mostly nonstationary or highly persistent. From Table 8.2, we find that for those variables, first order autocorrelation is usually above 0.8, especially for dividend yield and short term interest rate, whose values are very close to 1, when we usually could not reject the null hypothesis of unit root. On the contrary, for excess return and variance risk premium, first order correlations are 0.45 and 0.22, indicating weak persistence.

The correlation matrix from Table 8.3 supports the conclusion that excess return is strongly correlated with all the predictors. Finally, we observe that variance risk premium only weakly correlates with traditional predictors, indicating that although they all serve as predictors, their roles and characteristics may be quite different.

Table 8.3 Correlation matrix

	Correlation Matrix					
Correlation	EXRET	HVRP	Log(P/E)	DY	MMR	UVRP
EXRET	1 –					
HVRP	0.32 (3.67)	1 –				
Log(P/E)	0.32 (3.59)	0.21 (2.30)	1 –			
DY	0.24 (2.68)	−0.25 (−2.81)	−0.5 (−6.11)	1 –		
MMR	−0.54 (−6.96)	0.12 (1.32)	−0.13 (−1.38)	−0.62 (−8.44)	1 –	
UVRP	0.27 (2.97)	0.74 (11.69)	0.31 (3.54)	-0.26 (−2.84)	0.01 (0.10)	1 –

Note EXRET, HVRP, log(P/E), DY, MMR, UVRP denote the monthly excess return of Heng Seng index, variance risk premium for Hong Kong market, logarithm value of P/E ratio, dividend yield, Hong Kong money market rate and the variance risk premium for U.S. market, respectively

Table 8.4 Results for predicating monthly excess returns

Dependent variable is the monthly excess return								
Dep.Var.	(1)	(2)	(3)	(4)	(5)	(6)	(7)	(8)
HVRP	0.01 (5.98)					0.01 (2.16)		0.01 (5.23)
Log(P/E)		5.27 (2.15)					4.18 (2.43)	2.82 (2.82)
DY			1.19 (1.61)					
MMR				−1.01 (−6.48)			−0.95 (−5.74)	−1.05 (−7.38)
UVRP					0.024 (2.70)	0.01 (0.39)		
Constant	−2.65 (−5.14)	−16.89 (−2.48)	−6.19 (−0.80)	−0.001 (−0.002)	−2.67 (−5.32)	−2.67 (−5.20)	−11.58 (−2.28)	−7.79 (−2.68)
Adj.R^2	0.097	0.093	0.05	0.29	0.063	0.09	0.35	0.46

Note EXRET, HVRP, log(P/E), DY, MMR, UVRP denote the monthly excess return of Heng Seng index, variance risk premium for Hong Kong market, logarithm value of P/E ratio, dividend yield, Hong Kong money market rate and the variance risk premium for U.S. market, respectively. Constant,values in brackets and Adj.R^2 are constant terms, robust t-statistics using Newey–West autocorrelation consistent standard errors and adjusted R^2 statistics, respectively

Table 8.4 reports regression result using monthly excess return as explained variable. First, in univariate regressions, we identify the explanatory power for each predictors individually. Among them, the coefficients in front of variance risk premium of Hong Kong market and U.S. market are 0.01 and 0.02, respectively. Both of them are statistically significant with adjusted R^2 equal to 9.7 and 6.3%. When we add both of them into the same regression, the coefficient in front of variance risk premium in Hong Kong market remains unchanged while the coefficient for U.S. market turns into insignificance, showing that there may not be additional informational content in U.S. market.

The positive coefficients are in line with previous studies such as Bollerslev et al. (2009), Zhou (2010). According to the theoretical model of Bollerslev et al. (2009), variance risk premium is correlated with the systematic risk from the time-varying volatility of the volatility of consumption growth rate of representative agent and bearing high systematic risk demands high excess return as compensation.

Second, among those regressions, conventional predictors exhibit stable explanatory power: the coefficients in front of logarithms of P/E ratios are between 5.08 and 5.27; The coefficients in front of dividend yield are between 0.87 and 1.19; The coefficients in front of short term interest rate are between −1.01 and −0.75. Since dividend yield is only marginally significant and strongly correlated with logarithm P/E ratio, we drop dividend yield in last regression to avoid multicollinearity. In the regression considering all conventional predictors, adjusted R^2 reaches 35%, which is relatively high than studies by Bollerslev et al. (2009) and Zhou (2010). Third, after controlling for log(P/E) and short term interest rate, adding variance risk premium helps to increase the adjusted R^2 from 35 to 46%. All the explanatory variables are significant at the 5% level. In line with previous discussions, the variance risk premium as short-term predictors, is able to provide additional information to reflect changes in market risk aversion in short term in addition to other persistent variables.

8.3.5 Evidences During the Financial Crisis Period

The subprime crisis firstly appearing at the beginning of 2006 reached its summit at 2007 and 2008. During this period, Hong Kong market experienced a turbulent time along with international market, especially in the last half year of 2008 when the realized volatility climbed to historically high level. As is well known, financial crisis mostly reflects systematic risk associated with macroeconomic environment, especially in the short term, variance risk premium as a reflection of macro uncertainty, does it serve as predictors or indicators of market return?

To ensure reasonable sample length and coverage of financial crisis period, we choose the period spanning from January 2006 to September 2009 as sub-sample and repeat what we have done in Sect. 8.3.4. The correlation between excess return and variance risk premium is approximately 0.51, which is higher than 0.32 in full sample, indicating a much closer interaction during turbulent market period.

Table 8.5 Results during the financial crisis period

Dependent variable is the monthly excess return

Dep.Var.	(1)	(2)	(3)	(4)	(5)	(6)	(7)	(8)
HVRP	0.0122 (5.91)					0.01 (1.95)		0.012 (5.00)
Log(P/E)		2.94 (1.05)					4.86 (1.72)	2.88 (1.49)
DY			0.26 (0.29)					
MMR				−0.63 (−1.64)			−0.86 (−2.48)	−0.9 (−2.87)
UVRP					0.029 (2.95)	0.004 (0.22)		
Constant	−2.21 (−3.35)	−10.15 (−1.31)	−3.12 (−1.24)	−0.8 (−0.53)	−2.24 (−3.49)	−2.22 (−3.35)	−13.27 (−1.78)	−7.81 (−1.66)
Adj.R^2	0.24	0.02	−0.02	0.06	0.17	0.23	0.14	0.38

Note EXRET, HVRP, log(P/E), DY, MMR, UVRP denote the monthly excess return of Heng Seng index, variance risk premium for Hong Kong market, logarithm value of P/E ratio, dividend yield, Hong Kong money market rate and the variance risk premium for U.S. market, respectively. Constant,values in brackets and Adj.R^2 are constant terms, robust t-statistics using Newey–West autocorrelation consistent standard errors and adjusted R^2 statistics, respectively

Table 8.5 reports the regression result when monthly excess return during financial crisis period used as explained variable. In contrast to Table 8.4, we can obtain the following conclusions.

First, the predictive power of conventional predictors falls. In univariate regressions, log(P/E) and dividend yield become insignificant with a drop in adjusted R^2. In a regression considering all conventional predictors, the adjusted R^2 is only 14.4%, a significant drop compared with full sample adjusted R^2 as 34.8%. During financial crisis period, the volatility of stock market return, especially significant drop, reflects investors expectations. The risk averse investors would overreact, causing the stock return to drop more than corresponding actual change of the fundamental value. Under this circumstances, the dividend yield or P/E ratio reflecting the historical or current earnings information would predict future excess return to a smaller extent. We could conclude that conventional predictors perform well in the long-run or under stable economic condition when investors hold consistent and homogeneous expectations.

Second, during the financial crisis period, the explanatory power of variance risk premium of both Hong Kong market and U.S. market increases. In univariate regressions considering both premiums, the adjusted R^2 reaches 24.3 and 17.2%, which is a significant increase compared with the full sample adjusted R^2 of 9.7 and 6.3%. In addition, after adding other predictors, the adjusted R^2 is 37.5%, which is slight drop in comparison with full sample adjusted R^2 at 46.4%, mainly due to low predictive power of other variables. More importantly, during financial crisis period, compared with adjusted R^2 of 14.4% without considering variance risk premium, the variance risk premium does exhibit more predictive power. This further lends support to the conclusion that conventional predictors perform better in the long-run partially due to its high persistence. However, when macroeconomic uncertainty explodes, these variables are not sensitive enough to reflect the investors risk aversion embedded in model-free implied volatility derived from option prices. Variance risk premium is closely related to macroeconomic fluctuation and perform exceptionally well in the short term.

8.4 Conclusions

This chapter utilizes the model-free volatility method including the realized volatility and model-free implied volatility method to estimate the time-varying variance risk premium for both U.S. and Hong Kong market. The empirical analysis demonstrates that the variance risk premium in both markets follow similar trends. Meanwhile, controlling the traditional conventional stock return predictors such as dividend yield, log(P/E) and short term interest rate, variance risk premium in Hong Kong market predicts future return additionally, especially during financial crisis period. This support the theoretical conclusion that variance risk premium as a proxy of (short term) macroeconomic risk and investors' degree of risk aversion, captures the systematic risk related, thus economically significant.

Chapter 9
Predictability of VRP: Other International Evidence

9.1 Introduction

The intertemporal CAPM model of Merton (1973) demonstrates that the aggregate market risk premium is determined by the uncertainty of underlying returns, quantified by the return variance. When holding the market portfolio, however, an investor is also bearing the uncertainty of the variance itself. Just like that the equity premium demanded by investors is a result of fear to the uncertainty of future returns, the variance risk premium, defined as the difference between risk-neutral and physical expected variances, is also required to compensate for the risk of the uncertain variance. Several recent studies document the link between risk preference and variance risk premium. In particular, Bakshi and Madan (2006) argue that the variance risk premium is approximately determined by the risk aversion parameter and the higher order moments of underlying returns. In a similar vein, Bollerslev et al. (2011) assume an affine version of the stochastic volatility model in Heston (1993) and show that the variance risk premium is linearly related to the risk preference of individual agents. Other investigations in this area include Bekaert and Engstrom (2010), Todorov (2010), and Gabaix (2012).

Furthermore, with Epstein and Zin (1989)'s recursive utility function, Bollerslev et al. (2009) and Drechsler and Yaron (2011) extend Bansal and Yaron (2004)'s long-run risk model, and set up a theoretical relationship between variance risk premium and macroeconomic uncertainty. In their models, the time variation in economic uncertainty and a preference for early resolution of uncertainty due to the fear of future risks are required to generate a positive variance risk premium that can predict excess stock market returns.

In the empirical investigation, Bollerslev et al. (2009) and Drechsler and Yaron (2011) find evidences in the U.S. market that the variance risk premium has a stronger predictive power at the quarterly return horizons than traditional factors such as the P/E ratio, the consumption-wealth ratio, the short rate, and the price-dividend ratio. This finding has a meaningful implication for the stock return predictability literature. As an age-old but still mostly studied question in asset pricing, the prediction

J. Chen, *General Equilibrium Option Pricing Method: Theoretical and Empirical Study*, https://doi.org/10.1007/978-981-10-7428-8_9

of aggregate market returns has been studied by many papers, e.g., Fama and French (1988), Campbell and Shiller (1988), and Lettau and Ludvigson (2001). They adopt traditional persistent variables and find that the predictability is the strongest over long multi-year horizons. However, using highly persistent predictive variables can result in possible statistical inference problems discussed in Campbell and Yogo (2006), Ang and Bekaert (2007), Boudoukh et al. (2008), among many others. In particular, Boudoukh et al. (2008) find that the estimated R^2 based on regressions with highly persistent predictors and overlapping returns will automatically increase in proportion to the return horizons, even without any evidences showing an improvement of predictability. This issue highlights the important role of variance risk premium in predicting stock returns, since its first order correlation is much smaller than 1, which implies less effect of the persistent predictor problem. In addition, the variance risk premium has predictive power over monthly or quarterly horizons, in contrast to the long-run predictors.

In spite of the success of variance risk premium in predicting market returns, there are still some issues remained to be addressed. First, existing literature diverges on how to construct the measure of variance risk premium, especially on the calculation of expected physical variances. For example, Bollerslev et al. (2009) consider the lagged realized variance (RV) as a proxy of the expected variance and construct the variance risk premium measure accordingly, which is labeled as VRP1 in the following context. Bollerslev et al. (2013) further examine the in-sample performance of this measure in predicting market returns for international markets. Bali et al. (2011) also use it as a control variable to investigate the intertemporal relationship between volatility spreads and expected returns. Alternatively, Drechsler and Yaron (2011) suggest to use the lagged realized variance and the model-free implied variance (MFIV) to forecast the expectation of physical variance. This version of variance risk premium is referred as VRP2 in the remainder of this chapter. Bali and Zhou (2011) consider this measure as a proxy of economic uncertainty and Bailey et al. (2011) study its determinants in high frequency. It seems that the variance risk premium may become a commonly used control variable in predicting future excess stock returns, and thus a careful empirical comparison for these two measures employed in aforementioned studies is necessary. Second, Bollerslev et al. (2009) and Drechsler and Yaron (2011) argue that when investors perceive a much bigger shock than usual economic variation, they desire to pay more to hedge future uncertainties, therefore leading to a larger premium. Since the variance risk premium is highly related to investor's fear to unknown shocks, whether it has a predictive power during a market crash period, for instance, the recent financial crisis period, is also an interesting question for the empirical studies of asset pricing.

This chapter decides to shed lights on these issues and provides more empirical evidences to Bollerslev et al. (2009) and Drechsler and Yaron (2011). More specifically, our study compares two measures of the premium proposed by Bollerslev et al. (2009) and Drechsler and Yaron (2011) in respect of their in-sample predictability across different markets, including U.S., Netherlands, Belgium, France, Germany, U.K., Japan, Switzerland, and the Euro zone. In addition to the robustness check of in-sample stock return predictability for both measures using the international data, this chapter further carries out an investigation for the financial crisis period. We find that both measures have a robust in-sample predictability at monthly and quarterly horizons for the U.S. market, and the magnitude of such predictive power rises when the episode of financial crisis is included. Turning to international markets, both VRP measures perform similarly. Specifically, both of them show an in-sample predictability for all international markets with an exception of Japan, and this forecasting power becomes more significant during the financial crisis period than that of full sample.

In two closely related studies, Londono (2010) and Bollerslev et al. (2013) also consider the role of variance risk premium in predicting excess stock return in international markets. Instead of focusing on the verification of the statistical inference procedure as in Bollerslev et al. (2013) and the extension of the model in Bollerslev et al. (2009) to an international setting as in Londono (2010), our study aims to provide more extensive empirical evidences that have not been documented in the literature before. In particular, we explicitly compare the difference of two measures of VRP through the in-sample test, and emphasize the rising forecasting power during recent financial crisis period. These empirical results will not only have implications for empirical researcher but also highlight the stylized facts that are essential to further theoretical modeling.

The rest of this chapter is organized as follows. Section 9.2 introduces methods of constructing the variance risk premia and predicting excess stock return through the in-sample test. Section 9.3 presents data and summary statistics. Section 9.4 reports the in-sample assessment for all markets. Finally, Sect. 9.5 concludes.

9.2 Empirical Methodology

9.2.1 Variance Risk Premium

The variance risk premium (VRP) during a time interval $[t, t+1]$ is defined as the difference between expected future return variance under risk-neutral and physical measures, and takes the following form:

$$VRP_{t,t+1} = E_t^Q(Var_{t,t+1}) - E_t^P(Var_{t,t+1}), \tag{9.1}$$

where $E_t^Q(\cdot)$ and $E_t^P(\cdot)$, respectively, denote the expectation operators under risk-neutral and physical measures with the information set available at time-t. Because both expectations are not directly observable, we have to find their corresponding empirical proxies in practice.

According to Carr and Madan (1998), Barndorff-Nielsen and Shephard (2004a), and Jiang and Tian (2005), the model-free implied variance (MFIV) based on option prices can provide an unbiased empirical analog of the risk-neutral expected variance. Adopting this method, Chicago Board Options Exchange (CBOE) constructs the volatility index (VIX), which is widely used by investors and researchers. Similar to Bollerslev et al. (2009), we also use VIX to quantify the MFIV. On the other hand, the true variance $Var_{t,t+1}$ in Eq. (9.1) can be replaced by the realized variance $RV_{t,t+1}$. Andersen et al. (2001a), Andersen et al. (2001b,c), Andersen et al. (2003b), and Taylor (2005) define the realized variance as a summation of squared high frequency intra-day returns. Following Bakshi and Madan (2006), we use the daily returns within a month to construct the end-of-month realized variance, because there are minor discrepancies in using daily and intraday data to calculate realized variance at monthly frequency. However, methods of constructing the expectation under physical measure, $E_t^P(Var_{t,t+1})$, vary in empirical studies. Bollerslev et al. (2009) choose the realized variation over the time interval $[t-1, t]$, $RV_{t-1,t}$, as a proxy of the expected physical variance. Alternatively, Drechsler and Yaron (2011) calculate the expectation by forecasting the realized variance based on a regression on its lagged counterparts and the lagged MFIV. This method aims to explore the informational advantage of MFIV in predicting future realized variance (see, e.g., Taylor 2005). As mentioned in introduction, based on different proxies of expected realized variance, the measures of variance risk premium proposed by Bollerslev et al. (2009) and Drechsler and Yaron (2011) are referred as VRP1 and VRP2, respectively, in our following discussion.

9.2.2 *In-Sample Predictability Regression*

Bollerslev et al. (2009) and Drechsler and Yaron (2011) argue that the variance risk premium is induced by the uncertainty of consumption through a recursive utility framework, and therefore can be used to predict equity returns. We adopt the multi-period predictability regression as follows:

$$r_{t+1\to t+h} = \frac{1}{h}\sum_{i=1}^{h} exr_{t+i} = \alpha(h) + \beta(h)VRP_t + \varepsilon_{t+h}, \tag{9.2}$$

where exr_{t+i} is the excess stock market return over time interval $[t+i, t+i-1]$, $r_{t+1\to t+h} = \frac{1}{h}\sum_{i=1}^{h} exr_{t+i}$ represents the average return for next h periods, and h denotes the prediction horizon. Because the predictive power of VRP mainly exists in relatively short horizon within one year, h takes values between 1 and 12 on monthly basis. In the empirical study, we construct different VRP measures and report the coefficient estimates $\hat{\beta}(h)$ for different horizons. The significance of coefficient estimates and the adjusted R^2 are signs of predictability. In order to control the possible autocorrelation in the residuals induced by the overlapping nature of the excess returns, the Newey–West t-statistic is used, and the optimal lags are chosen according to the suggestion of Newey and West (1994).

Moreover, as a simple way to show the time-varying pattern of predictability, we also employ a rolling regression method for the U.S. market. According to Chen

(2009), as the rolling window changes, the regression coefficients and the *t*-statistics are less influenced by a small pocket of the data.

9.3 Data and Summary Statistics

With respect to the MFIV measure, the VIX launched by CBOE is used for the U.S. market. Since the introduction of VIX index, as listed in Andersen et al. (2011), many developed markets and several emerging markets have developed the corresponding volatility index for their own markets following the methodology of VIX. In this chapter, we select the volatility indices for S&P 500 (VIX) of U.S., the AEX (VAEX) of Netherlands, the BEL 20 (VBEL) of Belgium, the CAC 40 (VCAC) of France, the DAX (VDAX) of Germany, the Euro Stoxx 50 (VSTOXX) of the Euro zone, the FTSE 100 (VFTSE) of U. K., the Nikkei 225 (VXJ) of Japan, and the SMI (VSMI) of Switzerland. The VIX is obtained from CBOE, the VAEX, VBEL, and VCAC from Euronext, the VDAX from Deutsche Börse, the VSTOXX from STOXX Limited, the VSMI from Swiss Exchange, and the VXJ is downloaded from the Center for the Study of Finance and Insurance, Osaka University. The daily stock indices are obtained from CEIC database. In respect of the risk free interest rates, we use the three-month rates of Treasury bill for the U.S. market, LIBOR (London Interbank Offered Rate) for the U.K. market, TIBOR (the Tokyo Interbank Offered Rate) for the Japan market, and EURIBOR (Euro Interbank Offered Rate) for all other European countries and the Euro zone markets. The time span for U.S. extends from January 1990 through June 2011, and from January 2000 to June 2011 for other markets, as the volatility indices are available since 2000 for most of the developed markets. The Belgium market is the only exception because the Euronext stops to update the VBEL since October 2010.

The summary statistics for excess returns and the variance risk premia are presented in Table 9.1. As the sample covering more than 20 years, the average return for U.S. is positive. But, for all other markets with a shorter sample since 2000, the mean of return is negative, ranging from a high of -2.38% for DAX to a low of -8.81% for AEX. With respect to VRP, both measures show positive means for all markets except for the Belgium market whose average premium is slightly negative. We can also find in Table 9.1 that the average of both VRP measures are almost the same across markets, but the standard deviations of VRP2 are smaller than those of VRP1. It implies that using the forecasting variance instead of the lagged RV can reduce the time variation of VRP. This is also consistent with the time series plot of VRP in Figs. 9.1 and 9.2.

As demonstrated in Fig. 9.1, for the U.S. market, both measures display similar patterns and fluctuate significantly during the NBER recession episodes,[1] especially during the recent financial crisis period. However, consistent with the summary

[1]The NBER peak and trough dates that define the recession phases of the U.S. business cycles are available at http://www.nber.org/cycles.html.

Table 9.1 Summary statistics

Indices	Excess stock return				VRP1				VRP2			
	Mean	Std	Skew.	Kurt.	Mean	Std	Skew.	Kurt.	Mean	Std	Skew.	Kurt.
S&P 500	2.62	52.59	−0.79	1.56	11.03	26.33	−5.82	57.01	11.05	15.66	−1.42	19.54
AEX	−8.81	76.93	−1.02	2.14	7.14	42.47	−4.55	34.03	7.51	13.13	0.31	9.77
BEL	−5.03	68.54	−1.47	3.49	−1.01	42.14	−5.17	36.94	−0.48	13.64	−2.65	22.22
CAC 40	−6.39	66.87	−0.61	0.84	4.33	40.86	−5.07	42.47	4.55	12.06	−0.51	18.25
DAX	−2.38	80.94	−0.88	2.74	7.67	35.72	−3.25	18.31	8.13	3.30	4.14	22.27
Euro Stoxx	−7.61	69.18	−0.62	1.20	10.37	35.34	−2.43	18.18	10.60	11.66	2.75	10.81
FTSE 100	−5.42	52.71	−0.72	0.67	8.25	31.66	−5.74	50.90	8.47	10.06	0.69	6.66
Nikkei 225	−6.05	71.95	−0.81	1.87	13.18	38.09	−4.61	39.06	13.33	36.73	8.03	78.23
SMI	−4.64	52.18	−0.70	0.56	5.75	28.66	−4.27	30.86	5.97	11.86	2.45	6.77

Note This table reports the summary statistics for excess stock returns and two measures of variance risk premium for different indices. S&P 500, AEX, BEL, CAC 40, DAX, Euro Stoxx, FTSE 100, Nikkei 225, and SMI are indices of US, Netherland, Belgium, France, Germany, Euro Zone, UK, Japan, and Switzerland markets. The sample extends from January 1990 to June 2011 for US, and from January 2000 to June 2011 for other markets with an exception of ending in October 2010 for Belgium. The VRP1 and VRP2 are measures of variance risk premium defined in Bollerslev et al. (2009) and Drechsler and Yaron (2011), respectively. The monthly excess stock returns are in annualized percentage form and both measures are in monthly percentage-squared form

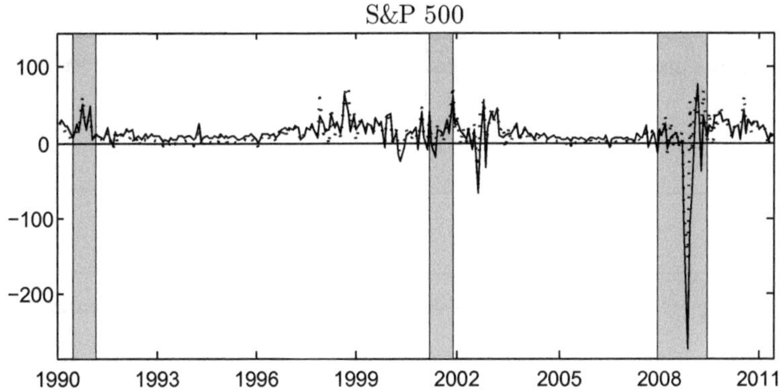

Fig. 9.1 Variance risk premia for the U.S. market
This figure plots the monthly variance risk premia for U.S. (S&P 500 index) from January 1990 to June 2011. The solid and dotted curves are the time series of VRP1 and VRP2, respectively. The VRP1 and VRP2 represent the measures of variance risk premium in Bollerslev et al. (2009) and Drechsler and Yaron (2011), respectively. The shaded areas stand for the NBER recession periods

statistics in Table 9.1, the variation of VRP2 is clearly smaller than that of VRP1. This is due to the fact that using the forecasts of realized variance from regression model can partially filter out the extreme changes as residuals, whereas VRP1 based on lagged RV still incorporates all variations of *ex post* RV series. As a result, the VRP1 displays peaks around 2008 while the magnitude of VRP2 is much smaller.

Further VRP series for AEX, BEL, CAC 40, DAX, Euro Stoxx 50, FTSE 100, Nikkei 225, and SMI indices are plotted in Fig. 9.2. Both measures exhibit similar patterns and fluctuate significantly during recessions. Similar to the case of U.S., the VRP2 shows less variations as employing the forecasting variance. In particular, VRP1 generates negative variance premium spikes around 2008 and 2011 in Japan, associated with the global financial crisis in 2008 and earthquake in March 2011. In contrast, VRP2 displays positive peaks at these two episodes, as the big shocks are not expected in the forward looking variance. Thus, the different ways to construct the expectation of physical variance may result in different implications for VRP and stock return predictability.

9.4 In-Sample Predictability Results

In this section, we estimate the regression model (9.2) at monthly horizons for $h = 1$, 2, 3, 4, 5, 6, 9, 12 using VRP1 or VRP2 as a single predictor. Empirical results for the U.S. market are presented in Table 9.2. We can find that, first, for the full-sample period from January 1990 till June 2011 in Panel A, the estimates of coefficients are highly significant at short monthly or quarterly horizons. The Newey–West t-statistics and adjusted R^2 statistics exhibit similar hump shapes, starting out relatively low,

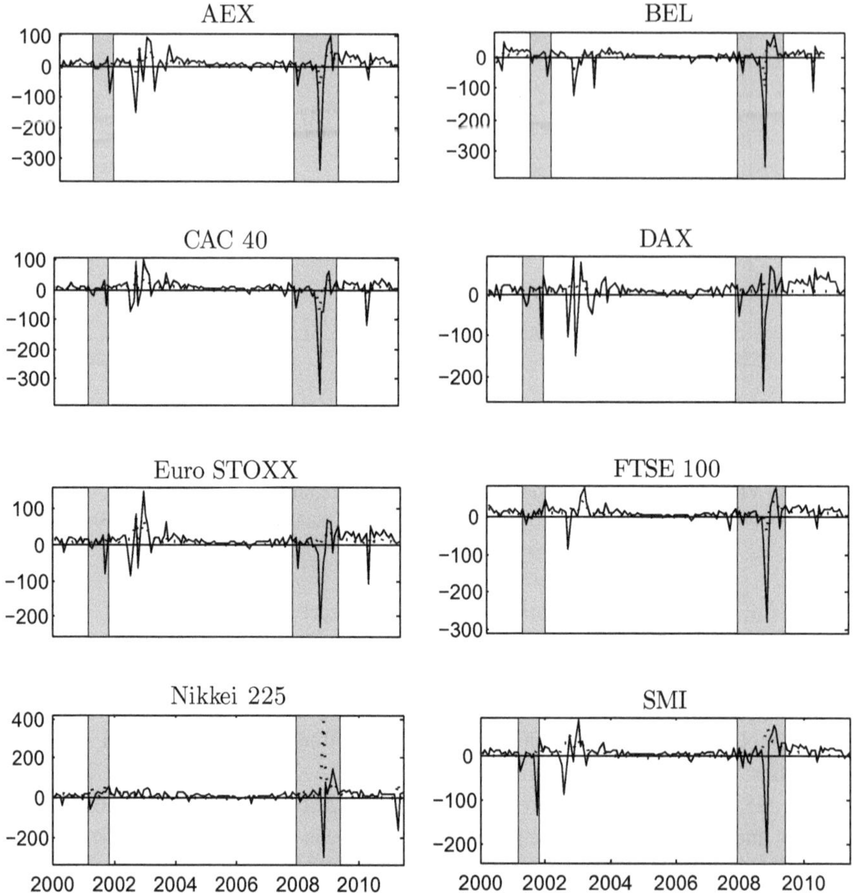

Fig. 9.2 Variance risk premia for international markets
This figure plots the monthly variance risk premia in international markets. The AEX, BEL, CAC 40, DAX, Euro Stoxx, FTSE 100, Nikkei 225, and SMI are indices of Netherland, Belgium, France, Germany, Euro Zone, U.K., Japan, and Switzerland markets. The sample extends from January 2000 to June 2011 for all the markets with an exception of ending in October 2010 for Belgium. The solid and dotted curves represent the time series of VRP1 and VRP2, respectively. The VRP1 and VRP2 are the measures of variance risk premium in Bollerslev et al. (2009) and Drechsler and Yaron (2011), respectively. The shaded areas stand for the NBER recession periods

rising to their largest values at the 3rd or 4th month, and gradually declining thereafter for relatively longer return horizons. In particular, the peak values of adjusted R^2 are 14.58 and 17.30% for VRP1 and VRP2 at the four-month horizon, respectively.

In spite of their similarities, there exists some differences between two measures in predicting the in-sample returns. First, the estimated coefficients of VRP2 are generally larger than those of VRP1. This finding is consistent with empirical results in the literature. For example, employing VRP1, Bollerslev et al. (2009) suggest the

Table 9.2 In-sample results for the U.S. market

Months	1	2	3	4	5	6	9	12
Panel A. Full sample (1990:01–2011:06)								
VRP1	0.49 (5.10)	0.49 (5.17)	0.45 (7.47)	0.41 (7.92)	0.32 (4.89)	0.23 (3.54)	0.09 (1.69)	0.06 (1.07)
Adj.R^2	5.75	10.97	13.99	14.58	10.59	6.05	1.12	0.31
VRP2	0.84 (4.10)	0.89 (7.23)	0.82 (8.48)	0.75 (7.32)	0.62 (6.66)	0.48 (5.38)	0.24 (2.54)	0.16 (1.81)
Adj.R^2	5.90	12.88	16.03	17.30	14.15	9.69	3.24	1.69
Panel B. First sub-sample (1990:01–2006:12)								
VRP1	0.40 (2.07)	0.62 (3.60)	0.42 (3.72)	0.40 (3.16)	0.38 (3.29)	0.29 (2.87)	0.17 (1.56)	0.13 (1.39)
Adj.R^2	0.97	6.80	4.63	5.49	6.59	4.49	1.89	1.40
VRP2	0.54 (2.31)	0.76 (3.67)	0.56 (3.34)	0.52 (2.94)	0.46 (2.91)	0.34 (2.43)	0.18 (1.20)	0.12 (0.94)
Adj.R^2	1.26	6.83	5.49	6.26	6.40	4.19	1.34	0.55
Panel C. Second sub-sample (2007:01–2011:06)								
VRP1	0.51 (4.46)	0.44 (4.54)	0.46 (5.21)	0.40 (6.97)	0.29 (4.10)	0.19 (2.61)	0.04 (0.73)	0.00 (−0.04)
Adj.R^2	13.16	15.31	24.42	23.32	12.25	4.98	−1.71	−2.44
VRP2	1.07 (3.71)	0.99 (5.10)	1.02 (5.82)	0.94 (7.17)	0.76 (4.46)	0.59 (2.98)	0.29 (1.49)	0.18 (0.94)
Adj.R^2	15.63	21.27	33.08	33.95	23.40	15.47	3.92	1.19

Note This table reports the estimation results for U.S. market of model $r_{t+1\rightarrow t+h} = \alpha(h) + \beta(h)VRP_t + \varepsilon_{t+h}$, where $r_{t+1\rightarrow t+h}$ is the average return for next h months, h equals to 1, 2, 3, 4, 5, 6, 9, 12. The constant term is also estimated but not reported. The VRP1 and VRP2 are the measures of variance risk premium in Bollerslev et al. (2009) and Drechsler and Yaron (2011), respectively, and are employed as a single predictor. The full sample period extends from January 1990 to June 2011, the first sub-sample from January 1990 to December 2006, and the second sub-sample from January 2007 to June 2011. The Newey–West t-statistics are reported in parentheses. The adj.R^2 denotes the adjusted R^2

coefficient estimates of 0.39 and 0.47 at $h = 1$ and $h = 3$, respectively, with U.S. data ending in December 2007; While Drechsler and Yaron (2011) report estimates of 0.76 and 0.86 using VRP2 at corresponding horizons, respectively, with U.S. data ending in March 2007. Second, the predictive power of VRP2 is slightly stronger than that of VRP1, especially for the relatively longer horizons. For instance, at the six- and twelve-month, the adjusted R^2 statistics are equal to 9.69 and 1.69% for VRP2 and statistically significant, compared with 6.05 and 0.31% for VRP1.

Second, we further divide the sample into two parts and the results are reported in Panel B and C of Table 9.2. In terms of the first sub-sample extending from January 1990 to December 2006 reported in Panel B, values of the Newey–West t-statistic are all significant at 5% level for prediction horizons less than six months and the adjusted R^2 statistics maximize at two-month horizon for both VRP measures. In particular, R^2 statistics vary between 0.97 and 6.80% for VRP1 when the prediction horizons are less than six months, which are similar to the values ranging from 1.07 to 6.82% reported in Bollerslev et al. (2009) using sample extending from January 1990 to December 2007, and start to decline when the horizon exceeds half a year. Overall, the R^2 statistics for VRP1 in Panel B also exhibit the hump-shaped pattern like in Panel A. Similar magnitude and pattern of R^2 statistics are also found for VRP2. These results confirm empirical findings in the literature that for both VRP measures constructed utilizing the pre-crisis data, the explanatory power is strong at the short monthly and quarterly horizons. Moreover, Panel C presents the result of the second sub-sample from January 2007 to June 2011, which incorporates the recent global financial crisis period. Clearly in Panel C, the adjusted R^2 statistics rise significantly at all horizons. The peak values of adjusted R^2 for VRP1 and VRP2 are, respectively, 24.42 and 33.95% at the three- and four-month horizons, which are much larger than their counterparts in first sub-sample and full sample.

A plausible explanation for this finding is linked to the more frequent and large jumps occurred in financial market during this period. Pan (2002) and Liu et al. (2005) argue that more frequently occurred jumps can result in a larger market risk premium. More recently, Todorov (2010) and Bollerslev and Todorov (2011) highlight the important role of jumps played on the dynamics of variance risk premium and market premium. In particular, Bollerslev and Todorov (2011) point out that the compensation for rare events accounts for a large proportion of the market premium and the variance risk premium. Therefore, due to the existence of the pronounced jump risk, the relationship between the market premium and variance risk premium becomes much closer during the financial crisis period.

As an alternative explanation, this finding is also consistent with the repeatedly reported observation in the literature that stock return predictability tends to increase during recessions relative to the normal times. For example, Rapach et al. (2010) observe that combining forecasts of the equity premium are closely related to NBER business cycles, and Henkel et al. (2011) find that in the G7 countries, the short-run forecasting ability of commonly used predictors such as the dividend yield and the short rate mainly exists during business contractions. Since the second sub-sample covers the longest NBER recession period in the sample, this period is overall considered as a recession one. Consistent with these two studies, our findings also support the view that increasing risk aversion during economic downturn requires a higher risk premium, which generates the link between countercyclical risk premium and return predictability.

The above finding can also be confirmed by a rolling regression technique. More specifically, we employ the VRP1 and VRP2 individually to forecast the four-month ahead excess returns of S&P 500 index with a sixty-month rolling window,[2] and plot the adjusted R^2 and Newey–West t-statistics in Fig. 9.3.

Clearly, the adjusted R^2 and Newey–West t-statistics are time-varying and show similar patterns for both VRP measures. In particular, the t-statistics in two panels are above the dashed line of 90% critical values during almost the whole period,

[2]Here, we predict the four-month ahead market returns, as the VRP always show a strong predictability at short horizons, say three- or four-month horizons in Table 9.2.

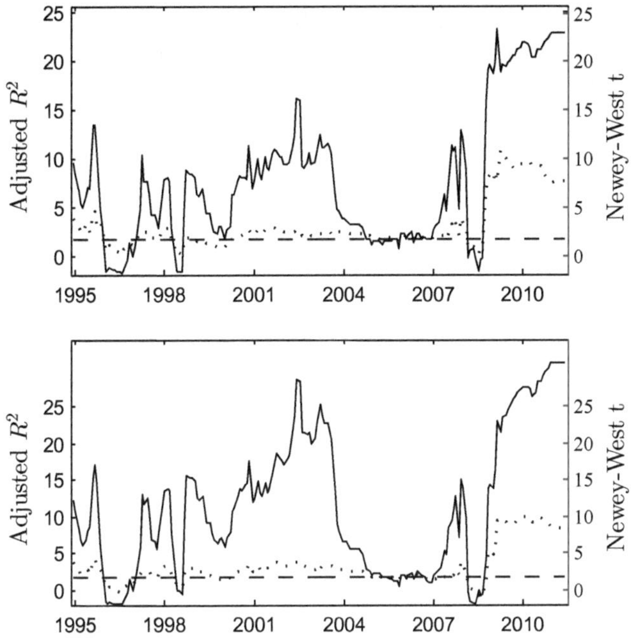

Fig. 9.3 The rolling regression for the U.S. market
This figure plots adjusted R^2 (left scale and solid curves) in percentage form and the Newey–West t-statistics (right scale and dotted curves) of the rolling regression with a window of 60 months. The top panel illustrates the results using VRP1 to predict four-month ahead excess returns of S&P 500 index and the bottom panel is for VRP2. The VRP1 and VRP2 are the measures of variance risk premium in Bollerslev et al. (2009) and Drechsler and Yaron (2011), respectively. The horizontal dashed line in each panel, fixed at 1.645, represents the 90% confidence boundary

and sharply increase during the recent financial crisis period, which implies that the estimates become more significant than before. The explanatory power of VRP2 tends to be stronger than VRP1 in view of the t-statistics and adjusted R^2 for both VRP measures. Overall, the rolling regression result confirms that the explanatory power of VRP does not come from a small portion of the data and rises significantly during the financial crisis period.

Further in-sample evidence for international markets are reported in Table 9.3. To save space, we only report regression results of predicting 1, 2, 4, 6 and 12 months ahead excess returns during the period from January 2000 to June 2011 and a sub-sample since January 2007. As is shown in Table 9.3, for the full sample, the t-statistics and the adjusted R^2 statistics show a hump-shaped pattern as the U.S. market. In particular, when employing VRP1, the Newey–West t-statistics reach the largest value at six-month horizon for AEX index and Euro Stoxx index, and at four-month horizon for other markets with only an exception of insignificant t-statistic for Nikkei 225 index. As indicated by the adjusted R^2, the maximum forecasting power of VRP1 exceeds 5% for markets of Belgium and France, varying between 2

Table 9.3 In-sample results for international markets

	Months	Full sample					Sub-sample				
		1	2	4	6	12	1	2	4	6	12
AEX	VRP1	0.11	0.18	0.15	0.14	0.04	0.27	0.25	0.26	0.18	0.03
		(0.58)	(1.26)	(1.98)	(2.45)	(0.64)	(2.22)	(3.06)	(3.63)	(1.98)	(0.31)
	Adj.R^2	−0.34	0.96	1.40	1.73	−0.47	1.56	2.71	6.71	3.03	−2.17
	VRP2	0.26	0.56	0.56	0.59	0.45	0.77	0.97	1.20	1.16	0.76
		(0.41)	(1.02)	(1.73)	(2.11)	(2.00)	(1.16)	(1.96)	(3.44)	(2.81)	(1.58)
	Adj.R^2	−0.54	0.89	2.07	3.50	3.60	0.24	3.65	12.03	14.00	11.37
BEL	VRP1	0.43	0.32	0.22	0.18	0.03	0.50	0.31	0.24	0.17	0.01
		(2.56)	(2.88)	(3.25)	(2.85)	(0.70)	(4.02)	(3.14)	(3.70)	(1.77)	(0.07)
	Adj.R^2	6.63	5.64	4.18	3.02	−0.65	11.98	5.67	6.51	1.98	−3.02
	VRP2	1.20	0.94	0.62	0.59	0.23	1.41	0.94	0.81	0.74	0.36
		(2.55)	(2.78)	(3.47)	(2.96)	(1.18)	(3.17)	(2.80)	(3.32)	(1.92)	(0.85)
	Adj.R^2	5.32	5.03	3.56	3.69	0.28	10.05	5.90	8.36	7.03	1.36
CAC 40	VRP1	0.23	0.25	0.22	0.13	0.03	0.26	0.24	0.24	0.11	−0.03
		(1.81)	(2.59)	(4.43)	(2.86)	(0.58)	(4.49)	(3.46)	(4.69)	(2.02)	(−0.78)
	Adj.R^2	1.21	3.53	5.37	1.91	−0.58	2.56	4.63	11.13	1.28	−1.92
	VRP2	0.80	0.85	0.75	0.50	0.26	1.11	1.20	1.23	0.85	0.24
		(1.77)	(2.35)	(2.78)	(2.15)	(1.30)	(3.67)	(3.15)	(4.38)	(2.13)	(0.71)
	Adj.R^2	1.36	3.58	5.44	2.86	0.88	3.09	7.85	18.16	9.84	−0.54
DAX	VRP1	0.01	0.19	0.22	0.10	0.03	0.11	0.18	0.34	0.13	0.07
		(0.06)	(0.99)	(2.26)	(1.16)	(0.65)	(0.85)	(1.93)	(5.57)	(1.30)	(0.65)
	Adj.R^2	−0.74	0.58	2.46	0.06	−0.63	−1.57	−0.19	10.16	0.17	−1.20
	VRP2	−0.49	−1.75	−1.80	−0.46	0.48	−1.70	−1.48	−2.57	0.20	0.99
		(−0.23)	(−0.86)	(−1.20)	(−0.38)	(0.68)	(−1.05)	(−1.66)	(−2.44)	(0.25)	(1.65)
	Adj.R^2	−0.70	0.21	1.09	−0.61	−0.50	−1.12	−0.92	3.92	−2.08	−0.21
Euro Stoxx	VRP1	0.10	0.20	0.21	0.14	0.05	0.22	0.24	0.32	0.16	0.00
		(0.50)	(1.36)	(2.28)	(3.01)	(0.92)	(1.61)	(2.37)	(3.52)	(2.30)	(0.05)
	Adj.R^2	−0.49	1.10	3.41	1.54	−0.25	−0.07	1.61	11.05	1.85	−2.44
	VRP2	0.18	0.43	0.42	0.40	0.37	0.64	1.30	1.72	1.91	1.43
		(0.34)	(0.98)	(1.28)	(1.19)	(1.64)	(0.66)	(1.54)	(2.82)	(3.46)	(3.81)
	Adj.R^2	−0.65	0.21	0.97	1.36	2.38	−1.19	3.10	15.14	23.68	27.98
FTSE 100	VRP1	0.01	0.09	0.17	0.12	−0.02	0.07	0.07	0.21	0.12	0.00
		(0.04)	(1.18)	(4.70)	(2.08)	(−0.34)	(0.65)	(1.06)	(4.87)	(1.78)	(−0.08)
	Adj.R^2	−0.74	−0.16	3.39	1.67	−0.73	−1.59	−1.43	7.04	1.15	−2.43
	VRP2	−0.14	0.26	0.47	0.43	0.15	0.02	0.32	0.98	0.89	0.55
		(−0.38)	(0.84)	(1.91)	(1.97)	(0.63)	(0.04)	(0.66)	(3.63)	(2.66)	(1.61)
	Adj.R^2	−0.66	−0.28	2.23	2.46	−0.11	−1.92	−1.27	10.36	9.99	6.48
Nikkei 225	VRP1	0.02	0.02	0.16	0.11	0.02	0.05	0.06	0.19	0.11	0.04
		(0.16)	(0.15)	(1.47)	(0.94)	(0.36)	(0.36)	(0.38)	(1.34)	(0.75)	(0.39)
	Adj.R^2	−0.73	−0.73	1.09	0.47	−0.68	−1.82	−1.65	2.78	0.20	−1.48
	VRP2	0.01	0.03	−0.06	0.04	0.03	0.03	0.08	0.02	0.13	0.13
		(0.07)	(0.47)	(−0.92)	(0.58)	(0.64)	(0.55)	(1.51)	(0.22)	(2.15)	(3.43)
	Adj.R^2	−0.74	−0.70	−0.47	−0.63	−0.55	−1.87	−1.37	−1.99	1.82	8.47
SMI	VRP1	0.02	0.15	0.22	0.18	0.10	0.15	0.26	0.38	0.26	0.11
		(0.15)	(1.28)	(2.54)	(2.44)	(1.60)	(1.11)	(2.44)	(5.24)	(2.21)	(0.88)

(continued)

Table 9.3 (continued)

	Months	Full sample					Sub-sample				
		1	2	4	6	12	1	2	4	6	12
	Adj.R^2	−0.72	0.36	3.22	2.62	0.90	−0.84	3.30	15.50	8.59	1.61
	VRP2	−0.73	−0.53	−0.34	−0.07	0.28	−0.89	−0.64	−0.33	0.30	0.73
		(−1.88)	(−1.35)	(−0.82)	(−0.20)	(1.25)	(−2.05)	(−1.33)	(−0.58)	(0.66)	(2.60)
	Adj.R^2	2.09	1.68	0.82	−0.68	1.57	3.38	2.45	−0.23	−0.10	20.44

Note This table reports the estimation results for international markets of model $r_{t+1\to t+h} = \alpha(h) + \beta(h)VRP_t + \varepsilon_{t+h}$, where $r_{t+1\to t+h}$ is the average return for next h months, h equals to 1, 2, 4, 6, 12. The constant term in is also estimated but not reported. The AEX, BEL, CAC 40, DAX, Euro Stoxx, FTSE 100, Nikkei 225, and SMI are indices of Netherland, Belgium, France, Germany, Euro Zone, U.K., Japan, and Switzerland markets. The VRP1 and VRP2 are the measures of variance risk premium in Bollerslev et al. (2009) and Drechsler and Yaron (2011), respectively, and are employed as a single predictor. The full sample period extends from January 2000 to June 2011 and the sub-sample extends from January 2007 to June 2011 for all the indices except for the BEL index. For BEL index, the full-sample period extends from January 2000 to October 2010 and the sub-sample extends from January 2007 to October 2010. The Newey–West t-statistics are reported in parentheses. The adj.R^2 denotes the adjusted R^2

and 5% for Germany, U.K., Switzerland, and Euro zone, and is lower than 2% for Netherlands and Japan. This implies that the VRP1 is able to predict the excess stock returns at short horizons for most selected markets.

On the other hand, the estimation results using VRP2 are mixed. For the Netherlands and Euro zone markets, the VRP2 is able to forecast excess returns at relatively longer monthly horizons, as the estimated coefficients remain significant and adjusted R^2 statistics are larger than 2% at twelve-month horizons for both markets. Values of the Newey–West t-statistic are the largest at four-month horizon for Belgium and France, and at six-month for U.K. with corresponding adjusted R^2 statistics between 2 and 6%. However, the evidence of predictability for other markets is relatively weak, because the adjusted R^2 is small and estimated coefficient is insignificant at all monthly horizons.

In comparison, the predictive power of both measures grows stronger during the sub-sample from January 2007 to June 2011, as values of adjusted R^2 increase significantly, with an exception for the Japan market where the coefficients of VRP1 remain insignificant. Overall, the empirical evidences presented in Table 9.3 support the legitimacy of using VRP to predict the excess returns in international markets and the sub-sample analysis confirms the close relationship between equity premium and variance risk premium during financial crisis period.

9.5 Concluding Remarks

A number of recent papers have studied the variance risk premium defined as the difference between risk-neutral and realized variances, and suggest that it reflects individual agent's risk aversion to economic uncertainty and therefore can be used to predict equity returns. Since the VRP gains popularity in recent asset pricing studies and may serve as a commonly used control variable ever since, a further and more extensive evaluation of its performance becomes a necessity. This chapter intends to fill in the gap by comparing the performance of VRP1 and VRP2 proposed by Bollerslev et al. (2009) and Drechsler and Yaron (2011), respectively.

Our empirical analysis is carried out through the in-sample predictability test using data from the U.S. market and other selected developed markets including Netherlands, Belgium, France, Germany, Euro zone, U.K., Japan and Switzerland. In the empirical study, we find that both VRP1 and VRP2 measures produce significant Newey–West t-statistics at shorter horizon for the U.S. market and most of the international markets except for Japan. Sub-sample analysis further reveals that the magnitude of in-sample predictability is strongest during the post 2007 period.

Chapter 10
Predictability of VRP: A Comparison Study

10.1 Introduction

The intertemporal CAPM model of Merton (1973) demonstrates that the aggregate market risk is determined by the uncertainty of the underlying return, quantified by the return variance. When holding the market portfolio, however, an investor is also bearing the uncertainty of the variance itself. Just like the equity premium demanded by investors is the result of fear to the uncertainty of future returns, a variance risk premium, defined as the difference between risk-neutral and physical expected variances is also required to compensate for the randomness of the unknown variance. Many recent studies document the link between risk preference and variance risk premium. In particular, Bakshi and Madan (2006) argue that the variance risk premium is approximately determined by the risk aversion parameter and the higher order moments of underlying returns. In a similar vein, Bollerslev et al. (2013) assume an affine version of the stochastic volatility model as in Heston (1993) and show that the variance risk premium is linearly related to the risk aversion parameter. Other investigations in this area includes Bekaert and Engstrom (2010), Todorov (2010), and Gabaix (2012).

Furthermore, with Epstein and Zin (1989)'s recursive utility function, Bollerslev et al. (2009) and Drechsler and Yaron (2011) extend Bansal and Yaron (2004)'s long-run risk model, and set up a theoretical relationship between variance risk premium and macroeconomic uncertainty. In their models, the time variation in economic uncertainty and a preference for early resolution of uncertainty due to the fear of future risks are required to generate a positive variance risk premium that can predict excess stock market returns.

In the empirical investigation, Bollerslev et al. (2009), Zhou (2010), and Drechsler and Yaron (2011) find evidences in U.S. market that the variance risk premium has a stronger predictive power at the quarterly return horizon than traditional factors such as P/E ratio and price-dividend ratio. This finding has a strong implication for the stock return predictability literature. As an age-old but still mostly studied question in asset pricing, the prediction of aggregate market returns has been studied

J. Chen, *General Equilibrium Option Pricing Method: Theoretical and Empirical Study*, https://doi.org/10.1007/978-981-10-7428-8_10

by many papers, e.g., Fama and French (1988), Campbell and Shiller (1988), and Lettau and Ludvigson (2001). They adopt persistent variables such as the P/E ratio, the price-dividend ratio, the default spread, or the consumption-wealth ratio as the predictor, and empirical evidences show that the predictability is the strongest over long multi-year horizons. However, using highly persistent predictive variables can result in the possible statistical inference problems, as discussed in Campbell and Yogo (2006), Ang and Bekaert (2007), Boudoukh et al. (2008), among many others. In particular, Boudoukh et al. (2008) find that the estimated R^2 based on regressions with highly persistent predictors and overlapping returns will automatically increase in proportion to the return horizons, even without any evidences showing an improvement of predictability. This issue highlights the importance of variance risk premium as an additional predictor, since its first order correlation is much smaller than 1, which implies less effect of the persistent predictor problem. In addition, the variance premium has predictive power over monthly or quarterly horizon, in contrast to the long-run predictors.

In spite of the success of variance risk premium in predicting market returns, there are still some remaining issues. First, existing literature diverges on how to construct the measure of variance risk premium, especially on the calculation of expected realized variances (RV). For example, Bollerslev et al. (2009) assume that the realized variance follows a unit root process, Carr and Wu (2009) propose an ex post forward realized variance, and Drechsler and Yaron (2011) suggest to use lagged realized variance and model-free implied variance to construct the expectation of realized variance. Second, till to now, previous studies mainly focus on U.S. evidence and the time span usually does not extend to the post subprime crisis period.

Therefore, we decide to shed lights on these two issues. More specifically, our study compares nine types of the premia according to different methods of constructing the expectation of realized variance, including measures related to those in Carr and Wu (2009), Bollerslev et al. (2009), Zhou (2010), and Drechsler and Yaron (2011), as well as some extensions. With data from U.S., U.K., Germany, Canada, and Hong Kong markets, we further examine the predictability in international markets, especially during the financial crisis period. Related to our study, Bollerslev et al. (2013) also investigate the international evidence using the variance premium proposed in Bollerslev et al. (2009), and find that the premium only play a dominant role in predicting U.S. market. But, a robust check of different premium measures for international markets is provided in this paper. The empirical result shows that almost all variance risk premia across different markets are significant and positive with exceptions of two spikes. In predicting aggregate returns of international markets, the measure based on ex post realized variance displays a stronger predictive power than other types of premia and this finding is robust for all selected markets. Using ex post information to construct the variance risk premium is first introduced by Carr and Wu (2009) and also mentioned in Zhou (2010). But its empirical predictability is first examined in this paper.

In addition, both Bollerslev et al. (2009) and Drechsler and Yaron (2011) suggest that when investors perceive a much bigger shock than usual economic variation, they desire to pay more premium to hedge future uncertainties, therefore leading to a larger premium. This idea motivates us to select the special period of subprime crisis and investigate whether the market crash during this time are foreseen by the variance risk premium in short horizons, since it can carry more predictability for excess returns comparative to the normal episode.

The rest of this paper is organized as follows. Section 10.2 introduces the construction of variance risk premia and the setup of predictability regressions. Section 10.3 presents the data and empirical results. Finally, Section 10.4 concludes.

10.2 Methodology

10.2.1 Construction of Variance Risk Premium

The variance risk premium (VRP) during time interval $[t,\ t+1]$ is defined as the difference between expected future return variance under risk-neutral and physical measures, and takes the following form:

$$VRP_{t,t+1} = E_t^Q(Var_{t,t+1}) - E_t^P(Var_{t,t+1}), \tag{10.1}$$

where $E_t^Q(\cdot)$ and $E_t^P(\cdot)$, respectively, represent the expectations under risk-neutral and physical measures based on the information set available at time-t. Because both expectations are not directly observable, we have to find their corresponding empirical proxies in practice, denoted by $\hat{E}_t^Q(\cdot)$ and $\hat{E}_t^P(\cdot)$, respectively.

According to Carr and Madan (1998) and Britten-Jones and Neuberger (2000), the model-free implied variance (MFIV) can provide an unbiased empirical analog to the risk neutral expectation of total return variation:

$$MFIV_{t,t+1} = \hat{E}^Q(Var_{t,t+1}) = 2\int_0^{\infty} \frac{c\left(t+1,\ \frac{K}{B(t,t+1)}\right) - c(t,\ K)}{K^2} \mathrm{d}K, \tag{10.2}$$

where $MFIV_{t,t+1}$ is the model-free implied variance from t to $t+1$, $c(t,\ K)$ and $c(t+1,\ K)$ are prices of European call options with strike price K and maturity at t and $t+1$ respectively, and $B(t,\ t+1)$ is the price of a time t zero-coupon bond maturing at time $t+1$. Because there is no assumptions of the specific option pricing model and the form of underlying process, this measure is model-free. Jiang and Tian (2005) further relax the restriction of zero interest rate and allow a jump that can occur on underlying prices. Thus, the discrete time analog of MFIV from 0 to T is given by:

$$MFIV_{t,t+1} \approx 2\sum_{i=1}^{m} \frac{e^{r}c(t+1, K_i) - (S_t e^{r} - K)^{+}}{K_i^2} \Delta K_i, \tag{10.3}$$

where r is the risk-free interest ratc, $\Delta K_i = (K_{max} - K_{min})/m$, $K_i = K_{min} + i\,\Delta K$, $(0 \le i \le m)$, m is the number of discretization intervals, and S_t is the stock price at time t. There exists two types of error in Eq. (10.3). First, a discretization error is produced by substituting the discrete summation for the continuous integration. Second, in practice, the strike prices of trading options are available only within a certain range, thus resulting in a truncation error. Fortunately, Jiang and Tian (2005) argue that both types of error can be satisfactorily controlled and Eq. (10.3) is a fairly accurate approximation of the risk neutral expected variance.

On the other hand, the true variance $Var_{t,t+1}$ in Eq. (10.1) can be replaced by the realized variance $RV_{t,t+1}$. Andersen et al. (2001a), Andersen et al. (2001b, c), Andersen et al. (2003b), and Taylor (2005) define the realized variance as a summation of squared high frequency intra-day returns. Following Bakshi and Madan (2006), we use the daily returns within a month to construct the end-of-month realized variance, because there is minor error in using daily and intraday data to calculate monthly variance.

However, methods of constructing the expectation under physical measure $E_t^P(\cdot)$ vary in empirical studies. Basically, according to the information used to construct the expected variance, they can be classified into two categories as listed in Table 10.1.

As is shown in Panel A, the first category is based on the realized variance. For example, Bollerslev et al. (2009) directly use the realized variation over the interval $[t-1, t]$, i.e., $RV_{t-1,t}$. This method is valid only under the assumption that RV_t follows a martingale process, namely $E_t^P(RV_{t,t+1}) = RV_{t-1,t}$. Zhou (2010) advocates the lagged RV ($RV_{t-2,t-1}$) and lagged RV forecasts based on full sample AR(12) ($RVf1_{t-1,t}$) as an expectation of RV. Drechsler and Yaron (2011) introduce a regression model that takes ARMA(1,1) structure to produce realized variance forecasts ($RVf2_{t-1,t}$). All these four types of measures are included in our study. A natural extension would be directly using $RVf1_{t,t+1}$ or $RVf2_{t,t+1}$ instead of their lagged counterparts. Moreover, Carr and Wu (2009) follow the usual practice in variance swap market to propose ex post forward realized variance from daily price. In this paper, we use the ex post realized variance instead. This method of constructing the expected realized variance and therefore the variance risk premium is also briefly mentioned in Zhou (2010).

The second category is based on the past RV and MFIV information. For instance, with the high frequency S&P 500 data, Drechsler and Yaron (2011) forecast the realized variance by projecting the realized variance itself on its lagged counterparts and the lagged model-free implied variance, which is referred as $RVf3_{t,t+1}$ in Panel B. We also include its lagged value, $RVf3_{t-1,t}$, as a robustness check in this paper. According to the all nine types of expectations of the realized variances, their corresponding measures for variance risk premium are also reported in Table 10.1.

Table 10.1 Measures for variance risk premium

	Expectations of future variance under physical measure	Variance risk premia measures	Related studies
Panel A: Expectations constructed from RV			
I	RV, $RV_{t-1,t}$	$MFIV_{t,t+1} - RV_{t-1,t}$	Bollerslev et al. (2009)
II	Ex post RV, $RV_{t,t+1}$	$MFIV_{t,t+1} - RV_{t,t+1}$	Carr and Wu (2009), Zhou (2010)
II	Lagged RV, $RV_{t-2,t-1}$	$MFIV_{t,t+1} - RV_{t-2,t-1}$	Zhou (2010)
IV	Lagged RV forecast based on full sample AR(12) model, $RVf1_{t-1,t}$	$MFIV_{t,t+1} - RVf1_{t-1,t}$	Zhou (2010)
V	RV forecast based on full sample AR(12) model, $RVf1_{t,t+1}$	$MFIV_{t,t+1} - RVf1_{t,t+1}$	This study
VI	Lagged RV forecast based on full sample ARMA(1,1) model, $RVf2_{t-1,t}$	$MFIV_{t,t+1} - RVf2_{t-1,t}$	This study
VII	RV forecast based on full sample ARMA(1,1) model, $RVf2_{t,t+1}$	$MFIV_{t,t+1} - RVf2_{t,t+1}$	Drechsler and Yaron (2011)
Panel B: Expectations constructed from RV and MFIV			
VIII	Lagged RV forecast based on regression model, $RVf3_{t-1,t}$ $RVf3_{t-1,t} = \widehat{RV}_{t-1,t}$, $RV_{t,t+1} = \alpha + \beta RV_{t-1,t} + \gamma MFIV_{t,t+1} + \varepsilon_t$	$MFIV_{t,t+1} - RVf3_{t-1,t}$	This study
IX	RV forecast based on regression model, $RVf3_{t,t+1}$ $RVf3_{t,t+1} = \widehat{RV}_{t,t+1}$, $RV_{t,t+1} = \alpha + \beta RV_{t-1,t} + \gamma MFIV_{t,t+1} + \varepsilon_t$	$MFIV_{t,t+1} - RVf3_{t,t+1}$	Drechsler and Yaron (2011)

Note This table reports nine measures for the physical expectation of realized variance, and their corresponding variance risk premia. $\widehat{RV}_{t,t+1}$ denotes the fitted value from the regression model: $RV_{t,t+1} = \alpha + \beta RV_{t-1,t} + \gamma MFIV_{t,t+1} + \varepsilon_t$, where $\widehat{RV}_{t-1,t}$ is the lagged counterparts

10.2.2 Stock Return Predictability Regression

According to Bollerslev et al. (2009), Zhou (2010) and Drechsler and Yaron (2011), the variance risk premium is induced by the uncertainty of consumption through a recursive utility framework, and therefore can be used to predict equity returns. In Bollerslev et al. (2009), they find that the implied slope coefficient of variance risk premia regressed on h months ahead future returns shows a monotonically decreasing pattern, and the model implied R^2 exhibits a humped shape where the peaks are around quarterly horizon. In order to check whether the above findings are robust to different measures of variance risk premia and international markets, we adopt the multi-period return predictability regression as follows:

$$\frac{1}{h}\sum_{i=1}^{h} exr_{t+i} = b_0(h) + b_1(h)\, VRP_t + \varepsilon_{t+h}, \tag{10.4}$$

where exr_{t+i} is the excess stock market return over time interval $[t+i,\ t+i-1]$, $\frac{1}{h}\sum_{i=1}^{h} exr_{t+i}$ represents the average return for next h periods, and h denotes the prediction horizon. In the empirical study, we construct different VRP measures and report the coefficient estimates $\hat{b}_1(h)$ for $h = 1, 2, 3, 4, 5, 6, 9, 12$. The significance of coefficient estimates and the adjusted R^2 are signs of predictability.

10.3 Data and Empirical Results

10.3.1 Data and Summary Statistics

Our study focuses on five financial markets, namely U.S., U.K., Germany, Canada, and Hong Kong. The corresponding daily indexes, including S&P 500, FTSE 100, DAX, S&P/TSX 60, and HSI are obtained from CEIC. In order to construct the variance risk premium, we first calculate the monthly realized variance using daily stock index prices. Next, we employ the VIX obtained from CBOE as a substitution for MFIV in terms of the U.S. market, following Bollerslev et al. (2009), Zhou (2010) and Drechsler and Yaron (2011). For other markets, the MFIV are calculated using their corresponding index option prices with different strike prices and time to maturity according to Eq. (10.3). We obtain FTSE 100 index option prices from LIFFE, DAX and S&P/TSX 60 index options from ivolatility, and HSI index options from Bloomberg. As not all option prices for each market are available during the same period, our data samples have different starting dates. The U.S. data extends from January 1990 through May 2010, U.K. data from April 1992 to May 2010, Germany data from May 2002 to May 2010, Canada data from September 2001 to May 2010, and Hong Kong data from December 1999 to October 2009. The LIBOR rates are used as risk free interest rates. Conventional rules are used to filter the option data. First, we delete the observations with option prices less than minimum trading tick, with zero trading volume, with time to maturity shorter than 7 days or longer than 365 days, and violating boundary conditions or put-call parity.

For U.S. market, the VIX index is publicly available and updated daily from CBOE. For other markets, we have to construct the MFIV through a complete data set of option prices. The procedure is described as follows. First, we back out the Black–Scholes implied volatility from option prices observed from the market. Second, we apply the cubic spline to fit and interpolate the implied volatility curve for options with same time to maturity. In particular, we define the moneyness of option as the ratio of strike price divided by current stock price (K/S) and divided into many small intervals with length equals to 0.01, called moneyness bin. Some bins may have more than one option while others none. An average value is taken for the bins with multiple options while the bins with no options are removed. After that, cubic spline is used to interpolate and produce a continuum of implied volatility as curves and repeat it for all time to maturity days. The curve is flat outside the moneyness region implied from option prices. Finally, we back up option prices from implied volatility using Black–Scholes models. Considering that the relationship between option price and strike price is non-linear, we interpolate the implied volatility rather than option prices. Note that we only use Black–Scholes as a one-to-one mapping tool from implied volatility to option prices and do not assume that option prices follow Black–Scholes models.

The summary statistics for excess returns and the variance risk premia are reported in Table 10.2. In Panel A, the average excess returns in the North America markets are all positive with values exceeding 2%, but negative in the European markets, in particular, −1.64% for U.K. and −0.66% for Germany. In Hong Kong, the average excess return is 0.64%. The standard deviations for Germany and Hong Kong are over 80%, which are higher than other markets. In panel B, the correlations for the returns are all fairly high. With an exception of slightly lower value of the correlation between DAX and HSI, all other values are in excess of 0.70. Panel C reports the summary statistics for different variance risk premia measures as listed in Table 10.1. In total, we construct nine types of variance risk premia for each market. They are all positive on average across markets and values for S&P/TSX 60 rank the first, followed by HSI, DAX, and S&P 500, and lowest for FTSE 100. In terms of individual market, the premia perform differently.

The time series of variance premia using measure I and II are plotted in Fig. 10.1. Clearly, both measures of VRP show significant time variation. Particularly, premia are almost positive during the most sample periods and meanwhile show spikes at special time.

We also consider a sub-sample extending from January 2008 to October 2009 for Hong Kong and May 2010 for other markets. During this episode, the financial markets around the world suffer a recession caused by subprime crisis. The summary statistics are reported in Table 10.3. Compared with full-sample distributions, all excess returns in Panel A exhibit negative means ranging from a high of −8.26% for Canada to a low of −14.96% for Germany and considerable standard deviations particularly exceeding 120% for HSI. Unlike the consistence of the average variance

Table 10.2 Summary statistics

Market	Index	Sample period	Panel A: Excess returns						Panel B: Correlations for excess returns				
			Mean	S.D.	Min.	Max.	Skew.	Kurt.	S&P 500	FTSE 100	DAX	S&P/TSX 60	HSI
U.S.	S&P 500	1990.01–2010.05	2.21	52.39	−223.47	122.88	−0.85	4.76	1	0.79	0.86	0.84	0.74
U.K.	FTSE 100	1992.04–2010.05	−1.64	50.53	−173.77	109.61	−0.72	3.75		1	0.86	0.78	0.70
Germany	DAX	2002.05–2010.05	−0.66	84.45	−355.28	229.93	−0.94	6.18			1	0.71	0.64
Canada	S&P/TSX 60	2001.09–2010.05	2.58	53.71	−218.16	121.40	−1.12	5.79				1	0.75
Hong Kong	HSI	1999.12–2009.10	0.64	82.89	−308.65	188.79	−0.62	4.08					1

Panel C. Variance risk premium

Measures	S&P 500				FTSE 100				DAX				S&P/TSX 60				HSI			
	Mean	S.D.	Skew.	Kurt.	Mean	S.D.	Skew.	Kurt.	Mean	S.D.	Skew.	Kurt.	Mean	S.D.	Skew.	Kurt.	Mean	S.D.	Skew.	Kurt.
I	11.50	26.56	−5.11	50.32	2.36	37.25	−6.21	61.17	7.85	61.06	−4.39	26.89	14.73	37.44	−5.84	46.77	13.22	85.92	−8.36	84.76
II	11.26	37.42	−7.48	85.87	2.37	41.37	−6.00	60.24	7.80	67.59	−4.28	27.59	15.07	62.85	−6.61	60.37	13.20	88.38	−8.16	81.60
III	11.55	33.51	−4.76	46.64	2.79	20.26	−3.32	36.15	8.74	29.82	−5.21	39.41	13.73	22.19	1.18	11.20	13.33	80.24	−8.04	79.89
IV	11.66	25.65	−0.74	20.32	2.70	36.84	−7.55	82.17	8.56	60.09	−5.39	38.13	14.83	34.32	−4.63	36.87	12.55	30.36	1.24	4.25
V	11.41	21.15	−1.29	16.82	2.89	20.22	−1.41	23.79	8.71	30.85	−3.11	19.57	14.02	30.72	−0.48	11.36	12.57	33.08	0.72	7.07
VI	11.69	25.99	−0.86	19.46	2.92	21.90	−2.59	30.07	8.60	30.34	−5.06	37.68	14.02	22.67	1.71	17.22	11.81	30.84	1.17	3.88
VII	11.44	19.11	−0.18	15.45	2.84	22.05	−0.87	20.29	8.53	32.17	−3.36	19.18	13.94	28.05	−0.19	13.47	11.82	33.79	0.73	6.24
VIII	11.67	24.61	−0.89	21.23	2.47	18.91	−6.04	64.79	7.77	31.55	−5.49	40.18	15.00	27.00	−0.52	11.69	12.70	19.14	−1.34	8.13
IX	11.48	15.87	−0.77	18.27	2.37	18.33	−4.27	42.82	7.80	29.90	−4.42	27.32	15.07	37.78	−0.47	12.62	13.20	15.63	−8.42	84.29

Note This table reports the summary statistics for excess return and variance risk premium for each market. The monthly excess returns are in annualized percentage form, and the variance risk premia are in monthly percentage-squared form

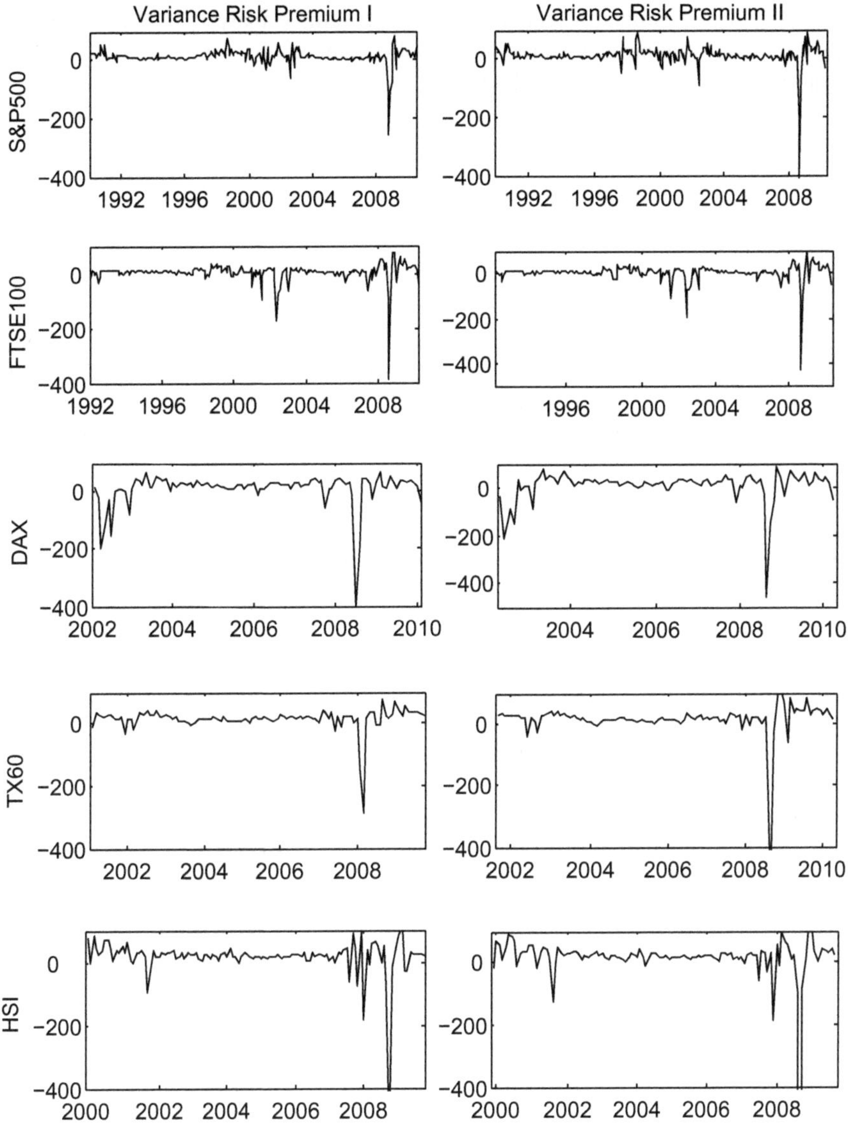

Fig. 10.1 Variance risk premium across markets
This figure illustrates the monthly variance risk premium for U.S. (S&P 500), U.K. (FTSE 100), Germany (DAX), Canada (S&P/TSX 60), and Hong Kong (HSI). The variance risk premia are constructed using measure I and II listed in Table 10.1

risk premia when using different measures in full-sample analysis, in Panel B, premia based on first three measures are much smaller than others across markets and even negative for S&P 500, DAX, and S&P/TSX 60.

10.3.2 Empirical Results from International Markets

We use the variance risk premium measures listed in Table 10.1 as the predictor[1] to forecast the aggregate international stock market returns.

Empirical results for international markets are reported in Table 10.4. First, results of the one-month horizon prediction show that, with comparative low values of adjusted R^2, the predicative power of VRP I is weak across international markets. The coefficient is significant only for U.S. but not for other markets. These findings are generally consistent for other VRP measures. The only exception is the VRP II that shows extremely better predictability than others, as values of adjusted R^2 are above 10% for all markets and even exceed 20% for S&P 500 and S&P /TSX 60. Second, turn to the multi-month horizon prediction results in Table 10.4, all coefficients of VRP measures for the U.S. market in Panel A are significant at quarterly horizon, and the predictive power as suggested by the adjusted R^2 begins to decline at longer horizons. Accordingly, the adjusted R^2 displays a humped shape pattern with peaks around quarterly horizon. This finding is consistent with Bollerslev et al. (2009) and also confirms that all these measures are robust for the U.S. market.

For other markets in Panels B to E, however, the forecasting performances are inconsistent. According to values of the adjusted R^2, all VRP with the exception of measures IV and VIII can predict future returns in German market at quarterly horizons; In Canadian market, the measures I, II, V, VII, and IX have predictive power within one to two quarters; When come to U.K. and Hong Kong markets, only the measure II performs relatively well.

All in all, it is very clear in Table 10.4 that adopting the variance risk premium constructed by ex post realized variance, namely VRP II, results in extremely higher values of the adjusted R^2 than other measures over the prediction horizons for each markets. This indicates a robust predictive power across markets. We further plot the estimated coefficients and adjusted R^2 over the prediction horizons in Fig. 10.2.

[1] We also consider several traditional long-run predictors, such as price-dividend ratio, price-earning ratio and short term interest rates. Their predictive power is relatively weak at short horizons and does not have major influence on the significance of VRP measures, and hence these results are not reported to save space.

Table 10.3 Summary statistics for sub-sample period

Panel A. Excess Returns

Market	Index	Sample period	Excess returns					
			Mean	S. D.	Min.	Max.	Skew.	Kurt.
U.S.	S&P 500	2008.01–2010.05	−13.00	80.61	−223.48	107.57	−0.69	3.05
U.K.	FTSE 100	2008.01–2010.05	−11.89	73.56	−173.77	96.49	−0.41	2.27
Germany	DAX	2008.01–2010.05	−14.96	93.26	−200.35	184.58	−0.16	2.78
Canada	S&P/TSX 60	2008.01–2010.05	−8.26	78.29	−218.16	121.40	−0.81	3.91
Hong Kong	HSI	2008.01–2009.10	−14.89	126.66	−308.65	188.79	−0.48	3.02

Panel B. Variance risk premium

Measures	S&P 500				FTSE 100				DAX				S&P/TSX 60				HSI			
	Mean	S.D.	Skew.	Kurt.	Mean	S.D.	Skew.	Kurt.	Mean	S.D.	Skew.	Kurt.	Mean	S.D.	Skew.	Kurt.	Mean	S.D.	Skew.	Kurt.
I	−1.62	66.60	−2.55	10.89	3.44	87.30	−3.56	17.91	−1.76	91.38	−3.62	17.46	8.58	68.74	−3.39	16.08	−24.33	190.70	−3.99	20.24
II	−2.63	98.82	−3.47	16.55	3.72	96.74	−3.45	17.73	−1.78	100.78	−3.62	18.54	8.84	118.41	−3.66	19.37	−19.79	197.87	−3.81	19.10
III	−0.53	84.42	−2.56	10.18	5.43	86.08	−4.47	22.03	1.04	90.86	−4.51	24.98	8.89	62.38	−2.69	13.07	−25.02	177.99	−3.76	15.68
IV	13.99	85.86	−1.80	9.18	19.71	42.80	−3.82	18.41	8.64	46.96	−4.32	24.11	23.93	36.07	0.26	5.46	31.09	41.80	0.03	3.07
V	12.98	44.24	−2.00	8.39	19.99	42.56	−2.21	12.99	8.61	47.75	−2.71	12.33	24.20	54.72	−0.90	2.02	35.62	53.16	−0.92	6.53
VI	15.20	59.23	−1.46	6.73	25.64	44.71	−3.84	21.74	9.37	47.20	−4.37	24.43	25.13	37.60	0.58	7.99	37.21	36.54	−0.04	4.08
VII	14.18	39.21	−1.22	7.88	25.92	44.90	−2.24	13.02	9.35	49.19	−2.96	12.62	25.40	49.12	−0.86	6.34	41.74	49.24	−1.29	8.77
VIII	13.44	57.15	−1.33	6.59	11.48	42.69	−4.52	25.88	4.93	48.06	−4.56	25.93	30.29	42.15	−1.57	6.55	−0.39	32.51	−0.64	2.57
IX	12.42	33.74	−1.49	8.36	11.75	41.53	−3.30	16.92	4.91	45.10	−3.66	14.71	30.56	65.63	−1.08	3.37	4.14	34.20	−3.94	19.84

Note The monthly excess returns are in annualized percentage form, and the variance risk premia are in monthly percentage-squared form. The data samples extend from January 2008 to October 2009 for Hong Kong and May 2010 for other markets

Table 10.4 Monthly regressions results

Panel A. Predicting S&P 500 index returns using different VRP measures

Month	VRP I	Adj. R^2(%)	VRP II	Adj. R^2(%)	VRP III	Adj. R^2(%)	VRP IV	Adj. R^2(%)	VRP V	Adj. R^2(%)	VRP VI	Adj. R^2(%)	VRP VII	Adj. R^2(%)	VRP VIII	Adj. R^2(%)	VRP IX	Adj. R^2(%)
1	0.49	5.79	0.64	20.64	0.18	0.86	0.09	−0.20	0.59	5.27	0.19	0.48	0.65	5.24	0.13	−0.06	0.80	5.48
	(4.00)		(8.03)		(1.76)		(0.72)		(3.82)		(1.48)		(3.81)		(0.92)		(3.89)	
2	0.51	11.92	0.51	23.64	0.25	4.36	0.26	2.50	0.56	9.04	0.32	4.17	0.75	13.09	0.29	3.01	0.91	13.33
	(5.83)		(8.75)		(3.48)		(2.69)		(5.02)		(3.41)		(6.15)		(2.92)		(6.21)	
3	0.45	13.61	0.39	20.95	0.20	3.99	0.24	3.30	0.48	9.60	0.25	3.62	0.64	14.46	0.22	2.45	0.78	14.78
	(6.28)		(8.10)		(3.33)		(3.05)		(5.19)		(3.19)		(6.50)		(2.67)		(6.58)	
4	0.40	14.07	0.35	21.41	0.11	1.26	0.14	1.26	0.48	12.52	0.14	1.29	0.59	15.41	0.11	0.48	0.71	15.69
	(6.40)		(8.21)		(2.03)		(2.03)		(5.99)		(2.05)		(6.74)		(1.48)		(6.81)	
5	0.32	10.26	0.33	22.64	0.05	0.00	0.08	0.24	0.41	10.88	0.08	0.30	0.49	12.85	0.06	−0.13	0.59	12.87
	(5.38)		(8.51)		(1.00)		(1.26)		(5.55)		(1.32)		(6.08)		(0.83)		(6.09)	
6	0.22	5.54	0.28	18.17	0.05	0.06	0.08	0.39	0.31	7.09	0.09	0.64	0.37	8.53	0.07	0.17	0.45	8.35
	(3.91)		(7.43)		(1.08)		(1.40)		(4.43)		(1.60)		(4.87)		(1.19)		(4.82)	
9	0.09	0.89	0.14	6.69	0.01	−0.39	0.04	−0.18	0.15	2.02	0.04	−0.09	0.18	2.65	0.04	−0.21	0.21	2.45
	(1.78)		(4.30)		(0.26)		(0.74)		(2.46)		(0.89)		(2.77)		(0.69)		(2.67)	
12	0.05	0.09	0.09	3.00	−0.01	−0.37	0.01	−0.38	0.01	0.94	0.01	−0.37	0.12	1.17	0.00	−0.41	0.13	1.03
	(1.10)		(2.92)		(−0.31)		(0.29)		(1.82)		(0.31)		(1.97)		(0.10)		(1.88)	

(continued)

Table 10.4 (continued)

Panel B. Predicting FTSE 100 index returns using different VRP measures

Month	VRP I	Adj. R^2(%)	VRP II	Adj. R^2(%)	VRP III	Adj. R^2(%)	VRP IV	Adj. R^2(%)	VRP V	Adj. R^2(%)	VRP VI	Adj. R^2(%)	VRP VII	Adj. R^2(%)	VRP VII	Adj. R^2(%)	VRP IX	Adj. R^2(%)
1	−0.06	−0.24	0.44	12.56	−0.02	−0.45	−0.25	0.53	−0.22	0.32	−0.14	−0.12	−0.20	0.27	−0.12	−0.28	−0.18	−0.02
	(−0.70)		(5.66)		(−0.18)		(−1.47)		(−1.30)		(−0.86)		(−1.26)		(−0.63)		(−0.97)	
2	−0.03	−0.39	0.20	4.80	0.06	−0.07	−0.07	−0.33	−0.19	0.58	0.01	−0.46	−0.13	0.11	0.04	−0.43	−0.10	−0.23
	(−0.41)		(3.45)		(0.92)		(−0.54)		(−1.50)		(0.04)		(−1.11)		(0.28)		(−0.71)	
3	0.04	−0.21	0.15	3.60	0.10	0.92	0.06	−0.32	−0.06	−0.29	0.08	−0.12	0.00	−0.46	0.12	0.11	0.05	−0.37
	(0.74)		(3.01)		(1.73)		(0.55)		(−0.60)		(0.86)		(−0.05)		(1.11)		(0.45)	
4	0.07	0.62	0.15	5.01	0.07	0.50	0.02	−0.44	0.03	−0.42	0.05	−0.25	0.06	−0.22	0.09	−0.03	0.12	0.28
	(1.53)		(3.52)		(1.44)		(0.22)		(0.32)		(0.68)		(0.73)		(0.97)		(1.26)	
5	0.05	0.18	0.14	5.49	0.03	−0.27	−0.05	−0.30	−0.02	−0.45	0.00	−0.46	0.03	−0.39	0.01	−0.46	0.08	−0.09
	(1.18)		(3.68)		(0.65)		(−0.60)		(−0.19)		(−0.05)		(0.40)		(0.12)		(0.89)	
6	0.03	−0.28	0.12	4.38	0.01	−0.45	−0.08	0.09	−0.04	−0.32	−0.03	−0.39	0.00	−0.47	−0.03	−0.41	0.03	−0.40
	(0.63)		(3.30)		(0.18)		(−1.09)		(−0.56)		(−0.41)		(−0.01)		(−0.36)		(0.37)	
9	−0.01	−0.41	0.06	1.49	−0.03	−0.18	−0.10	0.84	−0.08	0.25	−0.06	−0.01	−0.04	−0.28	−0.08	0.13	−0.03	−0.35
	(−0.36)		(2.07)		(−0.78)		(−1.68)		(−1.24)		(−0.99)		(−0.63)		(−1.13)		(−0.50)	
12	−0.02	−0.35	0.03	0.05	−0.02	−0.22	−0.06	0.15	−0.05	−0.07	−0.03	−0.28	−0.02	−0.37	−0.05	−0.11	−0.03	−0.34
	(−0.50)		(1.05)		(−0.72)		(−1.15)		(−0.92)		(−0.63)		(−0.45)		(−0.87)		(−0.51)	

(continued)

Table 10.4 (continued)

Panel C. Predicting DAX index returns using different VRP measures

Month	VRP I	Adj. R^2(%)	VRP II	Adj. R^2(%)	VRP III	Adj. R^2(%)	VRP IV	Adj. R^2(%)	VRP V	Adj. R^2(%)	VRP VI	Adj. R^2(%)	VRP VII	Adj. R^2(%)	VRP VIII	Adj. R^2(%)	VRP IX	Adj. R^2(%)
1	0.11	−0.38	0.53	16.96	0.25	2.07	0.28	−0.04	0.15	−0.76	0.45	1.58	0.21	−0.40	0.41	1.29	0.22	−0.43
	(0.80)		(4.52)		(1.73)		(0.98)		(0.53)		(1.59)		(0.79)		(1.49)		(0.77)	
2	0.19	2.68	0.32	11.61	0.18	2.24	0.23	0.15	0.27	0.73	0.33	1.66	0.36	2.55	0.28	1.13	0.39	2.62
	(1.90)		(3.67)		(1.78)		(1.07)		(1.30)		(1.61)		(1.87)		(1.44)		(1.89)	
3	0.19	4.42	0.31	16.11	0.17	3.23	0.27	1.60	0.30	2.48	0.31	2.61	0.38	4.83	0.24	1.43	0.39	4.45
	(2.32)		(4.39)		(2.04)		(1.60)		(1.85)		(1.88)		(2.41)		(1.54)		(2.33)	
4	0.19	5.89	0.28	16.78	0.13	1.81	0.16	0.11	0.37	5.40	0.23	1.39	0.39	7.00	0.20	1.35	0.40	6.11
	(2.63)		(4.49)		(1.66)		(1.05)		(2.53)		(1.53)		(2.86)		(1.51)		(2.68)	
5	0.15	4.47	0.25	17.97	0.04	−0.67	−0.02	−1.04	0.24	2.67	0.06	−0.83	0.30	4.94	0.03	−1.01	0.31	4.69
	(2.33)		(4.67)		(0.60)		(−0.15)		(1.90)		(0.46)		(2.44)		(0.25)		(2.33)	
6	0.08	0.99	0.21	15.08	0.03	−0.83	−0.01	−1.05	0.12	0.04	0.06	−0.85	0.19	1.78	0.00	−1.08	0.18	1.16
	(1.40)		(4.23)		(0.47)		(−0.11)		(1.02)		(0.45)		(1.65)		(0.01)		(1.45)	
9	0.01	−1.05	0.11	5.49	−0.04	−0.49	−0.09	−0.34	0.02	−1.04	−0.04	−0.90	0.06	−0.63	−0.08	−0.40	0.02	−1.01
	(0.12)		(2.55)		(−0.73)		(−0.82)		(0.16)		(−0.40)		(0.64)		(−0.79)		(0.23)	
12	−0.01	−0.99	0.05	0.68	−0.04	−0.09	−0.08	−0.08	−0.01	−1.05	−0.04	−0.78	0.03	0.92	−0.07	−0.13	−0.01	−1.04
	(−0.26)		(1.29)		(−0.96)		(−0.96)		(−0.11)		(−0.51)		(0.36)		(−0.94)		(−0.14)	

(continued)

Table 10.4 (continued)

Panel D. Predicting S&P/TSX 60 index returns using different VRP measures

Month	VRP I	Adj. R^2 (%)	VRP II	Adj. R^2 (%)	VRP III	Adj. R^2 (%)	VRP IV	Adj. R^2 (%)	VRP V	Adj. R^2 (%)	VRP VI	Adj. R^2 (%)	VRP VII	Adj. R^2 (%)	VRP VIII	Adj. R^2 (%)	VRP IX	Adj. R^2 (%)
1	0.32	4.13	0.41	23.25	0.10	−0.58	−0.07	−0.90	0.10	−0.67	−0.12	−0.72	0.22	0.38	−0.07	−0.87	0.18	0.62
	(2.33)		(5.67)		(0.64)		(−0.29)		(0.56)		(−0.51)		(1.18)		(−0.35)		(1.28)	
2	0.23	3.06	0.27	15.56	0.06	−0.70	−0.24	0.61	0.07	−0.74	−0.13	−0.50	0.12	−0.38	−0.04	−0.92	0.10	−0.24
	(2.06)		(4.47)		(0.53)		(−1.28)		(0.49)		(−0.70)		(0.78)		(−0.26)		(0.87)	
3	0.22	4.24	0.22	13.82	0.01	−0.98	−0.16	−0.07	0.08	−0.50	−0.13	−0.32	0.16	0.59	−0.01	−0.99	0.13	0.80
	(2.36)		(4.18)		(0.05)		(−0.97)		(0.70)		(−0.82)		(1.27)		(−0.07)		(1.35)	
4	0.22	5.23	0.22	15.73	−0.09	−0.15	−0.19	0.65	0.18	1.81	−0.17	0.33	0.24	3.12	−0.05	−0.85	0.18	3.26
	(2.59)		(4.50)		(−0.92)		(−1.29)		(1.70)		(−1.16)		(2.08)		(−0.38)		(2.12)	
5	0.16	2.75	0.20	16.27	−0.14	1.43	−0.18	0.74	0.18	2.18	−0.16	0.42	0.23	3.54	−0.07	−0.57	0.17	3.45
	(1.98)		(4.58)		(−1.58)		(−1.33)		(1.82)		(−1.20)		(2.19)		(−0.65)		(2.16)	
6	0.07	−0.04	0.16	11.62	−0.12	1.11	−0.13	0.00	0.12	0.68	−0.08	−0.52	0.16	1.55	−0.04	−0.85	0.12	1.42
	(0.98)		(3.81)		(−1.47)		(−1.00)		(1.30)		(−0.68)		(1.62)		(−0.38)		(1.58)	
9	0.00	−0.98	0.07	2.58	−0.08	0.58	−0.07	−0.54	0.04	−0.68	−0.03	−0.90	0.07	−0.26	−0.02	−0.95	0.05	−0.36
	(0.04)		(1.93)		(−1.26)		(−0.67)		(0.55)		(−0.29)		(0.85)		(−0.19)		(0.79)	
12	0.00	−0.97	0.04	0.80	−0.08	1.16	−0.07	−0.28	0.01	−0.96	−0.05	−0.52	0.01	−0.64	−0.04	−0.56	0.02	−0.73
	(−0.10)		(1.35)		(−1.49)		(−0.85)		(0.16)		(−0.68)		(0.58)		(−0.66)		(0.50)	

(continued)

Table 10.4 (continued)

Panel E. Predicting HSI index returns using different VRP measures

Month	VRP I	Adj. R^2(%)	VRP II	Adj. R^2(%)	VRP III	Adj. R^2(%)	VRP IV	Adj. R^2(%)	VRP V	Adj. R^2(%)	VRP VI	Adj. R^2(%)	VRP VII	Adj. R^2(%)	VRP VIII	Adj. R^2(%)	VRP IX	Adj. R^2(%)
1	−0.06	−0.42	0.41	18.49	−0.10	0.09	−0.43	1.72	−0.41	1.79	−0.50	2.67	−0.43	2.20	−0.82	2.87	−0.24	−0.65
	(−0.71)		(5.25)		(−1.05)		(−1.75)		(−1.77)		(−2.05)		(−1.91)		(−2.10)		(−0.49)	
2	−0.05	−0.35	0.19	6.42	−0.02	−0.82	−0.24	0.49	−0.25	0.76	−0.27	0.91	−0.29	1.45	−0.36	0.31	−0.22	−0.58
	(−0.77)		(3.01)		(−0.23)		(−1.26)		(−1.38)		(−1.44)		(−1.65)		(−1.17)		(−0.57)	
3	−0.02	−0.78	0.12	2.79	0.01	−0.85	−0.22	0.71	−0.18	0.40	−0.24	1.08	−0.21	0.88	−0.28	0.16	−0.03	−0.85
	(−0.30)		(2.09)		(0.11)		(−1.36)		(−1.21)		(−1.51)		(−1.43)		(−1.09)		(−0.11)	
4	0.00	−0.86	0.10	2.97	−0.01	−0.83	−0.24	1.64	−0.14	0.18	−0.26	2.02	−0.16	0.56	−0.23	0.00	0.06	−0.82
	(0.05)		(2.14)		(−0.18)		(−1.72)		(−1.10)		(−1.85)		(−1.29)		(−1.00)		0.23	
5	−0.01	−0.85	0.10	3.06	−0.06	0.26	−0.29	3.31	−0.16	0.68	−0.30	3.77	−0.18	1.06	−0.30	0.93	0.01	−0.86
	(−0.14)		(2.17)		(−1.14)		(−2.24)		(−1.34)		(−2.36)		(−1.50)		(−1.44)		(0.03)	
6	−0.04	−0.08	0.07	1.72	−0.08	1.54	−0.29	4.02	−0.20	1.98	−0.29	4.33	−0.22	2.45	−0.30	1.17	−0.18	−0.35
	(−0.95)		(1.74)		(−1.68)		(−2.43)		(−1.83)		(−2.51)		(−1.98)		(−1.54)		(−0.77)	
9	−0.06	1.58	−0.01	−0.83	−0.05	0.76	−0.33	8.45	−0.30	7.92	−0.32	8.28	−0.29	8.06	−0.08	−0.63	−0.27	0.70
	(−1.70)		(−0.20)		(−1.38)		(−3.43)		(−3.33)		(−3.40)		(−3.36)		(−0.52)		(−1.35)	
12	−0.05	1.01	−0.01	−0.82	−0.05	1.30	−0.38	15.26	−0.31	12.33	−0.36	14.61	−0.30	12.03	−0.11	−0.30	−0.17	0.05
	(−1.48)		(−0.22)		(−1.59)		(−4.70)		(−4.18)		(−4.58)		(−4.12)		(−0.81)		(−1.03)	

Note The estimation results for each market are based on regression model (10.4) and nine measures for the variance risk premium listed in Table 10.1. The prediction horizon is up to twelve months and t statistics are reported in parentheses. Adj. R^2 denotes the adjusted R^2. A constant is always included in the regression specification though it is not reported in the table

Table 10.5 Sub-sample analysis

	Month	1	2	3	4	5	6	9	12
S&P 500	VRP II	0.53	0.44	0.33	0.32	0.32	0.25	0.11	0.05
		(4.30)	(4.42)	(3.65)	(4.10)	(4.34)	(3.33)	(1.53)	(0.87)
	Adj.R^2(%)	37.65	38.96	29.82	35.29	38.10	25.87	4.45	−0.83
FTSE 100	VRP II	0.35	0.19	0.14	0.16	0.15	0.12	0.06	0.01
		(2.71)	(1.86)	(1.64)	(2.21)	(2.18)	(1.63)	(0.91)	(0.14)
	Adj.R^2(%)	18.46	8.06	5.65	12.15	11.88	5.57	−0.59	−3.63
DAX	VRP II	0.41	0.25	0.20	0.24	0.21	0.13	0.04	0.02
		(2.60)	(1.98)	(2.01)	(2.90)	(2.63)	(1.62)	(0.64)	(0.34)
	Adj.R^2(%)	17.05	9.48	9.81	20.90	17.44	5.47	−2.16	−3.25
S&P/TSX 60	VRP II	0.39	0.26	0.22	0.21	0.20	0.15	0.06	0.04
		(3.78)	(2.87)	(2.60)	(2.80)	(2.89)	(2.35)	(1.17)	(1.03)
	Adj.R^2(%)	32.19	20.57	17.07	19.60	20.77	13.94	1.28	0.25
HSI	VRP II	0.39	0.20	0.14	0.13	0.11	0.08	0.00	0.00
		(3.39)	(2.00)	(1.50)	(1.56)	(1.43)	(1.03)	(0.06)	(0.00)
	Adj.R^2(%)	33.29	12.56	5.56	6.34	4.70	0.32	−4.98	−5.00

Note This table reports sub-sample results during the episode of financial crisis from January 2008 to October 2009 for HSI and May 2010 for other markets. The estimation results for each market are based on regression model (10.4) and the second measure for variance risk premium listed in Table 10.1. The t statistics are reported in parentheses

As is shown, except for the Hong Kong market, all estimated coefficients are significant and display a monotonically decreasing pattern as the horizon increases when using measure II to predict aggregate returns in each market. On the other hand, values of the adjusted R^2 display a similar general pattern across markets, starting out high at the one-month horizon, then slightly going up for S&P 500 and down for other markets, staying at a relatively high level between one and two quarters, and thereafter decreasing. In particular, the value of adjusted R^2 is quite high at the shortest one-month horizon for each market, even exceeding 10% for all markets except for Hong Kong. This implies that the magnitude of predictability of VRP II is also strong at this one-month horizon. Our finding is comparable with Bollerslev et al. (2009)'s results in terms of the decreasing pattern of coefficient estimates and slightly humped shape for the adjusted R^2.

Finally, since the VRP II outperforms other measures, we use it to predict aggregate market returns during the special episode of financial crisis from January 2008 to October 2009 for HSI and May 2010 for other markets and investigate whether the crash is foreseen at short horizons. Empirical results are reported in Table 10.5. We can see that, both estimated coefficients and R^2 still exhibit the same pattern as found in full-sample investigation. In particular, the values of R^2 for all markets remarkably increase comparative to their corresponding estimates in Table 10.4. For example, the value of R^2 raises from 20.64 to 37.65% at the one-month horizon for S&P 500, and from 12.56 to 18.46% for FTSE 100. The evidence suggests that,

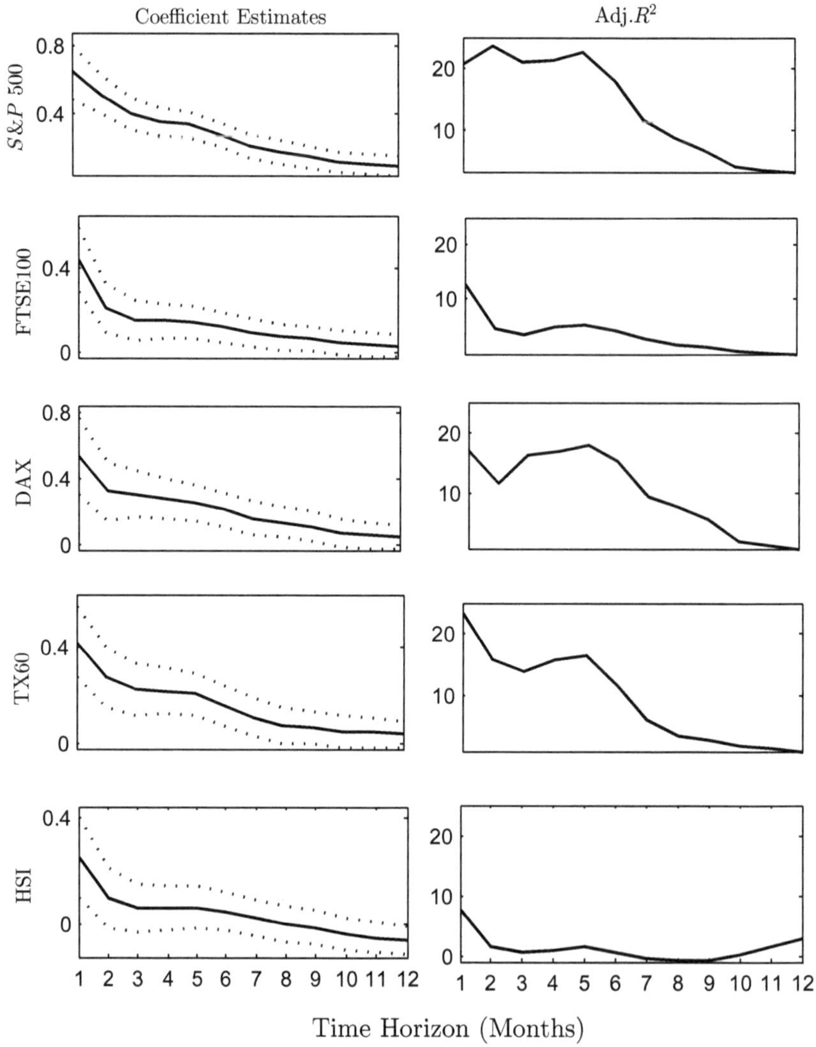

Fig. 10.2 Coefficients estimates and adjusted R^2 of return predictability regressions across markets The figure shows the coefficient estimates and adjusted R^2 statistics over prediction horizons for U.S. (S&P 500), U.K. (FTSE 100), Germany (DAX), Canada (S&P/TSX 60), and Hong Kong (HSI), based on results in Table 10.4 and measure II for the variance risk premium. In the left panel, the solid line depicts the estimated coefficients of variance risk premium and the dotted lines represent corresponding 95% confidence intervals

during the episode of high volatility and notorious spikes, the variance risk premium can predict equity returns better than normal episode.

10.4 Concluding Remarks

A number of recent papers have studied the variance risk premium defined as the difference between risk-neutral and realized variances, and suggest that it reflects investor's risk aversion to economic uncertainty and therefore can be used to predict equity returns. Existing literatures derive several measures of the variance premium due to different methods of calculating the expectation of realized variance. Introducing three alternative measures in this study, we totally construct nine measures of the variance risk premium. Their magnitudes of predictability for local stock markets is examined using U.S., U.K., Germany, Canada, and Hong Kong data.

Empirical results show that different measures of the variance risk premia have robust performance in the U.S. market, but not consistent in other markets. Comparing the empirical performances of all variance premia, we find that using the measure II clearly increases the values of adjusted R^2 and therefore the predicative power. A slightly humped shaped pattern of adjusted R^2 is also observed, and it implies a strong predictability at 1–2 months horizons, as well as a forecasting power at 1–2 quarters horizons which is consistent with previous findings. In addition, the subsample analysis suggests that the magnitude of predictability for the second premium is much stronger during a volatile period than normal times.

Chapter 11
Conclusions

11.1 Summary

Resorting to the general equilibrium model based on the fanning preference, this book obtains the market risk premium, jump risk premium, variance risk premium, and covariance risk premium in equilibrium. In particular, all these risk premiums are controlled by both the risk aversion and the fanning effect. Through the numerical and empirical studies, this book aims to investigate the role of fanning effect played in option pricing, and the predictability of the variance risk premium. The main results are summarized as follows:

(1) Based on the fanning preference, the equilibrium market prices for jump risk, variance risk, and covariance risk are obtained. In particular, the jump risk premium, variance risk premium, and covariance risk premium are controlled by both risk aversion and fanning preference. Remarkably, incorporating the fanning effect can reconcile the high market risk premium implicit in options with a moderate degree of risk aversion. The low degree of risk aversion results in a small amount of compensation paid for the jump risk, as indicated by the expected utility theory. However, the actual market risk premium is quite high in the presence of jump. To reconcile the high risk premium with a low degree of risk aversion, our model suggests that the objective probability is weighted by a weighting function driven by the fanning effect. As a result, a portion of the total market risk premium is captured by the agent's fanning out preference.

(2) Monte Carlo simulation is applied to compare the general equilibrium option pricing model with those based on no arbitrage (risk-neutral) method. Results show that the risk-neutral model is able to capture only a mild level of risk aversion and over-prices those options with moderate or high level of risk aversion. In addition, we simulates options over different underlying distributions for jump sizes and utility functions so as to emphasize their effects on option prices. Monte Carlo experiments report that using either the expected or the recursive utility function similarly reflects investor's aversion to jump risk when the fanning effect parameter is very close to zero; The choice between the log-normal

J. Chen, *General Equilibrium Option Pricing Method: Theoretical and Empirical Study*, https://doi.org/10.1007/978-981-10-7428-8_11

and the uniform distributions for jump sizes makes a big difference only if the standard deviation of the jump size is high in the magnitude.

(3) Empirical tests are carried out to evaluate the in-sample and out-of-sample performances of option pricing models based on the general equilibrium and the no arbitrage method. Empirical results reveal that the risk-neutral model overprices the short-term near-the-money options and underprices the short-term deep OTM call options when assuming that the jump risk premium is proportional to the risk factor itself. Allowing individual utility function to capture the jump risk, the general equilibrium model performs better to price short-dated options. In the absence of the stochastic volatility to capture the diffusive risks, however, the general equilibrium model of Ma and Vetzal (1997) overprices the long-term options.

(4) In order to examine the role of fanning out preference played in pricing options, we carry out numerical and empirical tests. Results show that the fanning out preference captures a significant portion of the total market premium, and it is also able to reconcile the moderate degree of risk aversion with the true premium implicit in the option market. Incorporating the fanning out preference, our model generates pronounced volatility smirks consistent with the post-1987 evidences on S&P500 index options, and fit the market observations better than the conventional expected utility model.

(5) In order to investigate the effect of jump size distribution on option smirk and risk-neutral stock return distribution, we consider a jump-diffusion model with Laplace jump size distribution in comparison with the conventional normal model. In addition, our analysis is built upon a general equilibrium framework, in which the representative agent's risk preference shows a fanning out characteristic. Results show that, when fanning effect is zero, both Laplace model and normal model price jump risk similarly, and generate relatively flat volatility smirks. Also, both models produce similar patterns of risk-neutral probability distribution. However, when fanning effect is present, Laplace model captures larger jump risk premium implicit in options than that of normal model. As a result, it generates more pronounced volatility smirks relative to normal model. On the other hand, imposing the Laplace distribution on jump sizes results in more remarkable left-skewed and heavy-tailed pattern of the risk-neutral distribution, in comparison to those generated by normal model.

(6) According to the departures between the risk-neutral and the physical volatilities proposed by Bakshi and Madan (2006), this book estimates the volatility spreads via the GMM and extracts the volatility risk aversion embedded in the FTSE-100 index returns. The empirical evidences show that the risk-neutral volatilities calculated by the model-free measure exceed their physical counterparts leading to positive volatility spreads. Further studying the volatility spreads reveals that the volatility risk aversion is around 3 and the annual distribution for index returns exhibits a heavy right-tail.

(7) As the variance risk premium (volatility spread) reflects the fear of investors to future variance risk, it can forecast expected excess stock returns. We use the model-free volatility method including the realized volatility and model-free

implied volatility method to estimate the time-varying variance risk premium for both U.S. and Hong Kong market. The empirical analysis demonstrates that the variance risk premium in both markets follow similar trends. Meanwhile, controlling the traditional conventional stock return predictors such as dividend yield, log(P/E) and short term interest rate, variance risk premium in Hong Kong market predicts future return additionally, especially during financial crisis period. This support the theoretical conclusion that variance risk premium as a proxy of (short term) macroeconomic risk and investors' degree of risk aversion, captures the systematic risk related, thus economically significant.

(8) A further and more extensive evaluation of the predictability of variance risk premium across different international stock markets is provided as well. Our empirical analysis is carried out through the in-sample predictability test using data from the U.S. market and other selected developed markets including Netherlands, Belgium, France, Germany, Euro zone, U.K., Japan and Switzerland. In the empirical study, we find that both VRP1 and VRP2 measures produce significant Newey-West t-statistics at shorter horizon for the U.S. market and most of the international markets except for Japan. Sub-sample analysis further reveals that the magnitude of in-sample predictability is strongest during the post 2007 period. This finding may be explained by the role of large jump risk on equity premium and it is also consistent with previous consensus on the link between countercyclical equity premium and business cycles.

(9) A similar study for different variance risk premium measures is also given. The existing literature proposes several measures of the variance premium due to different methods of calculating the expectation of realized variance. In this study, we totally construct nine measures of the variance risk premium. Their magnitudes of predictability for local stock markets is examined using the U.S., U.K., Germany, Canada, and Hong Kong data. Empirical results show that different measures of the variance risk premia have robust performance in the U.S. market, but not consistent in other markets. Comparing the empirical performances of all variance premia, we find that using the measure of Carr and Wu (2009) and Zhou (2010) clearly increases the values of adjusted R^2 and therefore the predicative power. A slightly humped shaped pattern of adjusted R^2 is also observed, and it implies a strong predictability at 1–2 months horizons, as well as a forecasting power at 1–2 quarters horizons which is consistent with previous findings. In addition, the sub-sample analysis suggests that the magnitude of predictability for the second premium is much stronger during a volatile period than normal times.

11.2 Future Research

For future research, studies in this book can be developed in the following directions.

First, this book shows the equilibrium prices for the market risks including jump risk, variance risk, and covariance risk. These premiums are driven by both the risk aversion and fanning preference. Recently, the two-parameters risk preference model becomes popular, for example, the model uncertainty model or ambiguity model. In the future research, one more parameter can be introduced to the risk preference, e.g. the disappoint aversion. Therefore, three parameters including risk aversion, fanning effect, and disappoint aversion drive the representative agent's risk preference.

Second, the recently developed variance risk premium show strong predictive power for the future stock returns. But, most papers focus on it's in-sample performance, few has done the out-of-sample predictability. Welch and Goyal (2008), Campbell and Thompson (2008), Rapach et al. (2010), among others concede in-sample analysis provides efficient parameter estimates and thus precise return forecasts by using all available data. However, they argue that out-of-sample tests are more important for assessing genuine return predictability in real time, by implicitly examining the stability of the data-generating process and guarding against in-sample over-fitting.

Third, up to now, the studies of variance risk premium focus on the aggregate stock market. Is there still a strong predictability for the individual equity? In our general equilibrium framework, we find that the variance risk premium for individual equity can be decomposed into the component related to the market variance risk premium and that only determined by the information implicit in the equity itself. We may refer the latter to an idiosyncratic variance risk premium. This separation can lead to many studies for the prediction of idiosyncratic variance risk premium and the role of fanning preference in the idiosyncratic variance risk premium.

Fourth, this book also derives the equilibrium price for the covariance risk. Since Driessen et al. (2009) propose the correlation risk premium, CBOE develop the correlation index for market investors. However, this correlation risk index is available for the aggregate stock market. The covariance risk premium derived in this book can be applied to individual stocks.

Appendix

A. Non-expected Recursive Utility

The utility aggregator function of Duffie and Epstein (1992a, b) is given by

$$f(c, \mathrm{v}) = \beta\left(\frac{c^{\zeta}}{\zeta} - \frac{\mathrm{v}^{\zeta}}{\zeta}\right) = \frac{\beta}{\zeta}\left(c^{\zeta} - \mathrm{v}^{\zeta}\right). \tag{A.1}$$

A monotonic transformation, $\mathrm{v} = \psi(\upsilon) \triangleq (\eta\upsilon)^{\frac{1}{\eta}}$, is applied and therefore

$$f(c, \upsilon) = \frac{\frac{\beta}{\zeta}[c^{\zeta} - (\eta\upsilon)^{\frac{\zeta}{\eta}}]}{(\eta\upsilon)^{\frac{\zeta-1}{\eta}}(\eta\upsilon)^{\frac{1}{\eta}-1}} = \frac{\beta[c^{\zeta} - (\eta\upsilon)^{\frac{\zeta}{\eta}}]}{\zeta(\eta\upsilon)^{\frac{\zeta}{\eta}-1}}, \tag{A.2}$$

which is the form presented in formula (2.6) and also same as the Eq. D.10 in Liu et al. (2005)'s paper.

On the other hand, the weighted utility's certainty equivalent satisfies the following condition (see Ma 2000; Epstein 1992 for more explanations),

$$H(x, y) = \frac{x^{\varphi}(x^{\alpha} - y^{\alpha})}{\alpha}, \tag{A.3}$$

in which $\eta \equiv \alpha + 2\varphi$ and measures the representative agent's local risk aversion. The $H(\cdot, \cdot)$ in Eq. (A.3) is defined in the betweenness utility studied by Chew (1989); Dekel (1986). More specifically, a betweenness certainty equivalent $CE(U_{t+1}|\mathcal{F}_t)$ is defined as the unique solution to $E_t[H(U_{t+1}, CE(U_{t+1}|\mathcal{F}_t))] = 0$, where function $H : \mathcal{R} \times R \to R$ is to be such that (i) $H(x, x) \equiv 0$, (ii) $H(\cdot, y)$ is strictly increasing, and (iii) $H(x, \cdot)$ is strictly decreasing.

According to Ma (2000, 2006), the $M(\cdot, \cdot)$ in Eq. (2.5) can be calculated as follows,

J. Chen, *General Equilibrium Option Pricing Method: Theoretical and Empirical Study*, https://doi.org/10.1007/978-981-10-7428-8

$$
\begin{aligned}
M(x, y) &= \frac{H((\eta x)^{\frac{1}{\eta}}, (\eta y)^{\frac{1}{\eta}})}{H_1((\eta y)^{\frac{1}{\eta}}, (\eta y)^{\frac{1}{\eta}})(\eta y)^{\frac{1}{\eta}-1}} \\
&= \frac{(\eta y)^{\frac{1}{\eta}}}{\alpha}\left[\left(\frac{x}{y}\right)^{\frac{\alpha+\varphi}{\eta}} - \left(\frac{x}{y}\right)^{\frac{\varphi}{\eta}}\right](\eta y)^{1-\frac{1}{\eta}} \\
&= \frac{\eta y}{\alpha}\left[\left(\frac{x}{y}\right)^{\frac{\alpha+\varphi}{\eta}} - \left(\frac{x}{y}\right)^{\frac{\varphi}{\eta}}\right]. \qquad (A.4)
\end{aligned}
$$

Let $\phi(z) = \frac{\eta}{\eta-2\varphi}[z^{1-\frac{\varphi}{\eta}} - z^{\frac{\varphi}{\eta}}]$ and the Eq. (A.4) can be written as $M(x, y) = y\phi(\frac{x}{y})$. Thus, we obtain the utility generator (2.6).

B. Jump Risk Premium

This appendix demonstrates the decomposition of total market premium (π). First, with $\phi(u^\eta) = \frac{\eta}{\eta-2\varphi}(u^{\eta-\varphi} - u^\varphi)$ and normal jump size distribution, Eq. (2.14) becomes $\pi = \pi_D + \pi_J^*$ and particularly

$$
\begin{aligned}
\pi_J^* = \lambda[g(1) - g(0)] - \frac{\lambda}{\eta - 2\varphi}&[(\eta - \varphi)(g(\eta - \varphi) - g(\eta - \varphi - 1)) \\
&-\varphi(g(\varphi) - g(\varphi - 1))], \qquad (B.1)
\end{aligned}
$$

where $g(\cdot)$ is the moment generating function for the normal distribution of the logarithm of jump size, and thus $g(x) = \exp\{\mu_J x + \frac{1}{2}x^2\sigma_J^2\}$, in which μ_J and σ_J are the average size and the standard deviation of normal distribution, respectively.

Second, let $A = \lambda[g(1) - g(0)]$ and $B = -\frac{\lambda}{\eta-2\varphi}[(\eta - \varphi)(g(\eta - \varphi) - g(\eta - \varphi - 1)) - \varphi(g(\varphi) - g(\varphi - 1))]$. Take the Taylor's expression for Eq. (B.1) at $\varphi = 0$,

$$
\pi_J^*(\varphi) = \pi_J^*|_{\varphi=0} + \varphi B'|_{\varphi=0} + \frac{1}{2}\varphi^2 B''|_{\varphi=0} + R\,, \qquad (B.2)
$$

in which, B' denotes the first order derivation, B'' means the second order derivation, and R represents the higher order terms.

Third, when $\varphi = 0$, π_J^* simplifies to

$$
\begin{aligned}
\pi_J^* &= \lambda[g(1) - g(0)] - \lambda[g(\eta) - g(\eta - 1)] \\
&= \lambda\left[\exp\left\{\mu_J + \frac{1}{2}\sigma_J^2\right\} - 1\right] - \lambda\left[\exp\left\{\mu_J\eta + \frac{1}{2}\eta^2\sigma_J^2\right\} - \right. \\
&\quad \left. \exp\left\{\mu_J(\eta - 1) + \frac{1}{2}(\eta - 1)^2\sigma_J^2\right\}\right]. \qquad (B.3)
\end{aligned}
$$

Let $\gamma = 1 - \eta$, for the consistent notation with Naik and Lee (1990); Liu et al. (2005),

$$\begin{aligned}
\pi_J^* &= \lambda\left[\exp\left\{\mu_J + \frac{1}{2}\sigma_J^2\right\} - 1\right] - \lambda\left[\exp\left\{(1-\gamma)\mu_J + \frac{1}{2}(1-\gamma)^2\sigma_J^2\right\}\right. \\
&\quad \left. -\exp\left\{-\gamma\mu_J + \frac{1}{2}\gamma^2\sigma_J^2\right\}\right] \\
&= \lambda\left[\exp\left\{\mu_J + \frac{1}{2}\sigma_J^2\right\} - 1\right] - \lambda\left[\exp\left\{\mu_J - \gamma\mu_J + \frac{1}{2}\sigma_J^2 - \gamma\sigma_J^2\right.\right. \\
&\quad \left.\left. + \frac{1}{2}\gamma^2\sigma_J^2\right\} - \exp\left\{-\gamma\mu_J + \frac{1}{2}\gamma^2\sigma_J^2\right\}\right] \\
&= \lambda\left[\exp\left\{\mu_J + \frac{1}{2}\sigma_J^2\right\} - 1\right] - \lambda\left[\exp\left\{\mu_J + \frac{1}{2}\sigma_J^2\right\}\exp\left\{-\gamma\mu_J + \frac{1}{2}\gamma^2\sigma_J^2\right\}\right. \\
&\quad \left. \exp\left\{-\gamma\sigma_J^2\right\} - \exp\left\{-\gamma\mu_J + \frac{1}{2}\gamma^2\sigma_J^2\right\}\right]. \qquad \text{(B.4)}
\end{aligned}$$

As defined in Naik and Lee (1990), the average percentage jump ($\bar{K}$) is equal to $\exp\{\mu_J + \frac{1}{2}\sigma_J^2\} - 1$, the risk-neutral counterpart ($\bar{K}^Q$) satisfies $\bar{K}^Q = (1 + \bar{K})\exp\{-\gamma\sigma_J^2\} - 1$, and the risk-neutral jump intensity (λ^Q) is determined by $\lambda^Q = \lambda\exp\{-\gamma\mu_J + \frac{1}{2}\gamma^2\sigma_J^2\}$. Therefore, Eq. (B.4) becomes

$$\pi_J^* = \lambda\bar{K} - \lambda\left[\frac{\lambda^Q}{\lambda}\left(1 + \bar{K}\right)\frac{1 + \bar{K}^Q}{1 + \bar{K}} - \frac{\lambda^Q}{\lambda}\right] = \lambda\bar{K} - \lambda^Q\bar{K}^Q = \pi_J\,, \qquad \text{(B.5)}$$

where π_J is the jump risk premium defined in Naik and Lee (1990), and is also the special case of Liu et al. (2005) in the absence of rare event premium.

Finally, the remaining terms on the RHS of Eq. (B.2) are determined by the fanning effect. We name them as the fanning effect premium denoted by π_F, and $\pi_F = \pi_J^* - \pi_J$. As a result, the total market premium (π) is decomposed into three components: the diffusive risk premium (π_D), the Naik and Lee (1990)'s jump risk premium (π_J), and the fanning effect premium (π_F),

$$\pi = \pi_D + \pi_J + \pi_F\,.$$

C. Variance Risk Premium

Let $y = \ln u$, and hence, $u = e^y$. In Eq. (2.24), the first integral becomes

$$
\begin{aligned}
\int_R (\ln u)^2\, \Pi(\mathrm{d}u) &= \int_R y^2 \frac{1}{\sqrt{2\pi}\sigma} \mathrm{e}^{-\frac{1}{2}\left(\frac{y-\mu}{\sigma}\right)^2} \frac{1}{\mathrm{e}^y} \mathrm{d}\,\mathrm{e}^y \\
&= \int_R y^2 \frac{1}{\sqrt{2\pi}\sigma} \mathrm{e}^{-\frac{1}{2}\left(\frac{y-\mu}{\sigma}\right)^2} \mathrm{d}y = \int_R y^2 f(y)\, \mathrm{d}y \\
&= g''(\mu,\ \sigma,\ 0) \\
&= \sigma^2 + \mu^2\,, \qquad \text{(C.1)}
\end{aligned}
$$

in which, $y \sim N(\mu,\ \sigma)$, and $g(\cdot)$ is the moment generating function for this normal distribution. With $\phi\,(z) = \frac{\eta}{\alpha}[z^{1-\frac{\delta}{\eta}} - z^{\frac{\varphi}{\eta}}]$ and $\eta = \alpha + 2\varphi$, the second integral in Eq. (2.24) becomes

$$
\begin{aligned}
&\int_R (\ln u)^2 \phi'(u^\eta)\, u^{\eta-1}\, \Pi(\mathrm{d}u) \\
&= \int_R (\ln u)^2 \left(\frac{\alpha+\varphi}{\alpha} u^{\alpha+\varphi-1} - \frac{\varphi}{\alpha} u^{\varphi-1}\right) \Pi(\mathrm{d}u) \\
&= \frac{\alpha+\varphi}{\alpha} \int_R (\ln u)^2 u^{\alpha+\varphi-1}\, \Pi(\mathrm{d}u) - \frac{\varphi}{\alpha} \int_R (\ln u)^2 u^{\varphi-1}\, \Pi(\mathrm{d}u)\,. \qquad \text{(C.2)}
\end{aligned}
$$

In Eq. (C.2), the first integral is determined by

$$
\begin{aligned}
&\int_R (\ln u)^2 u^{\alpha+\varphi-1}\, \Pi(\mathrm{d}u) \\
&= \int_R y^2 \mathrm{e}^{(\alpha+\varphi-1)y} \frac{1}{\sqrt{2\pi}\sigma} \mathrm{e}^{-\frac{1}{2}\left(\frac{y-\mu}{\sigma}\right)^2} \mathrm{d}y \\
&= \int_R y^2 \frac{1}{\sqrt{2\pi}\sigma} \mathrm{e}^{-\frac{1}{2\sigma^2}(y-\mu)^2 + (\alpha+\varphi-1)y} \mathrm{d}y \\
&= \int_R y^2 \frac{1}{\sqrt{2\pi}\sigma} \mathrm{e}^{-\frac{1}{2\sigma^2}\{y^2 - 2[\mu+(\alpha+\varphi-1)\sigma^2]y + \mu^2\}} \mathrm{d}y \\
&= \int_R y^2 \frac{1}{\sqrt{2\pi}\sigma} \mathrm{e}^{-\frac{1}{2\sigma^2}\{y-[\mu+(\alpha+\varphi-1)\sigma^2]\}^2 + \frac{1}{2\sigma^2}\{[\mu+(\alpha+\varphi-1)\sigma^2]^2 - \mu^2\}} \mathrm{d}y \\
&= \int_R y^2 \frac{1}{\sqrt{2\pi}\sigma} \mathrm{e}^{-\frac{1}{2\sigma^2}\{y-[\mu+(\alpha+\varphi-1)\sigma^2]\}^2 + \left[\mu(\alpha+\varphi-1) + \frac{1}{2}(\alpha+\varphi-1)^2\sigma^2\right]} \mathrm{d}y \\
&= \mathrm{e}^{\left[\mu(\alpha+\varphi-1) + \frac{1}{2}(\alpha+\varphi-1)^2\sigma^2\right]} \int_R y^2 \frac{1}{\sqrt{2\pi}\sigma} \mathrm{e}^{-\frac{1}{2\sigma^2}\{y-[\mu+(\alpha+\varphi-1)\sigma^2]\}^2} \mathrm{d}y \\
&= g(\mu,\ \sigma,\ \alpha+\varphi-1) \int_R y^2 f(y)\, \mathrm{d}y \\
&= g(\mu,\ \sigma,\ \alpha+\varphi-1)\, g''(\mu_1,\ \sigma,\ 0) \\
&= g(\mu,\ \sigma,\ \alpha+\varphi-1) \left(\mu_1^2 + \sigma^2\right)\,, \qquad \text{(C.3)}
\end{aligned}
$$

in which, $y \sim N(\mu_1,\ \sigma)$, and $\mu_1 = \mu + (\alpha+\varphi-1)\sigma^2$.

Similarly, the second integral in Eq. (C.2) is given by

$$\begin{aligned}\int_R (\ln u)^2\, u^{\varphi-1}\, \Pi(du) &= g(\mu,\ \sigma,\ \varphi-1) \int_R y^2 f(y)\, dy \\ &= g(\mu,\ \sigma,\ \varphi-1)\, g^{''}(\mu_2,\ \sigma,\ 0) \\ &= g(\mu,\ \sigma,\ \varphi-1)\left(\mu_2^2+\sigma^2\right), \qquad \text{(C.4)}\end{aligned}$$

in which, $y \sim N(\mu_2,\ \sigma)$, and $\mu_2 = \mu + (\varphi - 1)\sigma^2$. As a result, Eq. (C.2) can be obtained,

$$\begin{aligned}&\int_R (\ln u)^2\, \phi^{'}(u^\eta)\, u^{\eta-1}\, \Pi(du) \\ &= \frac{\alpha+\varphi}{\alpha}\int_R (\ln u)^2\, u^{\alpha+\varphi-1}\, \Pi(du) - \frac{\varphi}{\alpha}\int_R (\ln u)^2\, u^{\varphi-1}\, \Pi(du) \\ &= \frac{\alpha+\varphi}{\alpha} g(\mu,\ \sigma,\ \alpha+\varphi-1)\left(\mu_1^2+\sigma^2\right) - \frac{\varphi}{\alpha} g(\mu,\ \sigma,\ \varphi-1)\left(\mu_2^2+\sigma^2\right), \qquad \text{(C.5)}\end{aligned}$$

and variance risk premium is equal to

$$\begin{aligned}VRP_t &= \lambda \int_R (\ln u)^2\, \Pi(du) - \lambda \int_R (\ln u)^2\, \phi^{'}(u^\eta)\, u^{\eta-1}\, \Pi(du) \\ &= \lambda(\sigma^2+\mu^2) - \frac{\lambda}{a}\{(\alpha+\varphi)\left[g(\alpha+\varphi-1)(\mu_1^2+\sigma^2)\right] \\ &\quad -\varphi\left[g(\varphi-1)(\mu_2^2+\sigma^2)\right]\}, \qquad \text{(C.6)}\end{aligned}$$

in which, $\mu_1 = \mu + (\alpha + \varphi - 1)\sigma^2$ and $\mu_2 = \mu + (\varphi - 1)\sigma^2$.

D. Covariance Risk Premium

Let $y = \ln u_m$ and $x = \ln u_i$, and then $y \sim N(\mu_m,\ \sigma_m)$ and $x \sim N(\mu_i,\ \sigma_i)$. The first integral in Eq. (2.27), $\int\int_{R+} \ln u_m\ \ln u_i\ \Pi_{i,m}(du_i,\ du_m)$, is $\mathrm{E}[y\,x]$. According to the properties of covariance, we have

$$\begin{aligned}&\int\int_{R+} \ln u_m\ \ln u_i\ \Pi_{i,m}(du_i,\ du_m) \\ &\quad = \mathrm{E}[y\,x] = \mathrm{E}[y]\,\mathrm{E}[x] + \mathrm{Cov}(y,\ x) = \mu_m\,\mu_i + \sigma_m\,\sigma_i\,\rho_u, \qquad \text{(D.1)}\end{aligned}$$

where ρ_u is the correlation coefficient of jump sizes for the individual stock and the market portfolio.

With $\phi(z) = \frac{\eta}{\alpha}[z^{1-\frac{\varphi}{\eta}} - z^{\frac{\varphi}{\eta}}]$ and $\eta = \alpha + 2\varphi$, the second integral in Eq. (2.27) can be rewritten as

$$\int\int_{R+} \ln u_m \; \ln u_i \; \phi'(u_m^{\eta}) \, u_m^{\eta-1} \, \Pi_{i,m}(\mathrm{d}u_i, \; \mathrm{d}u_m)$$

$$= \int\int_{R+} \ln u_m \; \ln u_i \left(\frac{\alpha+\varphi}{\alpha} u_m^{\alpha+\varphi-1} - \frac{\varphi}{\alpha} u_m^{\varphi-1} \right) \Pi_{i,m}(\mathrm{d}u_i, \; \mathrm{d}u_m)$$

$$= \frac{\alpha+\varphi}{\alpha} \int\int_{R+} \ln u_m \; \ln u_i \; u_m^{\alpha+\varphi-1} \, \Pi_{i,m}(\mathrm{d}u_i, \; \mathrm{d}u_m) -$$

$$\frac{\varphi}{\alpha} \int\int_{R+} \ln u_m \; \ln u_i \; u_m^{\varphi-1} \, \Pi_{i,m}(\mathrm{d}u_i, \; \mathrm{d}u_m)$$

$$= \frac{\alpha+\varphi}{\alpha} \int\int_{R+} x \, y \, \mathrm{e}^{(\alpha+\varphi-1)y} \frac{1}{2\pi\sigma_m\sigma_i\sqrt{1-\rho_u^2}} \mathrm{e}^{-\frac{Z}{2(1-\rho_u^2)}} (\mathrm{d}x \; \mathrm{d}y) -$$

$$\frac{\varphi}{\alpha} \int\int_{R+} x \, y \, \mathrm{e}^{(\varphi-1)y} \frac{1}{2\pi\sigma_m\sigma_i\sqrt{1-\rho_u^2}} \mathrm{e}^{-\frac{Z}{2(1-\rho_u^2)}} (\mathrm{d}x \; \mathrm{d}y) \, , \tag{D.2}$$

where

$$Z = \frac{(x-\mu_i)^2}{\sigma_i^2} + \frac{(y-\mu_m)^2}{\sigma_m^2} - \frac{2\rho_u(x-\mu_i)(y-\mu_m)}{\sigma_m\sigma_i} \, .$$

In Eq. (D.2), the first integral is

$$\int\int_{R+} x \, y \, e^{(\alpha+\varphi-1)y} \frac{1}{2\pi\sigma_m\sigma_i\sqrt{1-\rho_u^2}} \mathrm{e}^{-\frac{Z}{2(1-\rho_u^2)}} (\mathrm{d}x \; \mathrm{d}y)$$

$$= \int\int_{R+} x \, y \frac{1}{2\pi\sigma_m\sigma_i\sqrt{1-\rho_u^2}} \mathrm{e}^{-\frac{Z}{2(1-\rho_u^2)}+(\alpha+\varphi-1)y} (\mathrm{d}x \; \mathrm{d}y)$$

$$= \int\int_{R+} x \, y \frac{1}{2\pi\sigma_m\sigma_i\sqrt{1-\rho_u^2}} \mathrm{e}^{-\frac{1}{2(1-\rho_u^2)}\left[Z-2(1-\rho_u^2)(\alpha+\varphi-1)y\right]} (\mathrm{d}x \; \mathrm{d}y) \, . \tag{D.3}$$

The exponential component can be calculated as

$$\frac{(x-\mu_i)^2}{\sigma_i^2} + \frac{(y-\mu_m)^2}{\sigma_m^2} - \frac{2\rho_u(x-\mu_i)(y-\mu_m)}{\sigma_m\sigma_i} - 2(1-\rho_u^2)(\alpha+\varphi-1)y$$

$$= \frac{(y-\mu_m)^2}{\sigma_m^2} - 2(\alpha+\varphi-1)y + 2\rho_u^2(\alpha+\varphi-1)y + \frac{(x-\mu_i)^2}{\sigma_i^2} -$$

$$\frac{2\rho_u(x-\mu_i)(y-\mu_m)}{\sigma_m\sigma_i}$$

$$= \frac{1}{\sigma_m^2}(y^2 - 2\mu_m y + \mu_m^2) - 2(\alpha+\varphi-1)y + 2\rho_u^2(\alpha+\varphi-1)y +$$

$$\frac{(x-\mu_i)^2}{\sigma_i^2} - \frac{2\rho_u(x-\mu_i)(y-\mu_m)}{\sigma_m\sigma_i}$$

$$= \frac{1}{\sigma_m^2}\left\{y^2 - 2[\mu_m + (\alpha+\varphi-1)\sigma_m^2]\,y + \mu_m^2\right\} + 2\rho_u^2(\alpha+\varphi-1)y +$$

$$\frac{(x-\mu_i)^2}{\sigma_i^2} - \frac{2\rho_u(x-\mu_i)(y-\mu_m)}{\sigma_m\sigma_i}$$

$$
\begin{aligned}
&= \frac{1}{\sigma_m^2}\left\{y^2 - [\mu_m + (\alpha+\varphi-1)\sigma_m^2]\right\}^2 - \\
&\quad 2\left[\mu_m(\alpha+\varphi-1) + \frac{1}{2}(\alpha+\varphi-1)^2\sigma_m^2\right] + 2\rho_u^2(\alpha+\varphi-1)y + \\
&\quad \frac{(x-\mu_i)^2}{\sigma_i^2} - \frac{2\rho_u(x-\mu_i)(y-\mu_m)}{\sigma_m\sigma_i}\,.
\end{aligned}
\tag{D.4}
$$

Let $\mu_m^* = \mu_m + (\alpha+\varphi-1)\sigma_m^2$, Eq. (D.4) becomes

$$
\begin{aligned}
&\frac{(y-\mu_m^*)^2}{\sigma_m^2} + \frac{(x-\mu_i)^2}{\sigma_i^2} - \frac{2\rho_u}{\sigma_m\sigma_i}(x-\mu_i)(y-\mu_m^*) - \\
&\quad \frac{2\rho_u}{\sigma_m\sigma_i}(x-\mu_i)(\alpha+\varphi-1)\sigma_m^2 + 2\rho_u^2(\alpha+\varphi-1)y - \\
&\quad 2\left[\mu_m(\alpha+\varphi-1) + \frac{1}{2}(\alpha+\varphi-1)^2\sigma_m^2\right] \\
&= \frac{(y-\mu_m^*)^2}{\sigma_m^2} - \frac{2\rho_u}{\sigma_m\sigma_i}(x-\mu_i)(y-\mu_m^*) - \\
&\quad 2\left[\mu_m(\alpha+\varphi-1) + \frac{1}{2}(\alpha+\varphi-1)^2\sigma_m^2\right] + \\
&\quad 2\rho_u^2(\alpha+\varphi-1)y + \frac{(x-\mu_i)^2}{\sigma_i^2} - \frac{2\rho_u\sigma_m}{\sigma_i}(x-\mu_i)(\alpha+\varphi-1) \\
&= \frac{(y-\mu_m^*)^2}{\sigma_m^2} - \frac{2\rho_u}{\sigma_m\sigma_i}(x-\mu_i)(y-\mu_m^*) - \\
&\quad 2\left[\mu_m(\alpha+\varphi-1) + \frac{1}{2}(\alpha+\varphi-1)^2\sigma_m^2\right] + 2\rho_u^2(\alpha+\varphi-1)y + \\
&\quad \frac{1}{\sigma_i^2}\left[x^2 - 2\mu_i x + \mu_i^2 - 2\rho_u\sigma_m\sigma_i(\alpha+\varphi-1)(x-\mu_i)\right] \\
&= \frac{(y-\mu_m^*)^2}{\sigma_m^2} - \frac{2\rho_u}{\sigma_m\sigma_i}(x-\mu_i)(y-\mu_m^*) - \\
&\quad 2\left[\mu_m(\alpha+\varphi-1) + \frac{1}{2}(\alpha+\varphi-1)^2\sigma_m^2\right] + 2\rho_u^2(\alpha+\varphi-1)y + \\
&\quad \frac{1}{\sigma_i^2}\{x - [\mu_i + \rho_u(\alpha+\varphi-1)\sigma_m\sigma_i]\}^2 - \rho_u^2(\alpha+\varphi-1)^2\sigma_m^2\,.
\end{aligned}
\tag{D.5}
$$

Let $\mu_i^* = \mu_i + \rho_u(\alpha+\varphi-1)\sigma_m\sigma_i$, Eq. (D.5) becomes

$$
\begin{aligned}
&\frac{(y-\mu_m^*)^2}{\sigma_m^2} + \frac{(x-\mu_i^*)^2}{\sigma_i^2} - \frac{2\rho_u}{\sigma_m \sigma_i}(x-\mu_i)(y-\mu_m^*) + \\
&\quad 2\rho_u^2(\alpha+\varphi-1)y - \rho_u^2(\alpha+\varphi-1)^2\sigma_m^2 - \\
&\quad 2\left[\mu_m(\alpha+\varphi-1) + \frac{1}{2}(\alpha+\varphi-1)^2\,\sigma_m^2\right] \\
&= \frac{(y-\mu_m^*)^2}{\sigma_m^2} + \frac{(x-\mu_i^*)^2}{\sigma_i^2} - \frac{2\rho_u}{\sigma_m \sigma_i}(x-\mu_i^*)(y-\mu_m^*) + \\
&\quad 2\rho_u^2(\alpha+\varphi-1)y - 2\left[\mu_m(\alpha+\varphi-1) + \frac{1}{2}(\alpha+\varphi-1)^2\,\sigma_M^2\right] - \\
&\quad \rho_u^2(\alpha+\varphi-1)^2\sigma_m^2 - 2\rho_u^2(\alpha+\varphi-1)(y-\mu_m^*) \\
&= \frac{(y-\mu_m^*)^2}{\sigma_m^2} + \frac{(x-\mu_i^*)^2}{\sigma_i^2} - \frac{2\rho_u(x-\mu_i^*)(y-\mu_m^*)}{\sigma_m \sigma_i} - \\
&\quad 2\left[\mu_m(\alpha+\varphi-1) + \frac{1}{2}(\alpha+\varphi-1)^2\,\sigma_m^2\right] + \\
&\quad 2\rho^2\left[\mu_m(\alpha+\varphi-1) + \frac{1}{2}(\alpha+\varphi-1)^2\,\sigma_m^2\right] \\
&= \frac{(y-\mu_m^*)^2}{\sigma_m^2} + \frac{(x-\mu_i^*)^2}{\sigma_i^2} - \frac{2\rho_u(x-\mu_i^*)(y-\mu_m^*)}{\sigma_m \sigma_i} - \\
&\quad 2(1-\rho^2)\left[\mu_m(\alpha+\varphi-1) + \frac{1}{2}(\alpha+\varphi-1)^2\,\sigma_m^2\right].
\end{aligned}
\tag{D.6}
$$

Substitute Eq. (D.6) into the integral (D.3), and then we have

$$
\begin{aligned}
&\int\int_{R+} x\,y\,\frac{1}{2\pi\,\sigma_m\sigma_i\sqrt{1-\rho_u^2}}\,\mathrm{e}^{-\frac{1}{2(1-\rho_u^2)}[Z-2(1-\rho_u^2)(\alpha+\varphi-1)y]}(\mathrm{d}x\,\mathrm{d}y) \\
&\quad = \int\int_{R+} x\,y\,\frac{1}{2\pi\,\sigma_m\sigma_i\sqrt{1-\rho_u^2}} \\
&\qquad \left[\mathrm{e}^{-\frac{1}{2(1-\rho_u^2)}\{Z^*-2(1-\rho_u^2)[\mu_m(\alpha+\varphi-1)+\frac{1}{2}(\alpha+\varphi-1)^2\,\sigma_m^2]\}}\right](\mathrm{d}x\,\mathrm{d}y) \\
&\quad = \int\int_{R+} x\,y\,\frac{1}{2\pi\,\sigma_m\sigma_i\sqrt{1-\rho_u^2}} \\
&\qquad \left[\mathrm{e}^{-\frac{Z^*}{2(1-\rho_u^2)}}\,\mathrm{e}^{\mu_m(\alpha+\varphi-1)+\frac{1}{2}(\alpha+\varphi-1)^2\,\sigma_m^2}\right](\mathrm{d}x\,\mathrm{d}y) \\
&\quad = \left[\mathrm{e}^{\mu_m(\alpha+\varphi-1)+\frac{1}{2}(\alpha+\varphi-1)^2\,\sigma_m^2}\right] \\
&\qquad \int\int_{R+} x\,y\,\frac{1}{2\pi\,\sigma_m\sigma_i\sqrt{1-\rho_u^2}}\,\mathrm{e}^{-\frac{Z^*}{2(1-\rho_u^2)}}(\mathrm{d}x\,\mathrm{d}y)
\end{aligned}
\tag{D.7}
$$

where

$$Z^* = \frac{(y-\mu_m^*)^2}{\sigma_m^2} + \frac{(x-\mu_i^*)^2}{\sigma_i^2} - \frac{2\rho_u(x-\mu_i^*)(y-\mu_m^*)}{\sigma_m\sigma_i} .$$

According to the definition of joint normal distribution, $y \sim N(\mu_m^*, \sigma_m)$ and $x \sim N(\mu_i^*, \sigma_i)$ in which $\mu_m^* = \mu_m + (\alpha+\varphi-1)\sigma_m^2$ and $\mu_i^* = \mu_i + \rho_u(\alpha+\varphi-1)\sigma_m\sigma_i$. Then, Eq. (D.7) can be regarded as

$$\begin{aligned} & g[\mu_m, \sigma_m, (\alpha+\varphi-1)]\,\mathrm{E}^*(y\,x) \\ & \quad = g[\mu_m, \sigma_m, (\alpha+\varphi-1)]\left[\mathrm{E}^*(y)\,\mathrm{E}^*(x) + \mathrm{Cov}(y, x)\right] \\ & \quad = g[\mu_m, \sigma_m, (\alpha+\varphi-1)]\left(\mu_m^*\,\mu_i^* + \sigma_m\,\sigma_i\,\rho_u\right) , \end{aligned} \tag{D.8}$$

where $g(\cdot)$ is the moment generating function for the normal distribution, $N(\mu_m, \sigma_m)$.

Similarly, the second integral in Eq. (D.2) can be solved,

$$\begin{aligned} & \int\!\!\int_{R+} x\,y\,\mathrm{e}^{(\varphi-1)y}\,\frac{1}{2\pi\,\sigma_m\sigma_i\sqrt{1-\rho_u^2}}\,\mathrm{e}^{-\frac{Z}{2(1-\rho_u^2)}}\,(\mathrm{d}x\,\mathrm{d}y) \\ & \quad = g[\mu_m, \sigma_m, (\varphi-1)]\left[\mathrm{E}'(y)\,\mathrm{E}'(x) + \mathrm{Cov}(y, x)\right] \\ & \quad = g[\mu_m, \sigma_m, (\varphi-1)]\left(\mu_m'\,\mu_i' + \sigma_m\,\sigma_i\,\rho_u\right) , \end{aligned} \tag{D.9}$$

where $y \sim N(\mu_m', \sigma_m)$ and $x \sim N(\mu_i', \sigma_i)$, in which $\mu_m' = \mu_m + (\varphi-1)\sigma_m^2$ and $\mu_i' = \mu_i + \rho_u(\varphi-1)\sigma_m\sigma_i$.

Now substitute Eqs. (D.8) and (D.9) into Eq. (D.2), we have the correlation risk premium as follow,

$$\begin{aligned} CRP = {} & \lambda\,(\mu_m\,\mu_i + \sigma_m\,\sigma_i\,\rho_u) - \\ & \frac{\lambda}{\alpha}\Big\{(\alpha+\varphi)\,g[\mu_m, \sigma_m, (\alpha+\varphi-1)]\left(\mu_m^*\,\mu_i^* + \sigma_m\,\sigma_i\,\rho_u\right) - \\ & \varphi\,g[\mu_m, \sigma_m, (\varphi-1)]\left(\mu_m'\,\mu_i' + \sigma_m\,\sigma_i\,\rho_u\right)\Big\} , \end{aligned} \tag{D.10}$$

where

$$\begin{aligned} \mu_m^* &= \mu_m + (\alpha+\varphi-1)\sigma_m^2 , \\ \mu_i^* &= \mu_i + \rho_u(\alpha+\varphi-1)\sigma_m\,\sigma_i , \\ \mu_m' &= \mu_m + (\varphi-1)\sigma_m^2 , \\ \mu_i' &= \mu_i + \rho_u(\varphi-1)\sigma_m\,\sigma_i . \end{aligned}$$

E. Observational Non-equivalence

Let $\hat{r}$ and $\hat{\Theta}(\cdot)$ be the corresponding equilibrium interest rate and the Θ-function for additive expected utility with parameters $(\hat{\beta}, \hat{\eta})$. According to Eq. (2.28), the condition under which the option pricing rule generated by (η, ϕ) is replicated by using the additive expected utility function with parameter $(\hat{\beta}, \hat{\eta})$ is

$$e^{-r}\Theta(s) = e^{-\hat{r}}\hat{\Theta}(s), \qquad \forall\, \mathrm{Re}(s) \in (x^*, -1), \tag{E.1}$$

since the Laplace transformation is invertible. Substituting Eq. (2.29) for $\hat{\Theta}$ and Θ into (E.1), and noting that $\hat{r} = \hat{\beta} - Q(\hat{\eta} - 1) - \int_0^\infty u^{\hat{\eta}-1}\Pi(du)$, we have

$$\begin{aligned} &\int_0^\infty u^{-s}u^{\eta-1}\phi'(u^\eta)\Pi(du) - \eta a^2 s - r - \hat{\lambda} \\ &\quad = \int_0^\infty u^{-s}u^{\hat{\eta}-1}\Pi(du) - \hat{\eta}a^2 s + Q(\hat{\eta} - 1) - \hat{\beta}, \end{aligned} \tag{E.2}$$

$\forall\, \mathrm{Re}(s) \in (x^*, -1)$, where $\hat{\lambda} = \int_0^\infty u^{\eta-1}\phi'(u^\eta)\Pi(du)$. Applying the Laplace inverse transformation to Eq. (E.2), we obtain

$$\begin{aligned} &\Pi(y)[\phi' e^{\eta y} e^{(\eta-1)y} - e^{(\hat{\eta}-1)y}] \\ &\quad = [Q(\hat{\eta} - 1) + r + \hat{\lambda} - \hat{\beta}]\delta_y[0] + (\eta - \hat{\eta})a^2\delta_y'[0], \end{aligned} \tag{E.3}$$

$\forall\, y \in \mathcal{R}$, where we notice that for the Dirac function $\delta_y[0]$ and its derivative we have $\mathcal{L}\{\delta_y[0]\}(s) = 1$ and $\mathcal{L}\{\delta_y'[0]\}(s) = s$.

First, we need to show that the above equality holds true when both conditions (i) and (ii) are violated. Notice that when conditions (i) and (ii) are violated, we have $a^2 = 0$ and $\frac{\ln\phi'(e^{\eta y})}{y}$ to be a constant on $y \in supp\{\Pi(\cdot)\}$. Therefore, the desired equality is achieved by setting $\hat{\eta} = \eta + \frac{\ln\phi'(e^{\eta y})}{y}$ and $\hat{\beta} = Q(\hat{\eta} - 1) + r + \hat{\lambda}$.

Second, we need to show that Eq. (E.3) must be violated when either (i) or (ii) holds true.

Case (i): When $a^2 > 0$, Eq. (E.3) reduces to the following three equalities: (a) $\hat{\eta} = \eta$, (b) $\hat{\beta} = Q(\hat{\eta} - 1) + r + \hat{\lambda}$, and (c) $\phi'(e^{\eta y}) = 1$ on $y \in supp\{\Pi(\cdot)\}$. The third equality violates the assumption that $\phi'(x) \neq 1$ for $x \neq 1$ since $supp\{\Pi(\cdot)\}$ contains non-zero supports.

Case (ii): When $a^2 = 0$ (the case of pure Poisson uncertainty), the second term on the right hand side of Eq. (E.3) disappears. Eq. (E.3) implies (a) $\hat{\beta} = Q(\hat{\eta} - 1) + r + \hat{\lambda}$, and (b) $\frac{\ln\phi'(e^{\eta y})}{y} = \hat{\eta} - \eta$ for all $y \in supp\{\Pi(\cdot)\}$. This last equality violates condition (ii) of the theorem.

F. Risk-Neutral MGF

Let $y_T = \ln \widehat{S}_T$ where $T > 0$, and the moment generating function (MGF) of a random variable is defined as the Laplace transform of the underlying probability density function. Then, the moment generating function for $y_T = \ln \widehat{S}_T$ exists, and is given by

$$\mathrm{E}\left[\widehat{S}_T^{-s} \mid \widehat{S}_0 = S\right] = S^{-s}\, \Theta^T(s)\,, \qquad Re(s) \in (s^*, -1)\,. \tag{F.1}$$

Consider the complex-valued stochastic process $\left\{z_t \equiv \widehat{S}_t^{-s}\right\}_{t \geq 0}$. Applying Ito's Lemma to Z_t, we have

$$\begin{aligned}\frac{\mathrm{d}z_t}{z_{t-}} &= [-(b + (\eta - 1.5)a^2)s + 0.5a^2\, s^2]\, \mathrm{d}t - a\, s\, \mathrm{d}B_t \\ &\quad + \int_0^\infty (u^{-s} - 1)\, \widehat{N}(\mathrm{d}t,\ \mathrm{d}u)\,,\end{aligned} \tag{F.2}$$

with $z_0 = S^{-s}$. For any $t \geq 0$, let $m(t) = E[z_t \,|\, z_0 = S^{-s}]$. Multiply both sides of Eq. (F.2) by z_t, integrate both sides from 0 to t, and take the expectation, to deduce

$$\begin{aligned} & m(t) - S^{-s} \\ &= \int_0^t m(\tau) \left\{-[b + (\eta - 1.5)a^2]s + 0.5a^2\, s^2 + \int_0^\infty (u^{-s} - 1)\, \widehat{N}(\mathrm{d}u)\right\} \mathrm{d}\tau \\ &= \ln \Theta(s) \int_0^t m(\tau)\, \mathrm{d}\tau\,, \end{aligned} \tag{F.3}$$

where $\Theta(\cdot)$ is defined by Eq. (2.29). The solution to this integral equation is given by $m(t) = S^{-s}\, \Theta^t(s)$, $\forall t \geq 0$.

G. Jump Size Distribution

We rewrite the Θ function defined in Eq. (2.29) as

$$\begin{aligned}\ln \Theta(s) &= -[b + (\eta - 1.5)a^2]s + 0.5a^2 s^2 + \int_0^\infty (u^{-s} - 1)\widehat{N}(\mathrm{d}t,\ \mathrm{d}u) \\ &= -[b + (\eta - 1.5)a^2]s + 0.5a^2 s^2 - \\ &\quad \int_0^\infty \widehat{N}(\mathrm{d}t,\ \mathrm{d}u) + \int_0^\infty u^{-s}\, \widehat{N}(\mathrm{d}t,\ \mathrm{d}u) \\ &= A(s) + \widehat{\lambda}\, m_u(s)\,. \end{aligned} \tag{G.1}$$

where $A(s) = -[b + (\eta - 1.5)a^2]s + 0.5a^2s^2 - \int_0^{\infty} \widehat{N}(\mathrm{d}t,\ \mathrm{d}u)$ and $m_u(s) = \int_0^{\infty} u^{-s}\, \widehat{\Pi}(\mathrm{d}u)$. Note, the risk-neutral moments of jump size distribution can be determined by $\mathrm{E}\,(u^n) = m_u(-n)$, in which n represents the nth order moment of risk-neutral jump size distribution.

According to Eq. (2.31), the risk-neutral skewness ($skew^*$) of log return distribution is

$$
\begin{aligned}
skew^* &= \{[A(-3) + \widehat{\lambda}\, m_u(-3)] - 3[A(-1) + \widehat{\lambda}\, m_u(-1)]\,[A(-2) + \widehat{\lambda}\, m_u(-2)] \\
&\quad +2[A(-1) + \widehat{\lambda}\, m_u(-1)]^3\}/\{[A(-2) + \widehat{\lambda}\, m_u(-2)] \\
&\quad -[A(-1) + \widehat{\lambda}\, m_u(-1)]^2\}^{3/2} \\
&= \frac{\widehat{\lambda}\,\{m_u(-3) - 3m_u(-1)\, m_u(-2) + 2[m_u(-1)]^3\} + B}{\widehat{\lambda}\,\{m_u(-2) - [m_v(-1)]^2\}^{3/2} + C} \\
&= \Psi \frac{m_u(-3) - 3m_u(-1)\, m_u(-2) + 2[m_u(-1)]^3}{\{m_u(-2) - [m_v(-1)]^2\}^{3/2}} + \Lambda \\
&= \Psi\; skew_u \; + \; \Lambda\,,
\end{aligned}
\tag{G.2}
$$

where $skew_u$ is the risk-neutral skewness of jump size distribution, Ψ is the coefficient, and Λ represents all remaining terms that affect the skewness of stock return distribution.

Similarly, we also can derive the risk-neutral kurtosis ($kurt^*$) of log return distribution according to Eq. (2.32). It follows

$$
kurt^* = \Upsilon\; kurt_u \; + \; \Gamma\,, \tag{G.3}
$$

where $kurt_u$ is the risk-neutral kurtosis of jump size distribution, Υ is the coefficient, and Γ represents all remaining terms that affect the kurtosis of stock return distribution.

References

Aït-Sahalia, Y., Lo, A., 2000. Nonparametric risk management and implied riskaversion. Journal of Econometrics 94, 9–51.

Allais, M., 1953. Le comportement de l'homme rationnel devant le risque: critique des postulats et axiomes de l'ecole americaine. Econometrica 21, 503–546.

Andersen, T., Bollerslev, T., Diebold, F., 2003a. Some like it smooth, and some like it rough: Untangling continuous and jump components in measuring, modeling, and forecasting asset return volatility, working Paper, Department of Economics, University of Pennsylvania.

Andersen, T., Bollerslev, T., Diebold, F., Ebens, H., 2001a. The distribution of realized stock return volatility. Journal of Financial Economics 61, 43–76.

Andersen, T., Bollerslev, T., Diebold, F., Labys, P., 2001b. The distribution of realized exchange rate volatility. Journal of the American Statistical Association 96, 42–55.

Andersen, T., Bollerslev, T., Diebold, F., Labys, P., 2001c. Exchange rate returns standardized by realized volatility are (nearly) gaussian. Multinational Finance Journal 4, 159–179.

Andersen, T., Bollerslev, T., Diebold, F., Labys, P., 2003b. Modeling and forecasting realized volatility. Econometrica 72, 579–625.

Andersen, T. G., Bondarenko, O., Gonzalez-Perez, M. T., 2011. Coherent model-free implied volatility: A corridor fix for high-frequency VIX. Working Paper, Northwestern University.

Ang, A., Bekaert, G., 2007. Stock return predictability: Is it there? Review of Financial Studies 20, 651–707.

Areal, N., Taylor, S., 2002. The realized volatility of FTSE-100 futures prices. Journal of Futures Markets 22, 627–648.

Bailey, W., Zheng, L., Zhou, Y., 2011. What makes the VIX tick? Working Paper, Cornell University.

Bakshi, G., Cao, C., Chen, Z., 1997. Empirical performance of alternative option pricing models. Journal of Finance 52, 2003–2049.

Bakshi, G., Cao, C., Chen, Z., 2000. Pricing and hedging long-term options. Journal of Econometrics 94, 277–318.

Bakshi, G., Kapadia, N., Madan, D., 2003. Stock return characteristics, skew law, and the differential pricing of individual equity options. Review of Financial Studies 16, 101–143.

Bakshi, G., Madan, D., 2006. A theory of volatility spreads. Management Science 52, 1945–1956.

Bakshi, G., Madan, D., Panayotov, G., 2010. Returns of claims on the upside and the viability of u-shaped pricing kernels. Journal of Financial Economics 97, 130–154.

Bali, T. G., Demirtas, K. O., Atilgan, Y., 2011. Implied volatility spreads and expected market returns. Working Paper, Georgetown University.

J. Chen, *General Equilibrium Option Pricing Method: Theoretical and Empirical Study*, https://doi.org/10.1007/978-981-10-7428-8

Bali, T. G., Zhou, H., 2011. Risk, uncertainty, and expected returns. Working Paper, Federal Reserve Board.

Ball, C. A., Torous, W. N., 1983. A simplified jump process for common stock returns. Journal of Financial and Quantitative Analysis 18, 53–65.

Bansal, R., Yaron, A., 2004. Risks for the long run: A potential resolution of asset pricing puzzles. Journal of Finance 59, 1481–1509.

Barberis, N., Huang, M., 2008a. The loss aversion/narrow framing approach to the equity premium puzzle, Handbook of the Equity Risk Premium, R. Mehra ed., North Holland, Amsterdam.

Barberis, N., Huang, M., 2008b. Stocks as lotteries: The implications of probability weighting for security prices,. American Economic Review 98, 2066–2100.

Barndorff-Nielsen, O., Shephard, N., 2002. Econometric analysis of realised volatility and its use in estimating stochastic volatility models. Journal of Royal Statistical Society Series B 64.

Barndorff-Nielsen, O., Shephard, N., 2004a. Econometric analysis of realised co-variation: High frequency based covariance, regression and correlation. Econometrica 72, 885–925.

Barndorff-Nielsen, O., Shephard, N., 2004b. Power and bipower variation with stochastic volatility and jumps. Journal of Financial Econometrics 2, 1C37.

Bates, D., 1991. The crash of 87: Was it expected? The evidence from options markets. Journal of Finance 46, 1009–1044.

Bates, D., 1996. Jumps and stochastic volatility: Exchange rate processes implicit in deutschemark option. Review of Financial Studies 9, 69–108.

Bates, D., 2000. Post-87 crash fears in the S&P 500 futures option market. Journal of Econometrics 94, 181–238.

Bates, D., 2008. The market for crash risk. Journal of Economic Dynamics and Control 32, 2291–2321.

Bekaert, G., Engstrom, E., 2010. Asset return dynamics under bad environment-good environment fundamentals. Working Paper, NBER.

Benzoni, L., Collin-Dufresne, P., Goldstein, R., 2011. Explaining asset pricing puzzles associated with the 1987 market crash. Journal of Financial Economics 101, 552–573.

Black, F., Scholes, M., 1973. The pricing of options and corporate liabilities. Journal of Political Economy 81(3), 637–654.

Bliss, R., Panigirtzoglou, N., 2004. Option-implied risk aversion estimates. Journal of Finance 59, 407–446.

Bollerslev, T., 1986. Generalized autoregressive conditional heteroskedasticity. Journal of Econometrics 31, 307–327.

Bollerslev, T., Todorov, V., 2011. Tails, fears, and risk premia. The Journal of Finance 66, 2165–2211.

Bollerslev, T. M., Gibson, H., Zhou, H., 2011. Dynamic estimation of volatility risk premia and investor risk aversion from option-implied and realized volatilities. Journal of Econometrics 160, 102–118.

Bollerslev, T. M., Marrone, J., Xu, L., Zhou, H., 2013. Stock return predictability and variance risk premia: Statistical inference and international evidence. forthcoming in Journal of Financial and Quantitative Analysis.

Bollerslev, T. M., Tauchen, G., Zhou, H., 2009. Expected stock returns and variance risk premia. Review of Financial Studies 22, 4463–4492.

Boudoukh, J., Richardson, M., Whitelaw, R. F., 2008. The myth of long-horizon predicability. Review of Financial Studies 21, 1577–1605.

Britten-Jones, M., Neuberger, A., 2000. Option prices, implied price processes and stochastic volatility. Journal of Finance 55, 839–866.

Brock, W., Lakonishok, J., LeBaron, B., 1992. Simple technical trading rules and the stochastic properties of stock returns. Journal of Finance 47, 1731–1764.

Cai, N., Kou, S. G., 2011. Option pricing under a mixed-exponential jump diffusion model. Management Science 57(11), 2067–2081.

Campbell, J., Thompson, S., 2008. Predicting excess stock returns out of sample: Can anything beat the historical average? Review of Financial Studies 21, 1509–1531.
Campbell, J. Y., 1991. A variance decomposition for stock returns. Economic Journal 101 (405), 157–179.
Campbell, J. Y., Cochrane, J. H., 1999. By force of habit: A consumption-based explanation of aggregate stock market behavior. Journal of Political Economy 107, 205–251.
Campbell, J. Y., Shiller, R. J., 1988. Stock prices, earnings, and expected dividends. Journal of Finance 43, 661–676.
Campbell, J. Y., Yogo, M., 2006. Efficient tests of stock return predictability. Journal of Financial Economics 81, 27–60.
Carr, P., Madan, D., 1998. Towards a Theory of Volatility Trading. Risk Books.
Carr, P., Wu, L., 2003. Finite moment log stable process and option pricing. Journal of Finance 58, 753–777.
Carr, P., Wu, L., 2004. Time-changed levy process and option pricing. Journal of Financial Economics 71, 113–141.
Carr, P., Wu, L., 2009. Variance risk premiums. Review of Financial Studies 22 (3), 1311–1341.
Chen, J., Liu, X., 2010. The model-free measure and the volatility spread. Applied Economic Letters 17, 1829–1833.
Chen, J., Ma, C., 2013. Risk aversion, fanning preference, and volatility smirk on S&P 500 index options, working paper, Xiamen University.
Chen, L., 2009. On the reversal of return and dividend growth predictability: A tale of two periods. Journal of Financial Economics 92, 128–151.
Chew, S. H., 1983. A generalization of the quasilinear mean with applications to the measurement of income inequality and decision theory resolving the allais paradox. Econometrica 51, 1065–1092.
Chew, S. H., 1989. An axiomatic utility theory with betweenness property. Annals of Operations Research 19, 273–298.
Chew, S. H., MacCrimmon, K., 1979a. Alpha-nu choice theory: a generalisation of expected utility theory, working paper 669, University of British Columbia.
Chew, S. H., MacCrimmon, K., 1979b. Alpha utility theory, lottery composition, and the allais paradox, working paper 686, University of British Columbia.
Christensen, B., Hansen, C. S., Prabhala, N. R., 2001. The telescoping overlap problem in options data, working Paper, University of Arahus and University of Maryland.
Cochrane, J. H., 1992. Explaining the variance of price-dividend ratios. Review of Financial Studies 5 (2), 243–280.
Cont, R., Tankov, P., Voltchkova, E., 2004. Option pricing models with jumps: Integro-differential equations and inverse problems, european Congress on Computational Methods in Applied Sciences and Engineering (ECCOMAS).
Cox, J., Ross, S., 1976. The valuation of options for alternative stochastic processes. Journal of Finanical Economics 3, 145–166.
Dekel, E., 1986. An axiomatic characterization of preferences under uncertainty. Journal of Economic Theory 40, 302–318.
Dierkes, M., 2009. Option implied risk attitude under rank dependent utility, working paper, Uniersity of Münster.
Drechsler, I., Yaron, A., 2011. What's vol got to do with it. Review of Financial Studies 24, 1–45.
Driessen, J., Maenhout, P., Vilkov, G., 2009. The price of correlation risk: Evidence from equity options. Journal of Finance 64, 1377–1406.
Du, D., 2011. General equilibrium pricing of options with habit formation and event risks. Journal of Financial Economics 99, 400–426.
Duffie, D., Epstein, L., 1992a. Asset pricing with stochastic differential utility. Review of Financial Studies 5, 411–436.
Duffie, D., Epstein, L., 1992b. Stochastic differential utility. Econometrica 62, 353–94.
Duffie, D., Pan, J., Singleton, K., 2000. Transform analysis and asset pricing for affine jump-diffusions. Econometrica 68, 1343–1376.

Dybvig, P. H., 1981. A practical framework for capital budgeting of projects having uncertain returns, working paper, Washington University.

Ebens, H., 1999. Realized stock volatility, working Paper, Johns Hopkins University.

Engle, R., 1982. Autoregressive conditional heteroscedasticity with estimates of the variance of united kingdom inflation. Econometrica 50 (4), 987–1007.

Engle, R., 2004. Risk and volatility: Econometric models and financial pratice. American Economic Review 94, 405–420.

Epstein, L., 1992. Behavior Under Risk: Recent Developments in Theory and Applications. Advances in Economic Theory – Sixth World Congress. Cambrige University Press.

Epstein, L., Zin, S., 1989. Substitution, risk aversion and the temporal behavior of consumption and asset returns: a theoretical framework. Econometrica 57, 937–969.

Epstein, L., Zin, S., 2001. The independence axiom and asset returns. Journal of Empirical Finance 8, 537–572.

Eraker, B., 2004. Do stock prices and volatility jump? Reconciling evidence from spot and option prices. Journal of Finance 59, 1367–1404.

Eraker, B., Johannes, M., Polson, N., 2003. The impact of jumps in volatility and returns. Journal of Finance 59, 1269–1300.

Fama, E. F., French, K. R., 1988. Dividend yields and expected stock returns. Journal of Financial Economics 22, 3–25.

Gabaix, X., 2012. Variable rare disasters: An exactly solved framework for ten puzzles in macro-finance. Quarterly Journal of Economics 127, 645–700.

Hansen, L., 1982. Large sample properties of generalized method of moments estimators. Econometrica 50, 1029–1084.

Henkel, S., Martin, J. S., Nardari, F., 2011. Time-varying short-horizon predictability. Journal of Financial Economics 99, 560–580.

Hess, J. D., Holthausen, D. M., 1990. Quantifying the allais paradox. Economics Letters 34, 21–25.

Heston, S., 1993. A closed-form solution of options with stochastic volatility with application to bond and currency options. The Review of Financial Studies 6, 327–343.

Hsu, M., Krajbich, I., Zhao, C., Camerer, C., 2009. Neural response to reward anticipation under risk is nonlinear in probabilities. Journal of Neuroscience 29, 2231–2237.

Huang, J., Wu, L., 2004. Specification analysis of option pricing models based on time-changed levy process. Journal of Finance 59, 1405–1439.

Jackwerth, J., Rubinstein, M., 1996. Recovering probability distributions from option prices. Journal of Finance 51, 1161–1631.

Jackwerth, J. C., 2000. Recovering risk aversion from options prices and realized returns. Review of Financial Studies 13, 433–451.

Jarrow, R., Rosenfeld, E., 1984. Jump risks and the intertemporal capital asset pricing model. Journal of Business 57, 337–351.

Jiang, G., Tian, Y. S., 2005. Model-free implied volatility and its information content. Review of Financial Studies 18, 1305–1342.

Jiang, G. J., Tian, Y. S., 2007. Extracting model-free volatility from option prices: An examination of the vix index. Journal of Derivatives 14 (3), 35–60.

Kocherlakota, N. R., 1990. Disentangling the coefficient of relative risk aversion from elasticity of intertemporal substitution : An irrelevance result. Journal of Finance 45, 175–190.

Kogan, L., Ross, S., Wang, J., Westerfield, M., 2006. The price impact and survival of irrational traders,. Journal of Finance 61, 195–229.

Kou, S. G., 2002. A jump-diffusion model for option pricing. Management Science 48, 1086–1101.

Kou, S. G., Wang, H., 2004. Option pricing under a double exponential jump diffusion model. Management Science 50, 1178–1192.

Lettau, M., Ludvigson, S., 2001. Consumption, aggregate wealth, and expected stock returns. Journal of Finance 56, 815–849.

Liu, J., Pan, J., Wang, T., 2005. An equilibrium model of rare-event premia and its implication for option smirks. Review of Financial Studies 18, 131–164.

Liu, X., Shackleton, M., Taylor, S., Xu, X., 2007. Closed-form transformations from risk-neutral to real-world distributions. Journal of Banking and Finance 31, 1501–1520.
Londono, J., 2010. The variance risk premium around the world. Working Paper, Tilburg University.
Lucas, R., 1978. Asset prices in an exchange economy. Econometrica 46, 1429–1445.
Lynch, D., Panigirtzoglou, N., 2003. Option implied and realized measures of variance, working Paper, Bank of England.
Ma, C., 1992. Two essays on intertemporal asset pricing and recursive utility, unpublished Ph.D. Thesis, University of Toronto.
Ma, C., 1998. A discrete-time intertemporal asset pricing model: Ge approach with recursive utility. Mathematical Finance 8, 249–275.
Ma, C., 2000. An existence theorem of intertemporal recursive utility in the presence of lévy jumps. Journal of Mathematical Economics 34, 509–526.
Ma, C., 2006. Intertemporal recursive utility and an equilibrium asset pricing model in the presence of levy jumps. Journal of Mathematical Economics 42, 131–160.
Ma, C., 2007. Preferences, lévy jumps and option pricing. Annals of Financial Economics 3, 1–39.
Ma, C., 2011. Advanced Asset Pricing Theory. Imperial College Press.
Ma, C., Vetzal, R., 1997. Pricing option on the market portfolio with discontinuous returns under recursive utility, university of Waterloo, mimeo.
Machina, M. J., 1982. Expected utility analysis without the independence axiom. Econometrica 50, 277–323.
Machina, M. J., 1987. Choice under uncertainty: Problems solved and unsolved. Journal of Econometric Perspectives 1, 121–154.
Madan, D., Carr, P., Chang, E., 1998. The variance gamma process and option pricing. European Finance Review 4, 125–144.
Menzly, L., Santos, T., Veronesi, P., 2004. Understanding predictability. Journal of Political Economy 112, 1–47.
Merton, R., 1976. Option pricing when the underlying stock returns are discontinuous. Journal of Financial Economics 4, 125–144.
Merton, R. C., 1973. An intertemporal capital asset pricing model. Econometrica 41, 867–887.
Naik, V., Lee, M., 1990. General equilibrium pricing of option on the market portfolio with discontinuous returns. The Review of Financial Studies 3, 493–521.
Newey, W., West, K., 1994. Automatic lag selection in covariance matrix estimation. Review of Economic Studies 61, 631–653.
Pan, J., 2002. The jump-risk premia implicit in options: Evidence from an integrated time-series study. Journal of Financial Economics 63, 3–50.
Polkovnichenko, V., Zhao, F., 2013. Probability weighting functions implied by options prices. Journal of Financial Economics 107, 580–609.
Quiggin, J., 1982. A theory of anticipated utility. Journal of Economic and Behavioral Organization 3, 323–343.
Rapach, D. E., Strauss, J. K., Zhou, G., 2010. Out-of-sample equity premium prediction: Combination forecasts and links to the real economy. Review of Financial Studies 23, 821–862.
Rosenberg, J., Engle, R., 2002. Empirical pricing kernels. Journal of Financial Economics 64, 341–372.
Rubinstein, M., 1994. Implied binomial trees. Journal of Finance 49, 771–818.
Santa-Clara, P., Yan, S., 2010. Crashes, volatility, and the equity premium: Lessons from S&P 500 options. The Review of Economics and Statistics 92, 435–451.
Shephard, N., Andersen, T. G., 2009. Stochastic volatility: Origins and overview. Handbook of Financial Time Series, 233–254.
Starmer, C., 2000. Developments in non-expected utility theory: The hunt for a descriptive theory of choice under risk. Journal of Economic Literature 38, 332–382.
Taylor, S., 2005. Asset Price Dynamics, Volatility, and Prediction. Princeton University Press.
Todorov, V., 2010. Variance risk premium dynamics: The role of jumps. Review of Financial Studies 23, 345–383.

Tversky, A., Kahneman, D., 1992. Advances in prospect theory: Cumulative representation of uncertainty. Journal of Risk and Uncertainty 5, 297–323.

Wang, S., 1993. The local recoverability of risk aversion and intertemporal substitution. Journal of Economic Theory 59, 333–363.

Weber, M., Camerer, C., 1987. Recent developments in modelling preferences under risk. OR Spektrum 9, 129–151.

Welch, I., Goyal, A., 2008. A comprehensive look at the empirical performance of equity premium prediction. Review of Financial Studies 21, 1455–1508.

Yaari, M., 1987. The dual theory of choice under risk. Econometrica 55, 95–115.

Yan, S., 2011. Jump risk, stock returns, and slope of implied volatility smile. Journal of Financial Economics 99, 216–233.

Yun, J., 2011. The role of time-varying jump risk premia in pricing stock index options. Journal of Empirical Finance 18, 833–846.

Zhang, J., Zhao, H., Chang, E., 2012. Equilibrium asset and option pricing under jump diffusion. Mathematical Finance 22, 538–568.

Zhou, H., 2010. Variance risk premia, asset predictability puzzles, and macroeconomic uncertainty. Working Paper, Federal Reserve Board.

MIX
Papier aus verantwortungsvollen Quellen
Paper from responsible sources
FSC® C105338

If you have any concerns about our products,
you can contact us on
ProductSafety@springernature.com

In case Publisher is established outside the EU,
the EU authorized representative is:
Springer Nature Customer Service Center GmbH
Europaplatz 3, 69115 Heidelberg, Germany

Printed by Libri Plureos GmbH
in Hamburg, Germany